Religion in Britain

Religion in Britain

A Persistent Paradox

SECOND EDITION

Grace Davie

WILEY Blackwell

This second edition first published 2015
© 2015 Grace Davie
Edition history: Blackwell Publishers (1e, 1994)

Registered Office
John Wiley & Sons, Ltd, The Atrium, Southern Gate, Chichester, West Sussex, PO19 8SQ, UK

Editorial Offices
350 Main Street, Malden, MA 02148-5020, USA
9600 Garsington Road, Oxford, OX4 2DQ, UK
The Atrium, Southern Gate, Chichester, West Sussex, PO19 8SQ, UK

For details of our global editorial offices, for customer services, and for information about
how to apply for permission to reuse the copyright material in this book please see our
website at www.wiley.com/wiley-blackwell.

Library of Congress Cataloging-in-Publication Data
Davie, Grace.
  [Religion in Britain since 1945]
  Religion in Britain / Grace Davie. – Second Edition.
     pages cm
  Includes bibliographical references and index.
  ISBN 978-1-4051-3595-5 (cloth) – ISBN 978-1-4051-3596-2 (pbk.)   1. Great Britain–
Religion–20th century.   2. Great Britain–Religion–21st century.   I. Title.
  BL980.G7 D38 2015
  200.941'09051–dc23

                                                                 2014032476

A catalogue record for this book is available from the British Library.

Cover image: St Paul's Cathedral, London, at night © Sack / iStockphoto

Set in 10/12pt Sabon by SPi Publisher Services, Pondicherry, India

Printed in Singapore by C.O.S. Printers Pte Ltd

1 2015

For the grandchildren

Contents

Contents

Figures and Tables

Figures

Tables

Preface

I was delighted to be asked by Wiley-Blackwell to consider a second edition of *Religion in Britain since 1945*, but re-reading a book written some 20 years ago is a strange experience – at one and the same time, it is both familiar and distant. Some of the themes introduced in the first edition have become central to my subsequent work; others have not – a division that could not have been predicted at the outset. I am struck, however, that a number of the questions introduced in the initial pages of the 1994 edition are as relevant to an understanding of religion in the second decade of the twenty-first century as they were in the 1990s. Two of them stand out: the first – the disjunction between believing and belonging – identified the core theme of the original book; the second – the unexpected prominence of religious issues in public debate – is even more significant now than it was then.

Believing without Belonging was the subtitle of *Religion in Britain since 1945* and, rightly or wrongly, became its defining feature. The idea as such was introduced as a question at the start of the original volume and was phrased as follows:

> Why is it … that the majority of British people – in common with many other Europeans – persist in believing (if only in an ordinary God),[1] but see no need to participate with even minimal regularity in their religious institutions? Indeed most people in this country – whatever their denominational allegiance – express their religious sentiments by staying away from, rather than going to, their places of worship. (Davie 1994: 2)

The notion of 'believing without belonging' caught the attention of a wide variety of readers and reviewers, and became very quickly a dominant theme in the sociological discussion about religion. It continues to resonate in the following pages, but is both refined and developed.

The second question captures the paradox that any serious scholar is obliged to address when contemplating the place of religion in twenty-first century Britain. In 1994 it was introduced as follows: 'we need to ask why the churches – as supposedly declining institutions – should have achieved in the 1980s and 1990s such a persistently high public profile'. To be honest, I find myself surprised that I considered this question so central some 20 years ago, in that it has become noticeably sharper in the intervening period. In terms of their statistical contours, the churches have continued to decline – a point that will become abundantly clear. In terms of the public presence of religion, however, the debate has intensified and includes not only the role of the churches as such, but a much wider discussion regarding the place of faith and faith communities in a liberal democracy. Much of this debate – it will be seen – reflects the changing nature of religion in modern Britain: a country with a deeply embedded Christian culture, which at one and the same time is becoming increasingly secular and increasingly diverse with regard to its religious profile.

Two further ideas are important, both of which were introduced as statements rather than questions in the original text. The first concerns the status of Britain as a European society; the second introduces the different parts of the United Kingdom. Since 1994 I have worked further on the European theme, looking at religion in Europe from the inside (Davie 2000, 2006), from the outside (Davie 2002) and in comparison with the United States (Berger, Davie and Fokas 2008). But one point remains constant. In terms of its religious institutions, Britain – most obviously in the cases of England and Scotland – is clearly a variation on the European theme. This finds expression in a historically dominant church which is organized on the basis of territory at every level of society: nation, diocese and parish. In terms of philosophical development, however, the story is a little different. In its understanding of the Enlightenment, Britain is closer to the United States than it is to continental Europe – an idea to be developed more fully in the chapters that follow. Both dimensions (institutional and philosophical) play a part in Britain's continuing ambivalence towards Europe, bearing in mind that the latter has also changed in nature.

The internal diversity of the United Kingdom remains crucial from a religious point of view. Here, however, there are new resonances given the changing situation in Northern Ireland (mostly for the better) and the relatively rapid process of devolution in Wales and Scotland, which has altered the status quo. Regarding the latter, the debate about independence has accompanied the writing of this edition. The referendum on: 'Should Scotland be an independent country?' took place on 18 September 2014, and resulted in a victory for the 'no' campaign. But whichever way the vote had gone, an important shift had already occurred. In 1994 it was still possible to argue that the General Assembly of the Church of Scotland offered the only forum where Scottish affairs could be addressed by Scottish people. That now happens in the Scottish Parliament – the national legislature of Scotland, which came into being in 1999 (see Chapter 5).

Bearing these points in mind, how should I organize a second edition of this book? Was it possible to do this within the framework of the original text? The answer was no. Certain themes – notably those outlined above – will of course continue, indeed they will be developed at some length. It is equally important, however, to introduce new ideas into the discussion – for three reasons. The first concerns the changing nature of religion and its place in British society. The second reflects not so much the evolution in religion as such, but the step change that has occurred in the study of this field – a story in its own right. The third draws on my own development as a scholar; 20 years of thinking and writing about religion in the modern world makes a difference, not least a growing capacity to see the British situation from the outside as well as from within.

The three are interrelated. Regarding religion as such, the central paradox has already been articulated. On the one hand the process of secularization continues; on the other, religion persists as a topic of discussion, indeed dispute, in the public sphere. The combination is hard to handle for an obvious reason: at precisely the moment when they are most needed, British people are losing the vocabulary, tools and concepts that they require in order to have a constructive conversation about faith. The result all too often is an ill-informed and ill-mannered debate about issues of extreme importance to the democratic future of this country. More heat than light is an understatement.

An important outcome of the growing prominence of religion has been a wide variety of publically funded research initiatives right across Europe, leading in turn to a veritable flood of publications. The logic is clear: if religion is to be effectively managed, it must be thoroughly researched. One of these initiatives – the widely acclaimed Religion and Society Research Programme – will be drawn on in many of the chapters that follow.[2] This £12 million venture, funded jointly by the Arts and Humanities Research Council and the Economic and Social Research Council, ran from 2007 to 2012 and was without precedent in Britain. The purpose of the programme was unequivocal: it existed in order to inform public debate and to advance understanding about religion in an ever more complex world. Specifically it aimed to further both research and research capacity in the field of religion (with a strong emphasis on training), to facilitate knowledge exchange between the academic community and a wide variety of stake-holders (including the religious communities themselves), and to make links with similar ventures in different parts of the world, especially Europe.

The external links are important and reflect both the similarities and differences. These are nicely exemplified in terms of new arrivals. Most, if not quite all, European societies have experienced considerable immigration in the latter half of the twentieth century, bearing in mind that the details (the timing, the nationalities involved, the precise faith communities) vary across the continent. More importantly what might be termed the 'pressure points' also differ – a feature that becomes clear when the interactions between the host society and the more recently arrived populations are examined in detail. A comparative perspective reveals the specificities of the British situation – an awareness that leads in turn to an appropriate caution with regard to policy-making. It is unwise to 'borrow' solutions from elsewhere, however attractive these may appear. It is more sensible to grasp the precise nature of the British case and to work constructively within this. The chapters that follow are written with this in mind. Their content is outlined in Chapter 1.

The third point – my own development as a scholar – is more personal. In many ways, however, it is inseparable from the reactions to the first edition of *Religion in Britain*, which took me a little by surprise; they also generated multiple invitations to a wide variety of seminars, meetings and conferences, both in this country and elsewhere. I have enjoyed these encounters enormously and learnt a great deal from them. It was these reactions, moreover, which encouraged me to explore further and to enlarge the scope and vision of my writing. Two themes have run parallel in this respect: I have paid attention not only to the evolving role of religion in different parts of the world but to the discipline (the sociology of religion) that purports to understand this better. Both are important and come together in the final chapter of this book.

More immediately I must thank the many individuals who have helped me in the preparation of the second edition, almost all of which is new. They are many, but the following should be noted in particular. David Voas, Peter Brierley and Callum Brown have gone a long way beyond the call of duty in helping me with the statistics. Peter Brierley kindly allowed me sight of new data prior to publication (see Figures 3.6 and 3.7); David Voas helped extensively with the presentation of these and other data. Callum Brown drew my attention to the facts and figures from Scotland. Judith Muskett offered hitherto unpublished information about cathedrals, Sylvia Collins-Mayo sent me additional material on street pastors and Paul Hammond provided early versions of a Ph D on fresh expressions. Padre Andrew Totten supplied valuable insights on military chaplains and helped me to understand this pivotal role rather better. David Voas, Peter Brierley, Robert Jackson, Marion Bowman, David Perfect and Paul Weller read through the drafts of various chapters and put me straight on a number of details David Perfect was also kind enough to help me with the proof reading.

In addition, I must thank the readers appointed by Wiley-Blackwell to check (most of) the typescript. Since I know who they are I can thank them by name for their time and for their comments. They are David Martin, who has inspired me over many years; Adam Dinham, who shares my passion for religious literacy; and Rebecca Catto, a former doctoral student, who was also the research associate for the Religion and Society Programme. All that said, the argument remains my own and I take full responsibility for it.

At the same time I have been grateful not only for the support of the editorial team at Wiley-Blackwell, but also for their patience. I have had a contract for a second edition for *Religion in Britain since 1945* for longer than I should have, during which time Justin Vaughan has remained not only gently persistent but warmly encouraging. It was moreover Justin who suggested that this edition should go to press simply as *Religion in Britain*. As before, the narrative starts in 1945, but the emphasis lies primarily on what has happened in more recent decades. Finally I must thank Ian Wallis for allowing me to reproduce the extract entitled 'Awakenings' on pp. xx.

My more personal debts reveal the passing of time. The first edition of this book was dedicated to my mother. This edition is dedicated to her great grandchildren, who provide a welcome distraction from things academic and restore a necessary balance to my life. My husband, as ever, remains the lynchpin.

Grace Davie
May 2014

Notes

1 The notion of an 'ordinary God' was introduced in the first chapter of the first edition. It comes from a study carried out in Islington in 1968. See Abercrombie *et al.* (1970) for more details.
2 See www.religionandsociety.org.uk (accessed 1 January 2013) for more details about the Religion and Society Programme itself and the very varied projects that contribute to this. See also Woodhead and Catto (2012).

Part I
Preliminaries

1

Introduction: A Framework for Discussion

The introduction to this book is divided into two sections. The first establishes the factors that must be taken into account if we are to understand the complexities of religion in twenty-first century Britain. In so doing, it draws extensively on two decades of research and writing in the field which began with the first edition of *Religion in Britain since 1945* and has continued since (see Davie 1994, 2000, 2002, 2006, 2007a). The second section sets out the plan for the book as a whole, indicating how the ideas already introduced reflect both the material covered in the first edition and more recent developments in the field.

Religion in Modern Britain: The Factors to Take into Account

There are six rather different features, which – taken together – contribute to a better understanding of the place of religion in modern Britain, seeing this as a distinctive variation on a European theme. The crucial point to remember is that they push and pull in different directions. The six factors are:

1. the role of the historic churches in shaping British culture;
2. an awareness that these churches still have a place at particular moments in the lives of British people, though they are no longer able to influence – let alone discipline – the beliefs and behaviour of the great majority of the population;

Religion in Britain: A Persistent Paradox, Second Edition. Grace Davie.
© 2015 Grace Davie. Published 2015 by John Wiley & Sons, Ltd.

3. an observable change in the actively religious constituencies of Britain, which operate increasingly on a model of choice, rather than a model of obligation or duty;
4. the arrival into Britain of groups of people from many different parts of the world, and with very different religious aspirations from those seen in the host society;
5. the reactions of Britain's secular elites to the increasing salience of religion in public as well as private life;
6. a growing realization that the patterns of religious life in modern Europe (including Britain) should be considered an 'exceptional case' in global terms – they are not a global prototype.

Each of these will be taken in turn in the paragraphs that follow. They will be drawn together in a short conclusion to this section.

Cultural heritage

The starting point reflects the undisputed role of Christianity in shaping British culture over the long term, remembering that other factors (notably Greek rationalism and Roman organization) must also be kept in mind. One example will suffice to illustrate this fact: the Christian tradition has had an irreversible effect in determining the most basic categories of human exist-ence (time and space) in this part of the world. Both week and year follow the Christian cycle, even if the major festivals of the Christian calendar are beginning to lose their resonance for large sections of the population. Many of them are nonetheless retained as a framework for public holidays. Sunday, moreover, remains distinctive despite the fact that the notion of a 'day of rest' has largely been discarded.

The same is true of space. Wherever you look in Britain, Christian churches predominate, some of which retain huge symbolic value for the populations that surround them. And from the largest city to the smallest village, British people orient themselves with reference to religious build-ings even if they seldom enter them for worship. The whole of Britain, moreover, is divided into parishes – a territorial model with civic as well as religious implications. For centuries, the parish determined the parameters of life for the great majority of British people from the cradle to the grave. Its significance has diminished over time, but the residues still resonate, sometimes in unexpected ways. This is not to deny that in some parts of the country (notably the larger cities) the skyline is fast becoming an indi-cator of growing religious diversity. Britain is changing, but the legacies of the past remain deeply embedded in both the physical and cultural environment.

The historic churches

The physical and cultural presence of the historic churches is one thing; a hands-on role in the everyday lives of British people quite another. Commentators of all kinds agree that the latter is no longer a realistic, or indeed a desirable, aspiration. That does not mean that these institutions have entirely lost their significance as markers of religious identity. But how should we understand their current role? It is at this point that I have drawn time and time again on one of the key themes of *Religion in Britain since 1945* – the notion of 'believing without belonging'. My thinking, however, has continued to develop, requiring a second conceptual tool, termed 'vicarious religion' (Davie 2000, 2007b, 2008). Both concepts have helped me to understand the continuing role of traditional religious institutions in a society which is both increasingly secular and increasingly diverse and will be developed at length. Only an outline is given here.

One of the most striking features of religious life in this country remains the mismatch between different measurements of religiousness. There exists, first of all, a set of indicators which measure firm commitments to (i) institutional life and (ii) *credal* statements of religion (in this case Christianity). These indicators, moreover, are closely related to each other in so far as institutional commitments – in the form of regular religious practice – both reflect and confirm religious belief in its 'orthodox' forms.[1] The believing Christian attends church to express his or her belief and to receive affirmation that this is the right thing to do. Conversely, repeated exposure to the institution and its teaching necessarily disciplines belief.

No observer of the current religious scene disputes the fact that these dimensions of British religion are interrelated and in serious decline. Fewer British people go to church than used to and fewer believe in a credal sense (see Chapters 3 and 4 for an extended discussion of these profiles). As a result, the idea of a common narrative (of Christian liturgy or of Christian language and metaphor) becomes more and more tenuous almost by the day. What, then, are the consequences of this situation? The complex relationship between belief in a wider sense and practice is central to this discussion, for it is abundantly clear that a manifest reduction in the 'hard' indicators of religious life has not, in the short term at least, had a similar effect on the less rigorous dimensions of religiousness. For the time being at least, the latter remain relatively strong though by no means immutable. Between half and two-thirds of British people assent to 'belief in God' in more general terms, and roughly similar proportions touch base with the institutional churches at some point in their lives, often at times of crisis. It is precisely this state of affairs which was captured by the phrase 'believing without belonging'. And given the rapidity with which this passed into both the sociological and pastoral literature, it clearly struck a chord.

Right from the start, however, I had misgivings – mainly because the expression 'believing without belonging' separates one kind of religiousness (belief) from another (belonging). It evokes less well the point already made: namely that both belief and belonging can be 'hard' or 'soft'. The notion of 'vicarious religion' was developed with this in mind. By vicarious is meant the notion of religion performed by an active minority but on behalf of a much larger number, who (implicitly at least) not only understand, but appear to approve of what the minority is doing. The first half of the definition is relatively straightforward and reflects the everyday meaning of the term 'vicarious' – that is, to do something on behalf of someone else. The second half is best explored by means of examples. It captures rather better than 'believing without belonging' the legacy of a historically dominant church.

Religion can operate vicariously in a wide variety of ways. For example, churches and church leaders perform ritual on behalf of others (at the time of a birth or a death for instance); if these services are denied, this causes offence – the more so amongst those who do not attend church with any regularity. Church leaders and churchgoers believe on behalf of others and incur criticism if they do not do this properly. Once again it is, very often, the occasional churchgoer who articulates this disquiet most clearly, and the more senior the church leader, the worse the problem gets. Third, church leaders and churchgoers are expected to embody moral codes on behalf of others, even when those codes have been abandoned by large sections of the populations that they serve. Churches, finally, can offer space for the vicarious debate of unresolved issues in modern societies. If the latter were not the case, it is hard to understand the persistent scrutiny of their positions on a wide variety of topical issues, from changing views regarding the nature of sexuality to the difficult moral questions surrounding birth and death – which reflect in turn the meaning of life itself. All of these points will be expanded in Chapter 4.

An alternative way of illustrating the nature of vicarious religion is to consider the place of religion and the continuing role of religious institutions in European societies when they face the unexpected or the tragic. The reactions provoked by the death of Princess Diana in August 1997 offer a revealing illustration: what happened in Britain in the week following the car accident in Paris cannot by any stretch of the imagination be described as either rational or secular, but nor was it conventionally religious. So what was it? One point is clear: a great deal of the improvised and markedly heterogeneous rituals that emerged at that time took place in the vicinity of centrally placed churches. It was these churches, moreover, that housed books of condolence and facilities for lighting candles – ordinary people queued for hours to make use of these resources – and it was the established church (the Church of England) that took responsibility for her funeral.

Even more important, however, is the fact that the reactions to Princess Diana's death (or any number of more recent equivalents) are simply 'writ-large' versions of what goes on in the everyday lives of individuals and communities all the time. People die, sometimes unexpectedly, and communities suffer, sometimes with little apparent justification. What is to be done on these occasions and who is to do it? Once again the taken-for-grantedness of this situation is the crucial point: the presence of the churches and their availability to ordinary people are simply assumed.

From obligation to consumption

Where, though, does this leave Britain's diminishing, but still significant churchgoers – those who maintain the tradition on behalf of the people described in the previous section? Here an observable change is clearly taking place, best summarized as a gradual shift from a culture of obligation or duty to a culture of consumption or choice. What was once simply imposed on substantial sections of the population (with all the negative connotations of this word), or inherited (which has a rather more positive spin), becomes instead a matter of personal choice. Religiously active individuals now go to a church or to another religious organization because they choose to, sometimes for a short period or sometimes for longer, sometimes regularly and sometimes occasionally, but they feel little *obligation* either to attend that church in the first place or to continue if they no longer want to.

As such, this pattern is entirely compatible with vicariousness: the historic churches need to be there in order that those who wish may attend them if they feel inclined. Their nature, however, gradually alters – a shift that is discernible in both practice and belief, not to mention the connections between them. There is, for example, an easily documentable change in the patterns of baptism in the Church of England. The overall number of baptisms has dropped dramatically in the post-war period, evidence once again of institutional decline. In England, though not yet in the Nordic countries, or indeed in parts of southern Europe, baptism is no longer seen as a ritual associated with birth, but has become increasingly a sign of membership in a chosen voluntary community. In other words membership of the historic churches is changing in nature. They are becoming more like the growing number of free or independent churches that can be found all over Britain, though more so in some places than in others. Voluntarism is beginning to establish itself *de facto*, regardless of the constitutional legacies of the church in question.

A second point follows from this. What are the most popular choices of twenty-first century Britons when it comes to religious attendance? The answers to this question are doubly interesting in the sense that they not only indicate the strengths and weaknesses of the present situation, but reveal that the predictions of an earlier generation (both scholars and church people) were largely incorrect. In the current period the actively religious are disproportionately drawn to two kinds of religious organization: charismatic evangelical churches on the one hand and cathedrals or city-centre churches on the other. The former epitomizes firm commitments, strong fellowship and conservative teaching, balanced by the warmth of a charismatic experience. The latter allows a much more individual (even anonymous) expression of religious commitment: in 'cathedral-type' churches the appeal is often associated with the beauty of the building, the quality of the music and the traditional nature of the liturgy. The important point to grasp is that in both cases there is a noticeable *experiential* element, albeit very differently expressed.

In the mid post-war decades, something rather different was envisaged. Conservative teaching was out of fashion and cathedrals were often classed as 'dinosaurs' – less and less relevant to the modern world and disproportionately expensive to maintain. They are still expensive to maintain, but the data indicate that they are increasingly attractive to late modern populations, whether they come as regular worshippers, less regular worshippers, tourists or pilgrims – noting that the lines between these categories are distinctly porous. Conversely, rather more liberal forms of Protestantism, noticeably fashionable in the 1960s, have not fulfilled their promise. There are, of course, important exceptions to this rule but by and large the purely cerebral has less appeal in the twenty-first century than many people thought would be the case.

It is abundantly clear, moreover, that a large sections of current 'religion' lies outside the churches altogether – indeed for growing numbers of people, even the word 'religious' is considered negatively. A new vocabulary has emerged. Specifically, the many and varied forms of the 'spiritual' now present in Britain must be taken into account, as indeed must the increasing tendency towards 'bricolage' – that is the building of individual packages (both religious and spiritual), which reflect the diversity of late modern lifestyles rather better than historic forms of religiousness. And once started, the logic of choice is relentless. It is almost certain to include a range of secular options which are as diverse as their religious counterparts. No longer are we in a situation where limited forms of religiousness confront their unbelieving alter egos. We find instead an almost infinite range of possibilities spreading along a continuum, which creeps incrementally from the religious or spiritual at one end to the more rather than less secular at the other. The grey areas towards the middle need very careful scrutiny.

A footnote concludes this discussion, which will be developed at length in Chapter 7. It raises an important conceptual question. To what extent can this situation be described as a 'market', and what are the implications of this vocabulary for our understanding of religion in modern Britain? Is it helpful to talk in these terms or do we need a more subtle frame of reference?

New arrivals

The fourth factor introduces a very different kind of diversity; it reflects the growing importance of other-faith populations now present in many parts of Britain, brought about by immigration. The initial influx was linked to an urgent need for labour in the mid post-war decades as west European economies, including Britain, expanded fast. Significantly this population is now in its third or fourth generation, to the extent that many of those who arrived as part of the labour force some 40 to 50 years ago are now about to retire. A second point should also be kept in mind. Compared with their counterparts in Europe, Britain's other-faith communities are relatively diverse and include Muslims, Sikhs and Hindus from the sub-continent as well as a distinctive group of Christians from West Africa and the Caribbean.[2] It is important to note that the small but significant Jewish population came earlier and for rather different reasons.[3]

An entirely different constituency found its way to Britain at a later stage. The 2004 (or in some cases 2007) enlargements of the European Union permitted the relatively easy movement of people from the east to the west of Europe which resulted in an influx of European workers, notably a size-able Polish contingent. Once again the motivation was largely economic and involved push as well as pull factors. Wages in the east remained low and, at least in the initial stages, Britain was noticeably more welcoming than the member states of continental Europe.[4] Polish migrants, moreover, were a relatively skilled group of workers who were able to make their way in Britain; many (if not all) of them weathered the dip in the economy following the 2008 financial crisis. That said the incentives to return home continue to grow as the Polish economy expands.

New arrivals, whatever their motivation, bring with them new ways of being religious – an argument that is more easily appreciated in a comparative perspective. The crucial point to grasp is that the consequences of growing religious diversity vary from place to place, and depend as much on the host society as on the new arrivals themselves. Britain and France offer an instructive example. As we have seen, immigration in Britain is relatively varied both in terms of provenance and in terms of faith communities. Britain is also a country where ethnicity and religion criss-cross each other in a bewildering variety of ways. Third, Britain has traditionally been more ready than many of her European neighbours, to embrace diversity – a tradition that stretches back to a colonial past where 'indirect rule', through or by means of a local elite, was the norm. The situation in France is different: here immigration has come largely from the Maghreb, as a result of which France houses one of the largest Muslim communities in Europe – an almost entirely Arab population. Rightly or wrongly, Arab and Muslim have become interchangeable terms in popular parlance in France. France, moreover, firmly rejects the notion of communitarianism (*communautarisme*), in the sense that French citizens are welcomed as such but their primary allegiance is to France, not to an intermediate group, be it religious or another. Once again the resonance with colonial policy is clear: French rule in the colonies meant 'direct rule' from Paris.

Beneath these differences lies however a common factor: the growing presence of other faith communities in general and of the Muslim population in particular, is challenging some deeply held assumptions. The notion that faith is a private matter and should, therefore, be proscribed from public life – notably from the state, from the education system, from the work place and from welfare – is widespread in Britain as it is in most of Europe. Conversely, many of those who are currently arriving in this part of the world have markedly different convictions, and offer – simply by their presence – a challenge to the status quo. The implications of this statement involve almost every aspect of British society, not least the law.

Secular reactions

The interactions between host society and the newly arrived described in the previous section raise an additional question: that is the extent to which secular elites make use of these sometimes difficult negotiations to articulate alternatives (ideological, constitutional and institutional) to religion. In order to understand this point fully, it is important to grasp three things. First, that the secular requires our attention as much as the religious; it is impossible to study one without the other. Second, that the more strident secular voices – often those of an atypical elite – have very largely emerged as a *reaction* to the renewed attention to religion in public debate. And third, that these groups, just like their religious counterparts, vary markedly from place to place – unsurprisingly given that the nature of the religious and the nature of the secular go hand in hand.

Key in this respect is an appreciation of the secularization process – specifically, an awareness that this has taken place differently in different European countries (Martin 1978). For example, what in Britain, and indeed in most of northern Europe, occurred gradually (starting with a de-clericalization of the churches from within at the time of the Reformation), became in France a delayed and much more ideological clash between a hegemonic, heavily clerical church and a much more militant secular state. The result was 'la guerre des deux Frances' (Catholic and *laïque*), which dominated French political life well into the twentieth century. The legacies still remain in the form of a self-consciously secular elite, and a lingering suspicion concerning religion of all kinds – the more so when this threatens the public sphere. The fact that these threats are no longer Catholic but Muslim does not alter the underlying reaction.

Britain has evolved differently and is on the whole more tolerant – a term to be explored in due course (pp. 177–78). But in Britain too can be found some sharply secular voices. The group that has become known as the 'new atheists' may not be all that numerous, but their voices are strident and at times dominate public debate. Two of their leading members – Richard Dawkins and the late Christopher Hitchens – are British.[5] For this reason alone, their claims require our attention. Equally noteworthy is the fact that their publications sell in millions. It should not be assumed that everyone who reads these books necessarily agrees with the argument, but a significant number do. It follows that the core argument of new atheism – that religion should not simply be tolerated but should be countered, criticized and exposed by rational argument – must be taken seriously. It has important implications for policy.

Is Europe an exceptional case?

The final factor in this section introduces a different perspective and is better addressed in European rather than British terms. It is however central to the argument of this book. It starts by reversing the core question: instead of asking what Europe (including Britain) is in term of its religious existence, it asks what Europe is not. It is not (yet) a vibrant religious market such as that found in the United States; it is not a part of the world where Christianity is growing exponentially, very often in Pentecostal forms, as is the case in the global south; it is not a part of the world dominated by faiths other than Christian, but is increasingly penetrated by these; and it is not for the most part subject to the violence often associated with religion and religious difference in other parts of the globe – the more so if religion becomes entangled in political conflict. Hence the inevitable, if at times unsettling conclusion: that the patterns of religion in this part of the world, notably its relative secularity, might be an exceptional case in global terms.

This inference is all the more disturbing if we remember that the paradigms of social science emerge from the European Enlightenment and are very largely premised on the notion that modern societies are likely to be secular societies. It follows that the traditional, European-based understandings of social science may be markedly less suitable for the study of religion in other parts of the world. Indeed they are not always helpful nearer home given the intricacies of religious life in the early years of the twenty-first century. It is this point that underpins the theoretical discussion found in the final chapter of this book.

Gathering the threads

Each of the above factors merits careful consideration in its own right – the purpose of the following chapters. One way of drawing them together, however, is to recall the two rather different things that are happening at once in twenty-first century Britain, an idea already introduced in the Preface (p. xiii). On the one hand are the increasing levels of secularity – or simply indifference – in modern Britain, which lead in turn to an inevitable decline in religious knowledge as well as in religious belief. On the other is a series of increasingly urgent debates about religion in public life, prompted by the need to accommodate new populations who bring with them very different ways of being religious. As we have seen, this largely unexpected combination is difficult to manage – unsurprisingly given the clashes of interest that are embedded in such encounters. How then can we proceed? The starting point resides in the clearest possible articulation of the present situation and a better appreciation of the pressures that lie beneath this. This book has been written with this in mind.

Religion in Britain: A Revised Road Map

The 1994 edition of *Religion in Britain since 1945* looked first at the changing economic, political and social context of modern Britain and then at the religious 'generations' that succeeded one another in the post-war period. This edition does likewise, bearing in mind that some of the material regarding the European context has already been covered and that the number of generations is growing. The final chapter of Part I (entitled 'Preliminaries') sets out the facts and figures relating to religion in this country. It is conceived primarily as a basis for operations but will also make reference to the media: as sources of information in their own right; as an indicator of change; and as a cautionary tale. We should not believe everything that we read in the papers.

The chapters that followed in the first edition formed the core of the original book, and dealt first with the religious constituencies found in modern Britain before looking in detail at the 'ordinary Gods' of British society – the luxuriant undergrowth of belief, much of which was far from orthodox. The subsequent chapter brought these points together in an extended discussion of believing without belonging. The later chapters dealt with a variety of topics: religious transmission, emphasizing the significance of age and gender and the place of religion in the school system; the ramifications of church and state as a framework for discussion; and the role of religious professionals, both lay and ordained. The book concluded with a theoretical discussion of the changing nature of a late modern society (in this case Britain) and the place of religion in this.

The substance of this edition is differently constructed. It derives from the material set out in the early part of this chapter and is divided into three parts. The first (Part II) concentrates on the 'old model': that is, the legacies of the past, recognizing that these still constitute the parameters of faith in this country. Such a statement does not mean that nothing has changed – it most certainly has; it does however recognize that our past is distinctive and continues to influence the present. For this reason, the initial chapter in this part of the book contains a fuller discussion of the cultural heritage of Christianity, and the frames of reference that have emerged from this: namely a tendency to believe without belonging and to engage vicariously both with religion and religious institutions.

The importance of territory and the links between church and state (the arrangement known as 'establishment' in England) are central to this discussion, in that they are part of the apparatus delivered to us by history and need to be recognized as such. Unsurprisingly, they are currently under strain given the changing nature of British – more specifically English – society. So what is to be done? A careful analysis of the pros and cons of the present situation is the obvious starting point. Only then will it be possible to think towards the future. The rather different situations in Scotland, Wales and Northern Ireland are equally important – all of them are evolving but not always in the same ways. The specificity of the Northern Irish case needs firm underlining; things are better than they used to be in this corner of the United Kingdom but sectarianism remains a salient theme. A more developed discussion of two selected localities (York and London) concludes this discussion.

Inevitably, debates about church and state spill over into other aspects of society. The role of chaplains offers an interesting starting point in this respect. To what extent is the 'representative' role traditionally associated with chaplaincy still viable in late modern society? Four examples will be taken to illustrate the changes taking place: health care, prisons, the military and higher education. The last of these raises the question of religious literacy and the role of the university in public debate, and in so doing it opens the discussion about the place of religion in education per se. A whole range of issues emerge at this point, including the desirability or otherwise of faith schools, the widely ignored legal requirement to hold a daily act of worship in all schools, and the role of religious education both in and beyond the classroom. The significance of religious education will be considered in the greatest detail, in light of the comments set out above. The essential point is easily summarized: is it, or is it not, possible to reverse the decline in religious knowledge that has become not only pervasive, but damaging to public discussion? What is the role of religious education in this process and can anything be done to make it more effective? It is almost impossible to overestimate the importance of these questions.

At least some reference must also be made to the continuing disputes regarding religious professionals. These will focus largely but not exclusively on the Church of England. It is abundantly clear that an exclusively male priesthood no longer fits current aspirations. The process of change, however, is far from smooth. Interestingly the first edition of *Religion in Britain* dealt at some length with the debates surrounding the ordination of women to the priesthood in the Church of England. The inevitable corollary – the expectation that women would in due course become bishops – constitutes an important theme in this one. It has provoked considerable public discussion both inside and outside the churches. Questions of sexuality are equally apposite; they are, however, distinct from questions of gender and must be considered in their own right. Both issues not only reflect the changing nature of British society, but the very different situation that pertains in those parts of the world where Christianity (including Anglicanism) is noticeably strong. The role of the Church of England as the mother church of the Anglican Communion will be pertinent at this point.

Parts III and IV look forward rather than back. Part III is concerned with the visible mutation that is clearly taking place in the religious life of this country, summarized above as a shift from a culture of obligation or duty to a culture of consumption or choice. This can be seen in any number of ways. The chapters that develop this discussion work outwards. They deal first with the options available in the Christian 'sector' of this country, recognizing that the range is almost as wide within the denominations in question as it is between them. 'Conservatives' exist in almost every branch of Christianity as indeed do liberals; alliances (at times unholy ones) are constructed accordingly. Who gains and who loses in this complicated network of interests? An answer has already been hinted at in the early part of this chapter but it needs to be interrogated in more detail. Why is it that conservative churches in almost all denominations are doing relatively well? And why is it that the experiential is noticeably more attractive than the cerebral to late modern worshippers? Attention must also be paid to the counter-intuitive nature of these findings and to the difficulties that they present for social science.

A second question follows from this. Given the growing significance of choice, how should these various churches react? Should they play to their respective strengths or should they continue to provide what might be termed a 'comprehensive' service? Should they all do the same thing? It is at this point that the past begins to resonate, in that churches that are locked into territory (the parish) are necessarily restricted. Have they, however, a corresponding advantage and how might this be exploited? Territory, moreover, has indirect as well as direct implications and at every level of society. Not only is it the organizational *raison d'être* of the historic churches, it also implies a certain way of working – one which is more like a public utility than a market. The tensions between the two models – the public utility on one hand and the market on the other – need careful scrutiny. They reveal a great deal about the religious life of this country.

The following chapter extends this discussion, finding its focus in what has become known as the spiritual, rather than the religious. A good place to start in this disparate field is to recognize the very different understandings of pluralism that can be found not only in the realities of religious and/or spiritual life in this country, but in the literature (both academic and other) that surrounds this. Once this is straight it will be easier to address the range of possibilities that are open to the British 'seeker' and how he or she might determine a spiritual pathway. A comprehensive coverage of all the options available is not possible – it would require a book in its own right – but consideration will be given to at least the more prominent new religious movements and to the huge variety of ideas that are subsumed under the rubric 'new age' (the most usual nomenclature in the 1990s).

Equally important, however, are the proliferations of the spiritual as they have developed in more recent decades and the hybrid cases that emerge as boundaries are crossed and re-crossed in this continually evolving field. The interesting, but sometimes delicate, relationships between the Christian churches and newer forms of spiritual life form one focus for this discussion. A second can be found in the tensions that arise between the material (i.e. the realities of everyday life) and the spiritual – strains that are captured in the following questions. To what extent is the market in the spiritual an extension of the market per se? Once material needs have been satisfied, individuals turn to the spiritual: the buying and selling continues. Or is it more accurate to see the spiritual as the obverse of the market in so far as it is indicative of non-material rather than material values? There is more to life than shopping. It might of course be possible to combine the two approaches, in the sense that individuals make use of the distinctively spiritual techniques to become more effective economic operators.

Part IV of the book introduces a different kind of religious diversity: namely the growing number of other-faith communities now present in many parts of Britain. Drawing on the facts and figures presented in Chapter 3, an accurate presentation of the current situation is a necessary starting point. It is true that the other-faith populations are growing in this country, but two points must be kept firmly in mind: these communities – though expanding – are both modest in size and varied in nature. Neither element is recognized in a great deal of public debate, which very quickly becomes confused. Inaccuracies, some of them deliberate, abound. Once the basics are in place, however, it will be possible to look more carefully at individual communities, paying particular attention to the Muslim minority for reasons that will be carefully explained. The discussion will be set within a wider consideration of the public and the private dimensions of religiousness and how these are evolving in twenty-first century Britain.

At this point, a clarification is helpful. It is not true that religion was once firmly privatized and has suddenly become a public phenomenon (it always has been). It is true that religion has become visible in new ways. The presence of other-faith communities in general and of Muslims in particular has acted as a catalyst in this respect. Unsurprisingly, this has provoked a wide variety of responses. One of these can be found in a re-affirmation of the secular, both in society as a whole and in the social scientific study of this, demonstrating a further slippage in the taken-for-granted. For the greater part of the post-war period, both policy-makers and analysts assumed that religion would gradually fade from public discussion but continue to exist in the private lives of significant numbers of individuals. To say that the reverse has happened is an over-simplification but there is truth in this. The crucial point is the following: fewer people are now religious, but those who are take their religious lives more seriously – a shift with important implications for public as well as private life. Hence a new configuration: one in which both the religious and the secular are more consciously articulated. Both, moreover, are varied. The preoccupations of the new atheists form one, but only one, focus for this discussion.

Chapter 10 considers the implications of diversity (both religious and secular) for a wide variety of public institutions. As ever the religious spills over into every aspect of economic and social life: it cannot be contained in a discrete or private sector however much the more extreme secularists might want this to be the case. How then should religion be managed in, say, economic life, including the everyday demands of the workplace? What is and is not 'reasonable' and (realistically) how far does this depend on the state of the economy, specifically the current rate of unemployment? The implications for politics, welfare and the health service are equally important and will be confronted in their turn. It is these issues, moreover, that lie behind the striking growth in the attention to religion by various branches of the law. Particular cases will be looked at to illustrate this point, which will also make reference to the European Court of Human Rights – raising once again the markedly ambiguous relationship between Britain and Europe.

This discussion reflects the necessarily arbitrary nature of the divisions within this book. It is clear that there is a new urgency in the debates about religion and public life, and that many of these have been triggered by a specific and relatively recent combination of events. It is equally clear that the manner in which these issues are addressed is framed by the legacies of the past – a point at which the distinctiveness of the United Kingdom, and within this, of England, Scotland, Wales and Northern Ireland must be taken into account. The law evolves in a particular context, one aspect of which concerns the links between church and state. It is for this reason that the 'pressure points' which emerge in Britain are noticeably different from those that have developed in other European countries, not to mention the United States. This means – inevitably – that the fourth section of this book builds very directly on the second and that the divisions between them are somewhat artificial. The discussion of the law could equally well follow that on church and state; the discussion of welfare could be joined to that on education. Most importantly of all, the material in both sections must take account of the fact that religion as such is changing in nature – a situation in which paradoxes abound. At one and the same time, religion is both more diffuse and more controlled, more experimental and more constrained, more personal and more exposed.

How then can we make sense of this complex phenomenon, which persists despite the predictions of social science? The final chapter of the 1994 edition of this book contained a theoretical discussion of the (then) current situation, as I understood this. In itself, it provoked considerable debate. This edition does likewise, but the theoretical content is noticeably different – a fact that reflects both the changing situation as such and the development of debate in the field. Both, moreover, must take into account an enormous amount of new material, which will be fully referenced as the chapters develop. The step-change represented by the Religion and Society Programme and its European equivalents (introduced in the Preface – p. xiii) is central to this discussion, recognizing that these initiatives are themselves part of the story. Why they took place at the time that they did is as significant as the abundance of material that emanated from them. A second theme runs parallel: that is the noticeably Eurocentric nature of the paradigms that have emerged in this field. To what extent are these adequate in a world in which religion grows, at times exponentially – a fact with inevitable consequences for the situation in Britain, the primary focus of this book?

Notes

1 'Orthodox' at this point means the mainstream doctrine in the church in question.
2 The Christians who came from West Africa and the Caribbean are not of course other-faith communities, though they are distinct from the host population. Their place in the religious life of Britain is important and will be discussed at some length.
3 The Jewish story is particular (see Chapter 3 and Graham 2012). Significant sections of this community arrived in Britain to escape persecution, in the nineteenth century from Russia and in the twentieth century from Germany.
4 The controversies surrounding the right of entry of Romanians and Bulgarians to live and work in the United Kingdom have been noticeably sharper. These were provoked by the ending of temporary controls in place between January 2007 and December 2013.
5 The remaining two – Daniel Dennett and Sam Harries – are American.

2

Contexts and Generations

This chapter provides a framework within which to consider the subsequent material on British religion. It starts by locating Britain in a global context. Attention has already been paid to the European dimension: the six factors set out in the previous chapter can be applied to almost all European societies, albeit weighted variously. Britain is nonetheless distinct for a variety of reasons. One of these concerns cultural rather than structural features: specifically the nature of the Enlightenment. It is very clear, for example, that Enlightenment thinking, as understood in Britain, was markedly less opposed to religion than its equivalent in France. It was, in fact, more akin to the interpretations discovered in the United States – this is one reason for a persistent pull across the Atlantic. A third influence reflects the New Commonwealth and its continuing significance for British religion. Substantial sections of this entity lie in the global south where religion is diverse, vibrant and, in general, conservative – a far cry from northern indifference. It is hardly surprising therefore that British people are brought up short when vociferous Christians from this part of the world challenge the views of their co-religionists regarding (say) the place of women in church leadership, or when new and differently configured faith communities disturb the status quo.

The second section has a rather different focus: it outlines some of the most salient economic, political and social changes in post-war Britain. In so doing, it pays particular attention to the long period of Conservative dominance at the end of the last century and the subsequent shift to New Labour. Given the extent of political change (as measured in electoral terms), it is easy to miss the underlying continuities – seen particularly in more positive approaches to the market and a systematic rolling back of the state.

Religion in Britain: A Persistent Paradox, Second Edition. Grace Davie.
© 2015 Grace Davie. Published 2015 by John Wiley & Sons, Ltd.

The impact of demography on the latter, specifically the demands of an age-ing population, is given due weight. The section ends by noting the shifting moral climate in twenty-first century Britain – a debate that brings to the fore new understandings of sexualities and the dilemmas that these present for religious constituencies.

The final section introduces the notion of generational change, taking the evolving economic and political moods already outlined as a starting point. The stress at this point lies on the reactions of both religious people and religious organizations to these changes. An emphasis on rehabilitation in the aftermath of war gave way to radical change in the 1960s, a shift with profound effects on the churches. Global uncertainties in the following decades were equally disconcerting but in differing ways. At a more general level, however, it is possible to discern the two relatively long-term and seemingly contradictory processes that underpin this book: continuing secularization on the one hand, alongside increasing attention to religion in public life on the other.

Britain in a Global Context

A European variant

Some 30 years ago, Halsey (1985) summarized the position of the British *vis-à-vis* the majority of Europeans in the following terms: 'though by no means outlandish from the European culture to which they belong, the British are to be seen and see themselves as a relatively unchurched, nation-alistic, optimistic, satisfied, conservative, and moralistic people' (1985: 12). In making these remarks, Halsey was commenting on one of the first surveys to be carried out under the auspices of the European Values Study (EVS) – the data that provide the starting point for many of the ideas set out in Chapter 1.[1] The EVS material clearly reveals the mismatch between the two types of variable that run through this analysis: on the one hand are the variables concerned with feelings, experience and the more numinous religious beliefs; on the other are those which measure religious orthodoxy, ritual participation and institutional attachment. It is the latter which display, most obviously, an undeniable degree of secularization across most of Europe. The former are more likely to persist.

Stepping back a little, two themes run through the EVS enquiries. The first concerns the substance of European values and asks, in particular, to what extent they are shared; the second takes a more dynamic approach, asking to what extent they are changing. Both involve a religious element. The first, for example, leads very quickly to questions about origins. If values in Europe are to any extent held in common, how had this come about?

The answer lies in deep-rooted social and cultural influences which have been formative for all European societies. A shared religious heritage is one such influence. On that we can agree. As soon as the idea of value change is introduced, however, the situation becomes contentious. How far is the primacy given to the role of religion, and more especially Christian religion, in the creation of values still appropriate? Has this role not been undermined by the twin processes of secularization and pluralization? Can we really maintain in the early twenty-first century that the Christian religion remains a central element of our value system? Its influence is becoming, surely, increasingly peripheral within European – including British – society. Or is it? It was these questions that set up the argument for the first edition of this book. Some 20 years later, they continue to resonate, albeit in different ways.

If the disjunction between indices of religious belief and those pertaining to religious practice forms a pattern across most of Europe, are there variations within this which have particular significance for an analysis of religion in Britain? The first and most obvious of these points towards the notably more religious countries of the Catholic south and the much lower indices of religious activity discovered further north. There can be no doubt where Britain belongs in this respect – it is firmly part of the Protestant north. A further variation should also be noted. In the 1981 EVS enquiry, there was a higher than average incidence of no religion, or at least no denominational affiliation in France, Belgium and the Netherlands than in most west European societies. It is becoming increasingly clear that Britain should also be included in this category – a fact endorsed by a whole series of subsequent enquiries, not least the 2011 British Census.[2]

The real key to understanding the distinctive nature of Britain as a European variant lies, however, in the specificities of history. The argument is drawn from the work of David Martin and starts from the following premise:

> Europe is a unity by virtue of having possessed one Caesar and one God i.e. by virtue of Rome. It is a diversity by the virtue of the existence of nations. The patterns of European religion derive from the tension and the partnership between Caesar and God, and from the relationship between religion and the search for national integrity and identity. (Martin 1978: 100)

Martin's thinking in this respect provides the necessary background both for a rounded discussion of church and state and for a proper understanding of the religious situation in the different parts of the United Kingdom, an argument that will be engaged in full in Chapter 5. The crucial point to grasp is that the process of secularization is historically patterned and takes place differently in different places – an analysis that can applied at different levels.

Transatlantic ties

As will become clear in this discussion, England, Scotland and to an extent Northern Ireland are similar, in that each has its own version of a national, territorially based, majority church within which the parish system persists. The United States does not. Across the Atlantic, the free-standing, voluntary congregation constitutes the essential building block for religious life. Congregations aggregate themselves into denominations, none of which receives support from the state. This is a matter of principle. The separation of church and state is carefully articulated in the founding documents of the federal state – specifically in two clauses of the First Amendment to the American Constitution. These have become known as the establishment clause and the freedom clause and read as follows: 'Congress shall make no law respecting an establishment of religion or prohibiting the free exercise thereof.' Both are fundamental to American self-understanding.

This is one reason for the marked difference between Europe and America in terms of religion. A second can be found in interpretations of the Enlightenment. In Europe, or more precisely in France, the Enlightenment embraced an attitude to religion which can be summarized as a 'freedom from belief' – meaning effectively a freedom from the obscurantism of the Catholic Church (Voltaire's famous 'écrasez l'infâme'). By the time that Enlightenment ideas had made their way across the Atlantic, however, a 'freedom from belief' had mutated into a noticeably different formulation: a 'freedom to believe'. In the United States, moreover, such ideas were very largely carried by (not against) the many different versions of Christianity that were establishing themselves at the end of the eighteenth century. A more developed discussion of these fundamental differences and their implications for religious vitality can be found in Berger, Davie and Fokas (2008). The point to be grasped here concerns the significance of Britain in this process.

Gertrude Himmelfarb's *The Roads to Modernity: The British, French and American Enlightenments* (2004) is an innovative, controversial and widely read book, which engages this question directly. Himmelfarb's essential claim is the following: that the influence of the French Enlightenment (based on reason) has been vastly overrated, at the expense of the British and American variants, which have much more in common. Both the British, characterized by virtue, and the American, characterized by political liberty, must be restored to their rightful position, not only in terms of the historical account but with reference to their influence on modern political thinking. Himmelfarb's well-known 'neo-conservatism' is immediately evident in this analysis, which strongly endorses American rather than French understandings of democracy. Reviewers have reacted accordingly, sometimes very sharply.

Beneath the polemic, however, the key question remains unchanged: where is the dividing line in this sequence? Is it between France and Britain, or between Britain and America? Without doubt, Himmelfarb locates this between France and Britain: hence her desire to rehabilitate the British Enlightenment at the expense of the French and to draw together the British and the American cases. In terms of the argument in this chapter, the implications are considerable. One of these concerns the tendency to over-emphasize the French understanding of the Enlightenment, including its marked secularism. It is for this reason that the assumption of secularization has become normative in social-scientific discourse. Britain, however, is different from France – a fact increasingly recognized.[3] But is it sufficiently different in terms of its approach to religious liberty to outweigh the territorial constraints of the parish system common to Europe as a whole?

'Up to a point' is the most likely answer, bearing in mind a number of other factors. Among the latter is the notion of a 'special relationship' between Britain and the United States – an idea formulated by Winston Churchill in the immediate post-war period, but hardly new even then.[4] The special relationship can, moreover, be expressed in a multiplicity of ways: economic, political, diplomatic, military, historical, cultural and linguistic. A degree of religious affinity should be seen in this light, bearing in mind that the fascination with America is stronger for some religious constituencies than for others. It is a tendency seen most obviously in the evangelical world, a part of the church that is growing in confidence. Interestingly, even in the Church of England evangelicals sit more lightly to the parish structure than many of their co-religionists and for this reason link easily to their counterparts in the United States. It is important to remember, however, that like-mindedness in theology does not imply the wholesale embracing of associated political ideals. There is no equivalent in British evangelical circles to America's New Christian Right.[5]

Global connections

Episcopalians (i.e. American Anglicans) are part of the Anglican Communion – and at times a very influential part. The Anglican Communion as a whole, however, is rather differently shaped. Its contours were formed by the rapid expansion of the British Empire in the eighteenth and nineteenth centuries – a truly global development. For better or worse, the missionary thrust of the Anglican Church was part of this endeavour, meaning that the Communion brings together churches from all over the world, notably (but not exclusively) from the countries of the New Commonwealth. Churches in the different global regions are grouped into Provinces, which are largely autonomous – unlike their equivalents in the Catholic Church. There is, however, agreement on essential doctrines, at least in principle. Membership of the Anglican Communion is currently estimated at around 80 million members worldwide and continues to grow.

A short paragraph can hardly do justice to the subtleties of these arrangements, nor to the implications of global affinities for decision-making in the Church of England. These will be dealt with at a later stage. It is also important to note that almost all Christian churches in Britain have continuing and effective links with their co-religionists in different parts of the world – this is not exclusive to Anglicanism. The point to grasp, moreover, is the same in every case: namely that global Christianity is changing in nature. No longer are the churches in the northern hemisphere calling the shots, though they still possess disproportionate amounts of power and money, largely for historical reasons. But when it comes to numbers, the picture looks very different. The vast majority of the world's Christians live in the global south and exert simply by their presence considerable pressure on their fellow believers further north. Here is a vibrant, growing, enthusiastic and largely conservative body of people who are no longer the passive recipients of mission (Sanneh 2004; Jenkins 2012). They, as much as anyone else, are senders as well as receivers, and look with alarm at the levels of secularity that they see in Europe. The notion of 'reverse mission' is an oversimplification which begs many questions, but as a phrase it captures an important aspect of these developing relationships (Catto 2008).

The geographical reach of the Commonwealth accounts finally for the distinctive religious diversity discovered in modern Britain. It is true that immigration from the West Indies and West Africa is predominantly Christian. Those arriving from the Indian subcontinent, however, are different. From this part of the world have come not only significant numbers of Muslims, but important populations of Hindus and Sikhs. It is clear, moreover, that links with the place of origin (mostly Commonwealth countries) remain a crucial element in the self-understanding of these communities. Each of these points is significant and will be expanded in Chapter 3.

Economic, Political and Social Transformations

Placing the countries of the United Kingdom within a global context provides one frame of reference within which to consider the religious situation in modern Britain. Equally important is the changing nature of British society itself. The first edition of this book focused on the transformation that occurred in the latter part of the twentieth century as a predominantly industrial society mutated into something rather different: production was giving way to consumption as the dominant economic metaphor, and (to use the jargon current at the time) modernity was transforming into late or post-modernity. Patterns of employment and residence were evolving fast as late modern individuals reshaped their working lives, discovered new kinds of leisure activity, and decided differently about where and with whom they wanted to live. These were lively debates with important implications for religion. The timing, moreover, is important: the book went to press when John Major was still Prime Minister. The Conservative Party had been in power since 1979. New Labour was barely invented as a concept, much less as the defining feature of British government for more than a decade.[6]

So what has happened since? In political terms, 1997 was undoubtedly a watershed: the moment when the Labour Party emerged from almost 20 years in the wilderness to win three elections in a row. For most of this time Tony Blair was Prime Minister. In many ways highly successful, Blair's reputation was tarnished for many (including large numbers within the churches) by his support for American policies in the Middle East – a good illustration of the 'special relationship' outlined above, and expressed most clearly in the invasion of Afghanistan in 2001 and of Iraq in 2003. The grounds for the latter were controversial and provoked widespread opposition both inside and outside Parliament. On one point, however, everyone can agree: the balance of power had changed decisively. Comprehensive electoral defeat meant that it was the turn of the Conservatives to languish on the sidelines: an almost total reversal of the Thatcher years.

In economic terms, however, there was greater continuity than the electoral narrative implies. In this respect, the 1980s were pivotal. This was the decade in which neo-liberalism triumphed and attempts by the opposition to turn back the tide were simply ineffectual. New Labour, moreover, was very different from Old Labour: the former looked for new ways to achieve their goals; the latter clung firmly to post-war policies, expressed most obviously in the nationalization of major industries. The shift can be captured in one of Tony Blair's first acts as leader: the re-wording of Clause IV, which liberated the Party from one of its core policies – common ownership of the means of production. The change was accepted in 1995. It is not for nothing that the phrase 'a Clause IV moment' has come to mean a decisive break with the past. This was the moment when the Labour Party endorsed a fundamental shift in outlook, accepting the market as a legitimate means to the end. The policy worked: New Labour won by a landslide in 1997.

The change in government coincided with a marked upturn in the economy. The recession in the early 1990s should not be forgotten – it was profoundly damaging for many people – but from the middle of the decade onwards there was an unprecedented period of economic growth. This continued until 2008 – the moment when Britain, together with most of the western world, experienced the most serious global recession since the 1920s. The bubble burst spectacularly. By this time, Tony Blair had handed the leadership of the Labour Party to Gordon Brown, who was Prime Minister from 2007 to 2010. An initial lift in the opinion polls following Brown's succession was short-lived. Both Gordon Brown's and the Party's popularity declined rapidly as the recession took its toll, leading to defeat in 2010.

What emerged was a hung parliament: specifically an uneasy coalition between the Conservatives and the Liberal Democrats. Beneath these shifts, moreover, an important point was becoming clear: the conventional divisions of right and left (i.e. of capital and labour) are less and less relevant to British politics. The underlying continuities are as significant as the changes in political fortune.

One of these can be found in a steady retrenchment of the state, a thread that runs right through this narrative. Frequently associated with the Thatcher years, the contraction began earlier – under a Labour rather than Conservative government; it was a direct result of the 1973 oil crisis and the economic uncertainty that followed. The trend continued inexorably as it became increasingly clear to all parties that it was no longer possible for the state to provide from the cradle to the grave, reversing the assumptions of the immediate post-war period. It was Mrs Thatcher, however, who made a virtue of necessity. 'Thatcherism' became a clearly articulated ideology which brought together a cluster of ideas: low inflation, the rolling back of the state, advocacy of a free market and corresponding restrictions on wage-bargaining. And like it or not, the decades that follow are 'post-Thatcherite'. To a large extent, the policies set out above remain in force; they ebb and flow but do not disappear.

A second, very different factor should also be kept in mind in understanding these shifts in policy: that is the changing demographic profile of Britain. The state can no longer provide from the cradle to the grave for the simple reason that there are more and more people who require support. Britain, in line with the developed economies of the western world, is an ageing society in every sense of the term. Both the absolute numbers and the proportion of elderly people are growing, as is the median age of the population as a whole, with the effect that most of us are likely to live well beyond retirement age.[7] At the same time, the prolongation of education for significant numbers of younger people and the difficulty of finding work mean that earning – and therefore taxation – is correspondingly deferred. It follows that the dependent sections of the population are growing at the expense of the independent to the point that there is insufficient income to sustain the services to which we have become accustomed. The imbalance, moreover, is exacerbated by rising unemployment. It was hardly surprising, therefore, that the situation became acute following the financial crisis of 2008, precipitating a prolonged period of austerity in an attempt to balance the budget.

A whole series of measures follow from this, ranging from the financing of higher education by fee-paying rather than by grant-giving, to the step-by-step increase in the age at which an individual is entitled to a pension. It is equally clear that care as such is being systematically outsourced – away from the state to the for-profit and non-profit sectors, a situation in which religious organizations of many different kinds are finding new roles (see Chapter 10). Questions of entitlement, very often directed at those who have arrived in this country relatively recently, are central to these discussions – repeating a pattern that occurred in the later twentieth century. Populations that were welcomed in the post-war period as the economy expanded rapidly were viewed rather differently in the decades of uncertainty that followed (i.e. the 1970s and 1980s). By this stage unemployment was on the increase, leading to resentment towards non-white populations who might be given preference in terms of jobs, housing or education. The cycle began again in the 1990s: new arrivals were welcomed – or at least more easily absorbed – as the economic indicators begin to rise. Post 2008, austerity set in bringing with it rising levels of hostility. Since this date, immigration has dominated the political agenda.

The first edition of *Religion in Britain since 1945* reflected on these issues and their implications – both direct and indirect – for the religious life of this country. The discussion will continue in this book. The same will be true with respect to family life. In the 1994 edition a cluster of issues emerged, which revolved around the formation, attrition and dissolution of households, noting not only the 'cultural, social, economic and biological salience' of these moments in the life course (Hobcraft and Joshi 1989: 1), but the place of the churches in them. Changing gender roles were central to these debates, notably the increasing tendency for women to participate in the workforce for the greater part of their adult lives and to adapt their domestic responsibilities accordingly.

Closely associated with this shift was the almost universal assumption that women should be able to control their own fertility. By the mid postwar decades, sexual activity had been definitively divorced from conception, with profound effects not only for the onset of such activity, but for the age of marriage, which was increasingly delayed.[8] A second question followed from this: that is, the possibility of conception without sexual activity. My remarks in this respect were more tentative – unsurprisingly given that the necessary technology was relatively new (the first 'test tube baby' was born in 1978). Some 20 years later, the consequences are clearer: a medical technique, which is welcomed as a resolution for those unable to conceive children, has immense implications (medical, familial, social, moral and religious) for late modern societies as a whole. To give but one example, if a child can be conceived outside the womb it follows that same-sex couples can (and do) become parents.

A marked shift in the understanding of sexualities is part and parcel of this discussion. An indication of the rapidity of change in this respect can be found by comparing the heated debates surrounding 'Section 28' in 1988 with the discussion of the marriage of same-sex couples in 2013. 'Section 28' was shorthand for an amendment to the 1988 Local Government Act, which stated explicitly that that a local authority 'shall not intentionally promote homosexuality or publish material with the intention of promoting homosexuality', or 'promote the teaching in any maintained school of the acceptability of homosexuality as a *pretended family relationship*' (my italics).[9] Always controversial, the clause was eventually repealed in 2003. In the intervening years, public opinion on same-sex relationships had begun to alter decisively and continues to do so. The latter point is nicely illustrated by the change in views of the present Prime Minister. In 2003, David Cameron (newly elected as Leader of the Conservative Party) resisted the repeal of Section 28, a gesture for which he publicly apologized in 2009.[10] Some four years later, Cameron strongly endorsed the Marriage (Same-Sex Couples) Act, which received parliamentary approval in July 2013. The wheel, it seems, has turned full circle.

Not quite. At its first reading in February 2013, more Conservative MPs voted against the Bill than for it – the Party, and the sections of the population that it represents, were (and still are) deeply divided. It is equally clear that many within the churches are discomfited by this legislation and are formally opposed to it.[11] That said, the situation continues to evolve. It would be incorrect, for example, to assume that all religiously active people are of the same opinion in this respect. There are significant elements in almost all religious denominations who favour the acceptance of marriage between same-sex couples and who would welcome the opportunity to celebrate such partnerships within their churches.[12] In short the situation is complex, much as it was in 1994. The presenting issues may be different but the underlying questions remain the same. How should religious organizations – as guardians of the sacred – respond to these profound, delicate and, for many people, disturbing social and cultural shifts? It is not entirely clear. The situation is rendered more difficult in so far as the requirements of 'truth' as this is variously understood very often pull in one direction, whereas pastoral sympathies lead in another.

Generational Changes Since 1945

Any attempt to suggest particular periods of time within post-war religious development must to some extent be arbitrary; it is always possible to offer alternative and equally plausible sets of dates. Nor are such periods, however decided upon, tidy or self-contained units – the thread of events will be continuous whatever the shifts in mood and emphasis. This section attempts, nonetheless, to outline a series of 'generational' shifts, selected primarily because they reflect significant changes in the way that the religious dimension of society relates to the wider economic, political or social environment. The notion of a 'generation' has been chosen for two reasons: on the one hand it conveys a period of time, and on the other, it evokes the idea of handing on a tradition (a body of knowledge) from one generation to the next. The extent to which this does or does not happen becomes a central theme in the process of secularization.

1945–1960: Post-war reconstruction

Six years of war left Europe as a whole in ruins: Britain was no exception. Not only was the need for material reconstruction obvious, there was, in addition, the task of reconstituting the whole fabric of political, economic and social life. In the Diocese of London only 70 out of 700 churches remained unscathed after the bombing and many had been completely destroyed. At the same time the need to provide new church buildings and personnel to keep pace with post-war housing programmes was all too plain. And if London was to some extent a special case, similarly daunting figures could be quoted for a number of other Church of England dioceses, particularly those containing the larger cities. Faced with the enormity of the challenge, most people agree that the churches managed pretty well. In the 1950s at least, there was a distinct feeling of well-being, of revival even, within church circles. Adrian Hastings describes this as follows:

> The general feeling of religious revival or, perhaps better, of restoration, continued for about a dozen years. It fitted well with the dominant mood of the fifties, its politicians, its literary figures, its art. 'The church', declares a character in Pamela Hansford Johnson's novel, *The Humbler Creation*, 'is respectable again. People have to say they believe in God.' (Hastings 1986: 444)

Above all, however, the 1950s were an Anglican decade, in which the social role of the church was confirmatory rather than confrontational. The sacred (at least in its Anglican forms) synchronized nicely with the secular in this predominantly Conservative period.

The moment which caught this sense of restoration – symbolic as well as material – most vividly was the Coronation of Elizabeth II in June 1953, described by Jenkins as 'the most universally impressive ceremonial event in history' (Jenkins 1975: 74). Whatever the case, it undoubtedly brought together the Church of England, the monarchy and the nation in an act of sacralization, witnessed for the first time by a television audience numbered in millions. For many (myself included), the Coronation became a crucially remembered event for precisely this reason; it was their first experience of television. Not surprisingly it also caught the attention of contemporary sociologists who, predictably, were divided in their interpretations. Did the Coronation reflect the values of British society current at the time, or was the ceremonial a conscious effort to *construct* a consensus whose existence should not be assumed at the outset? Bocock and Thompson (1985: 214–218) outline the contours of this particular controversy. But whatever the sociologists conclude, the Coronation undoubtedly embodied in high-profile form what might be termed the establishment spirit of the 1950s.

It was not to last. The gradual realization that the old order could not be rebuilt and that a majority in the nation remained largely indifferent to what was going on in the churches required a very different type of response. Such indifference was unevenly spread, but there was a growing awareness that the industrialized parts of the country were slipping away from the churches' influence. Wickham's important study of church life in Sheffield was published in 1957. Its message about the effectiveness – or rather ineffectiveness – of the churches in many working-class areas was hardly reassuring (Wickham 1957). Exactly what form this 'slipping away from the churches' influence' took, however, was more problematic. Richard Hoggart's celebrated *The Uses of Literacy*, also published in 1957, offered a more nuanced account (Hoggart [1957] 1984). Practice was unusual except in pockets, but Hoggart affirmed very strongly the working-class hold on what G.K. Chesterton called 'the dumb certainties of existence' or Reinhold Niebuhr's 'primary religion'. Nor should such beliefs be taken lightly, for in coming to their religious institutions at the important moments of life or in times of personal crisis 'they [the working class] are not simply taking out a saving policy; they still believe underneath, in certain ways. At least, middle-aged people do, and here I am thinking chiefly of them' (Hoggart [1957] 1984: 113). Two themes crucial to the first edition of this book were already evident: the mismatch in belief and practice in this country and the generational factor. They are, of course, related.

1960–1979: Radical change

The churches were in for a bumpy ride in the 1960s. The world into which they appeared to fit so well was challenged on every front. Not everything happened at once, but by the end of the decade a profound and probably irreversible revolution in social and, above all, sexual attitudes had taken place. Significant immigration had occurred and expectations of and about the role of women were evolving fast. Traditional, often Christian-based, values were no longer taken for granted; questioned by many, they were abandoned by increasing numbers. Given changes of such magnitude, a loss of confidence on the part of those in the churches was hardly surprising, a collapse that provoked in the first instance considerable confusion. Bit by bit, however, the emphasis changed and confusion gave way to calls for an equally radical reaction. Such sentiments took a variety of forms: intellectual, organizational and liturgical. The underlying motive, however, was the same in every case. All might still be well if the churches could shake off their image of belonging essentially to the past; instead they must present themselves as modern, up to date and, above all, relevant. The emphasis lay on 'breaking down the walls of partition between the sacred and the secular', or more directly still, on removing 'the dead hand of traditionalism' (Welsby 1984: 104).

Relevance was indeed the order of the day. The churches looked to the secular world for a lead and borrowed, in some cases rather uncritically, both its ideas and forms of expression. The desire to be modern, to be in rather than out of step with the world, lay behind a raft of 'reforms' within the Anglican and the free churches: intellectually, in the theological and moral debates of the period (notably the *Honest to God* controversy);[13] organizationally in the rearrangement of parishes, priests and people (in which the commissioning of the explicitly sociological *Paul Report* should not be overlooked);[14] liturgically, in the 'modernizing' of scripture and worship (new translations of the Bible and the steady – some would say relentless – revision of the Prayer Book); and ecumenically in a variety of attempts at greater ecclesiastical collaboration (notably the Anglican–Methodist Unity Scheme). No church involved in this process was going to be quite the same again, for important and lasting shifts were undoubtedly taking place.

It could be argued, however, that such changes pale almost into insignificance compared with the transformation in Roman Catholicism brought about in this decade by the Second Vatican Council (1962–1965), in that Vatican II altered the framework of ecclesiastical life on a global scale for Protestants and Catholics alike, in an enormous variety of ways and in a remarkably short time. It was, Hastings argues, the most important ecclesiastical event of the century, never mind the 1960s. 'It so greatly changed the character of by far the largest communion of Christendom ... that no one has been left unaffected' (Hastings 1986: 525). Not only did the Council alter very tangibly the ordinary practice of parochial life, it set in motion a whole process of discussion and renovation which very quickly assumed a momentum of its own. In Britain, an unprecedented degree of social and geographical mobility for large numbers of Catholics interacted with internal *aggiornamento* brought about by Pope John XXIII to produce far-reaching changes (Hornsby-Smith 1989). *Aggiornamento* (literally the bringing up to date) of the Catholic Church – the more dramatic because it had been longer delayed than in other churches – sums up better than anything else the religious mood of the 1960s.

Since the first edition of this book, three contributions have appeared which put these changes in perspective. The first is Callum Brown's *The Death of Christian Britain* (first published in 2001), which argues that the story of secularization in Britain pivots on what happened in the 1960s. Until then, Brown argues, indices of religion were relatively stable; thereafter decline sets in. The reason for the shift lies in the changing roles of women, which transformed definitively in this decade. No longer were women prepared to sustain traditional models of religion on behalf of everyone else; they had instead lives of their own to live and aspirations to strive for.[15] The second text is Hugh McLeod's *The Religious Crisis of the 1960s* (McLeod 2007), which offers a more rounded account. Meticulously researched, McLeod's analysis looks both at the decade itself and at the ways in which the 1960s as a whole fit into a much longer-term narrative regarding secularization, both in Britain and elsewhere. One point is particularly striking: that is, the noticeably different time periods *within* what McLeod calls the 'long 1960s'. Until 1963, the questioning of the status quo within the churches was relatively cautious; it grew bolder thereafter, until (following 1966) a more conservative reaction asserted itself once again.

The third contribution takes a different view. In a prize-winning essay, Sam Brewitt-Taylor (2013) argues that '[a]t some point some point between 1961 and 1964, the received wisdom about British religiosity abruptly changed'.[16] Almost overnight, educated opinion convinced itself that British society was no longer Christian but secular. Brewitt-Taylor considers the reason for this shift, arguing – innovatively – that the secularization discourses that emerged in the early 1960s originated not from secular sociology as is often assumed but from within British Christianity itself. This new way of thinking was moreover endorsed by senior Christian leaders, anxious to overcome the barriers between church and society. In other words it was a Christian, rather than secular, re-imagining of British religion that accounted for the rapid change in perspective. The statistical decline in church-going – often seen as the trigger for change – came later. Interestingly, an essay by David Martin, first published in *The Listener* in 1968, strongly endorses this view (Martin 1969).

One further factor is worth noting. It concerns the huge expansion of higher education in the 1960s and the place of the economic and social sciences within this. This was the moment when these relatively new disciplines came of age. And given that the 1960s – for whatever reason – exuded a degree of secular confidence hitherto unknown, it was hardly surprising that the social sciences followed suit. The future, it was assumed, would be secular – an attitude with far-reaching consequences.[17] It was, moreover, an understandable assumption. Standards of living were rising fast and, it seemed, would continue to do so. But, like all good things (or at least things that were good for some), the 1960s came to an end. Within a few short years, the oil crisis was dominating the world scene. The economic situation in Britain wavered accordingly: the currency was in difficulties, inflation was rising and unemployment began to climb. From 1969, moreover, the troubles in Northern Ireland – within which the religious factor has an undoubted significance – were becoming depressingly prominent. Above all, there was a manifest lack of political will about how to resolve these difficulties.

The religious constituency reacted variously. While changes set in motion in the 1960s continued to run their course, at least some both within and beyond the churches were beginning to think differently. More rather than less distinctive forms of religious life were making their presence felt. New religious movements epitomized this trend. Such movements are infinitely variable in type but are in the main exclusivist, meaning that they stand 'in some degree of protest against the dominant traditions of society' (Wilson 1990: 1). A rather similar stance could be found in the 'house church' movement, reflecting a comparable demand among Christians (usually evangelicals) for a more conscious commitment to religious life (Walker 1985). A third, and in the long term much more significant shift, concerned the growing number of other-faith communities in Britain. By this stage, it was increasingly clear that these communities were not only becoming a permanent feature of British society, but were anxious to retain their own forms of religious expression. Pressures to adapt to British ways of behaving, not least the markedly understated religiousness of the host population, were strongly resisted.

Each of these phenomena will be documented in detail in the following chapters, but taken together they evoke an important shift in emphasis. Over the top of widespread indifference a gradual but relentless change in religious activity was taking place: it can be summarized as a shift from contracting out to contracting in across many forms of religious life – a theme to be developed in Part III.

1979–1997: Reacting to Conservatism

The evident lack of political will regarding the multiple problems of the 1970s came to an abrupt end in 1979, the date which marks Margaret Thatcher's arrival as Prime Minister. No one, not even her worst enemies, could call Mrs Thatcher indecisive. Setting about her task with legendary determination, she introduced a series of political and economic initiatives with the specific aim of reversing what she perceived as Britain's calamitous national decline. The essence of Mrs Thatcher's policies has already been introduced and need not be repeated here, except to emphasize once again her commitment to the market as the key to economic growth. It is also important to recall that the Labour Party had more or less collapsed in terms of effective opposition, leaving a potentially dangerous void in political life. Who in this situation could speak on behalf of those who were caught at the sharp end of these far-reaching economic and social transformations, and on what authority?

Into this situation stepped the churches, specifically the Church of England, which in 1985 produced *Faith in the City*, the report of the Archbishop of Canterbury's Commission on Urban Priority Areas (*Faith in the City* 1985). Much has been written about this document,[18] which has become a touchstone for debate about the churches' role in welfare, as both advocate and provider – a topic to be developed in due course. The point to be made in this chapter is relatively specific and concerns, once again, the relationship between the church and its context. It recognizes in particular the capacities of an established church to defend those parts of society, notably urban priority areas, which were perceived as victims of economic change. Rubbished even before publication as 'pure Marxist theology', *Faith in the City* made its mark, reminding the nation as a whole that it could not simply forget the areas of society which were paying the price for economic regeneration. The state, the Report declared, was as responsible for the inner cities of Britain as it was for its more leafy suburbs.

That was one interpretation of the facts. Unsurprisingly Mrs. Thatcher thought otherwise, drawing at least in part on her Methodist upbringing (Filby 2015). Self-improvement, she argued, was the responsibility of the individual, not of the state – a view strongly supported by a close friend, the then Chief Rabbi, Immanuel Jakobovits.[19] A fuller and even more explicit articulation of Mrs Thatcher's own position can be found in her address to the General Assembly of the Church of Scotland in May 1988. Known colloquially as the 'Sermon on the Mound' this was effectively a theological justification of the market and laid great emphasis on the significance of individual choices. The assembled company – once again the representatives of a parochially organized national church – was not on the whole impressed. The moderator of the Church of Scotland responded to Mrs Thatcher's address by handing her recent reports from the churches on poverty, housing and a fair social benefit system. The gesture was interpreted as an implied rebuke.

An important point is already becoming clear: that there is no necessary connection between Christian theology as such and its political interpretation. At the same time, there is considerable evidence for the continuing role of the historic churches as the spokespersons for the less advantaged. In a sense, moreover, this connection captures an earlier relationship between the Conservative Party and the Church of England – in that both were seen as representatives of 'one nation'. One-nation Conservatism, an essentially Victorian idea, has ebbed and flowed in popularity within the Conservative Party.[20] It is favoured by those who advocate a non-ideological approach to politics and who prefer consensus to confrontation; it aims to be inclusive rather than exclusive. This was the preferred line of thought in the early post-war decades and precisely for this reason became a scapegoat for the economic ills of the 1970s. As Mrs Thatcher so forcefully argued, Keynesian economics, and the dependency culture associated with it, were not the solution, but the root of the problem. It followed that a return to the values of individualism was the only answer.

Her view prevailed. What became the New Right dominated British politics for the best part of 20 years, within which the Thatcher decade became a benchmark – one moreover which drew Britain away from Europe and towards the United States. Nothing comparable to Thatcherism occurred in continental Europe until at least a decade later; conversely Mrs Thatcher's empathy with both the person and the politics of Ronald Reagan is well known. The special relationship became noticeably stronger in this period.

In terms of religious life, the final decade of the twentieth century is significant for two further reasons. The first was the fall of the Berlin Wall in November 1989. The detail of this pivotal episode in European, indeed global, affairs lies beyond the limits of this chapter, except to note that the collapse of the Soviet Union implied – amongst many other things – the collapse of communism, an aggressively secular ideology. This had not been anticipated and set in train a re-alignment of the global order. The second is captured by the episode known as the Rushdie controversy, an event – or rather a whole series of events – which marks a visible shift in the focus of public debate. The full story will be developed in Part IV but an initial point is immediately clear: the furore surrounding the *The Satanic Verses* (first published in 1988) acted as a powerful catalyst provoking renewed attention to religion. The explanation lies not so much in the growing minorities of modern Britain, which were now in their third or fourth generation, but in the ways in which they were perceived. Constituencies that were initially identified in terms of race or ethnicity were increasingly labelled in terms of religion. The implications were multiple: for the communities themselves, for the nature of public discussion, for politicians and policy-makers, and for social science.

1997–2010: Understanding New Labour

Electorally the shift to New Labour was decisive, but there was no going back to pre-Thatcherite days; the country as well as the Labour Party had changed definitively. In terms of style, moreover, there is a recognizable affinity between Mrs Thatcher and Tony Blair – both enjoyed a certain charisma that translated easily into a 'presidential' way of doing politics. And both were motivated at least in part by Christian principles. Mrs Thatcher drew on her Methodist upbringing to hone her ideas on individualism; Tony Blair found inspiration in Christian Socialism. His religious predilections were well known at the time of his election, but were seldom articulated during his time as Prime Minister. Interestingly, they have become noticeably more prominent since retirement, and include his conversion to Catholicism.

That said many of the policies that dominated the Blair years have – implicitly or explicitly – a religious dimension. These include his persistent and largely successful attention to Northern Ireland, culminating in the Good Friday Agreement in 1998 (see Chapter 5), as well as his much more ambiguous forays into the Middle East (see below). Regarding the central theme of this section, however – that is, the changing emphases in the religious life of Britain more generally – it is helpful to look at two rather different episodes, neither of which is related to policy. The first was totally unexpected and happened within a few months of the 1997 election. At the end of August, Princess Diana (the ex-wife of the heir to the throne) was killed in car crash in Paris, provoking an outpouring of grief on a scale and in a manner hitherto unknown in Britain.

The episode has already been evoked as evidence of vicarious religion (see pp. 6–7). But quite apart from this, it revealed a significant shift: a rather different way of being religious which was markedly more expressive than had previously been the case. Above all, it was spontaneous. The response to the news was immediate and involved a complex mix of private emotion and public spectacle as people came together to express their feelings. Symbols, Christian and other, were readily juxtaposed in improvised rituals which more often than not took place in or near traditional religious buildings. In retrospect, the episode changed very little in terms of organized religious activity. It revealed, however, an enormous amount about the ways in which British people wished to express themselves when faced with disaster or crisis, and at every level of society. The change since the immediate post-war period was profound. The Prime Minister's description of Princess Diana as 'The People's Princess' caught the moment nicely. The Royal Family, conversely, were badly wrong-footed in their formal, and seemingly rather cold, approach both to the event as such and to the public's reaction.

The second episode occurred towards the end of Blair's term as Prime Minister. This was the long-expected death of Pope John Paul II in April 2005. John Paul II was not only a remarkable pope, but a global figure in every sense of the term: one of the best known individuals in the modern world. He was instantly recognized wherever he went and routinely followed by the world's press. No one was surprised therefore when the world turned towards Rome as it became clear that the Pope was dying. Few people, however, anticipated the scale of the reaction that followed, as almost every country suspended 'normal' activities in order to mark the occasion. The strange juxtaposition of events in Britain in the first week of April is instructive in this respect. Indeed the activities suspended in this case were hardly normal in that they included the marriage of Prince Charles to Camilla Parker-Bowles.[21] Remarkably, the ceremony was simply postponed in order that Prince Charles himself, Tony Blair (as Prime Minister) and Rowan Williams (as Archbishop of Canterbury) should attend the funeral. But no Prime Minister, or Archbishop of Canterbury, or heir to the throne had ever been to a papal funeral before, much less prioritized it over a royal wedding – a gesture that symbolized the wholly different alignments that were beginning to emerge in terms of global religion. Politicians, it was clear, were obliged to respond accordingly. The mourners on this occasion included four American presidents.

Entirely different was the devastating attack on the Twin Towers in New York in September 2001; an event which has become known as 9/11. This, once again, was a pivotal moment in the re-ordering of the modern world that cannot be discussed in detail. Both the event itself and its aftermath have, however, been so far-reaching that they have altered the entire context within which we think about religion. In global terms, the attack on the Twin Towers was a major factor in the 'war on terror', strengthening Britain's relationship with the United States, but at the same time damaging Blair's reputation. His controversial interventions in Afghanistan and in Iraq are clearly connected to this. At the same time, the perception of Muslims has shifted accordingly both in Britain as elsewhere. Rightly or wrongly, host populations have become much more wary of minorities, which are increasingly constructed in religious terms. The frequently negative consequences can be seen on a daily basis.

At this stage, therefore, something new is beginning to emerge. Britain remains a Christian country in terms of its culture and history. Nothing will alter that. Significant sections of the population are, however, becoming not only more secular but noticeably more critical of religion. An interesting indicator of a subtle but persistent adjustment in this respect can be found in the ways that different groups of people react to religious controversy. In the 1980s, the discussion was largely about socio-economic issues and found its focus in the negative consequences of an over-rigorous application of monetarist policies. The 'attack' was directed at the New Right, some of whom reacted sharply to what was considered an unwarranted intrusion by churches and church people in political affairs. Those on the political left, though largely side-lined from political activity, were unlikely to object. A generation or so later, things are different. Religious controversy continues but for different reasons. In the main it concerns the competing rights of secular and religious constituencies, recognizing that the latter are not only much more varied, but are more ready to press their claims in public as well as private life. Exactly how will become clear in Part IV, but the crucial point can be made already: the ruffled feathers are found this time amongst increasingly self-conscious secularists, often but by no means only on the political left. An important reason for this shift lies in a point already made: it concerns the evolving constructions of the minorities currently present in Britain. Those whose political predilections led them to defend minority groups disadvantaged by racial or ethnic factors are far less likely to defend the religious aspirations of the self-same people. Why not is an interesting question.

Moving forwards

What can be said of the present period? The detail will become clear as the narrative unfolds. The inherent complexity can however be captured in an interesting episode that took place in London in the autumn of 2011. 'Occupy London' is an activist movement concerned about economic inequalities, notably corporate greed. Thwarted in their original plan to camp outside the Stock Exchange, the focal point for the 2011 protest became St Paul's Cathedral. The Dean and Chapter were divided in their reactions: should they or should they not sympathize with the protestors, and more immediately, should they or should they not close the Cathedral on health and safety grounds? The eventual decision to close the building (for the first time since 1945) provoked public consternation: yet another example of vicarious religion. A number of resignations from the Cathedral Chapter followed, albeit for different reasons. Equally pertinent, however, were the responses of the protestors. The religiously literate among them saw an opportunity. 'What would Jesus do?' was prominently displayed on tents and banners in the vicinity and rapidly relayed around the world. What indeed?[22]

Notes

1   More details about the European Values Study can be found at http://www.europe-anvaluesstudy.eu/evs/about-evs/ (accessed 5 August 2014). See also the discussion in Chapter 3.
2   For more details about the 2011 Census and its coverage of religion, see Chapter 3.
3   As are Germany and Scandinavia. Indeed on some readings it is the French Enlightenment which is not only disproportionately influential, but atypical, even in Europe.
4   The phrase 'a special relationship', meaning a particular bond between the United Kingdom and the United States, was coined by Winston Churchill in a speech delivered in 1946. The occasion was his 'Sinews of Peace Address' in Fulton, Missouri.
5   See the report published by Theos (2013a), which argues against the exaggerated claims of some commentators regarding the possibility of a New Christian Right in Britain. For a start, there are insufficient evangelicals on this side of the Atlantic to make a political impact.
6   The label 'New Labour' dates from a conference slogan first used by the Labour Party in 1994.
7   The UK Census is the most obvious source of information in this respect. In 2011, the median age of the population in England and Wales was 39. In 1911, it was 25. The percentage of the population aged 65 and over was the highest seen in any census at 16.4 per cent, that is one in six people in the population was 65 and over. There were 430 000 residents aged 90 and over in 2011 compared with 340 000 in 2001 and 13 000 in 1911. For more information, see http://www.ons.gov.uk/ons/dcp171776_258607.pdf (accessed 5 August 2014).

8   It is equally important to note the economic motives for delaying marriage; there are multiple reasons for this change.

9   Local Government Act 1988, Section 28, see http://www.legislation.gov.uk/ ukpga/1988/9/contents for the full text (accessed 5 August 2014).

10 See, for example, *The Guardian*, 1 July 2009, http://www.guardian.co.uk/ politics/2009/jul/02/david-cameron-gay-pride-apology (accessed February 25 2013).

11 The position of the churches and religious professionals is protected by the Act. For more information, see the relevant pages of the Equality and Human Rights Commission website: http://www.equalityhumanrights.com/your-rights/equal-rights/sexual-orientation/marriage-same-sex-couples-act-2013-guidance (accessed 19 August 2014). There is separate legislation for Scotland: the Marriage and Civil Partnership (Scotland) Bill was passed in February 2014 and contains similar protection for the churches.

12 See, for example, the discussion of this issue in Westminster Faith Debates, 18 April 2013: http://www.religionandsociety.org.uk/faith_debates-2013/do_christians_ oppose_gay_marriage (accessed 5 August 2014). See also Woodhead with Winter (2013) and Woodhead (2014a).

13 *Bishop John Robinson's Honest to God* was published in 1963. Its questioning of traditional Christian teaching provoked a storm of controversy.

14 This was the work of Leslie Paul. It was a comprehensive report on 'The Deployment and Payment of Clergy' (Paul 1964). For more details, see Hastings 1986: 535ff.

15 Brown's thesis regarding the changing role of women as the key to religious change is controversial. In my view, it tells the truth, but not the whole truth (Davie 2013). A revised edition of *The Death of Christian Britain* was published in 2009, in which Brown responds to a number of his critics.

16 This essay is based on an Oxford DPhil. See Brewitt-Taylor (2012). A book will emerge in due course.

17 This point will be raised again in Chapter 11; it has become increasingly important given the growing prominence of religion in the modern world order.

18 An interesting development in this respect can be found in subsequent 'witness seminars', which look at *Faith in the City* with hindsight. See, for example, http://www.timeshighereducation.co.uk/story.asp?storyCode=204583&section code=26. See also the initiative known as Together for the Common Good: togetherforthecommongood.co.uk.Both websites accessed 1 August 2014.

19 Arguing thus, Lord Jacobovits controversially recalled the capacities of individual Jewish immigrants to work their way out of poverty; he expected those more recently arrived to do the same regardless of their background – a view that directly challenged *Faith in the City*, which recognized the plight of ethnic minorities as a whole.

20 The phrase 'One-nation Tory' is associated with Benjamin Disraeli and dates from the mid-nineteenth century. It emphasizes the reciprocal bonds between different members of society.

21 Camilla Parker-Bowles was a divorcée. For this reason, the marriage itself was a secular ceremony, but was followed by a blessing in St George's Chapel in Windsor.

22 A fascinating account of Christian involvement in the St Paul's Occupy movement can be found in Winter (2013).

3
Facts and Figures

Introduction

The aims of this chapter are straightforward. First and foremost it provides a basis for operations – in other words sufficient factual information about the religious constituencies in this country to permit an informed discussion about faith and the issues that this raises. The second aim follows from this – that is to highlight the changes that have taken place since the 1990s, taking care to set these in a longer term perspective. Both of these goals depend on adequate sources, a remark which leads immediately to an important reflection: the availability of material, including statistical data, has increased hugely in recent decades. Asking why this is so constitutes an important part of the discussion.

The first edition of *Religion in Britain* drew heavily on the data produced by Christian Research and its predecessor Marc Europe. This work has continued, though its organizational base has altered.[1] Particularly noteworthy are the seven editions of *Religious Trends*, published between 1998 and 2008, all of which were compiled and edited by Brierley.[2] A selection of the material contained in these publications is now available via a relatively new and very useful resource: an online collection of data known as 'British Religion in Numbers' (BRIN), an initiative which grew out of the Religion and Society Programme.[3] Frequently updated, this website provides a huge amount of information about religion in Britain, and includes some helpful professional commentaries. Amongst many other things are selections of data from the 2001 and 2011 Censuses. The fact that a question on religion was included in the 2001 Census (and was continued in 2011) is, once again,

Religion in Britain: A Persistent Paradox, Second Edition. Grace Davie.
© 2015 Grace Davie. Published 2015 by John Wiley & Sons, Ltd.

of significance in itself. The possibility of detailed comparisons between 2001 and 2011 is particularly helpful.

With this in mind, this chapter will be structured as follows. It will start with an overview of the current situation, drawing mainly on the 2001 and 2011 British Censuses and noting the changes that occurred in the intervening decade. It will continue with a more detailed consideration of the dominant religious constituencies in this country, updating and extending the pen portraits provided in the 1994 edition. The final section (effectively a postscript) will introduce a different perspective. It will consider the portrayals of religion in the media, underlining the rather different profiles that all too often dominate the headlines. An inevitable question follows from this: what can be done to correct some of the worst distortions that are discovered in this field?

A note regarding coverage completes this introduction. More detail about Scotland, Wales and Northern Ireland can be found in Chapter 5. Statistics about belief will be introduced in Chapter 4 as a preliminary to the discussion about 'believing without belonging'. At the same time this introduces the rather more amorphous category known as the 'spiritual'. The size and characteristics of the secular constituency are part and parcel of the same discussion, and will be developed in Chapter 9.

Religion in the Census: 2001 and 2011

What might be termed the 'story' of the religious question in the 2001 British Census has been admirably told by Francis (2003) and Weller (2004). It is important to reflect upon this narrative. In itself the decision to include such a question reveals a growing awareness that accurate religious statistics are significant for a wide variety of people, both inside and outside the churches, with the strong implication that religion is indeed a public matter about which we need precise information. This is all the more necessary in a religiously diverse society. The latter point is displayed in the following. Among those campaigning most vociferously for a question about religion in the Census were individuals from the other-faith communities in this country, notably the Muslims. As we shall see, the Muslim community in Britain is diverse in terms of ethnicity and nationality. It follows that statistics based on either of these indicators disperse an important religious identity and downplay for Muslims the most significant factor in their lives: their faith. British Muslims want to be known as Muslims in public as well as private life, in order that provision for their needs is met on these terms. Appropriate policies should be worked out on a secure statistical base not on estimates or extrapolations from other variables.

What then did the Census set out to do and what can it tell us about the religious profile of this country? The Census uses 'self-identification' as a measure of religiousness. In terms of the factors introduced in Chapter 1, this is a 'soft' rather than 'hard' indicator of religious attachment and needs to be interpreted accordingly. In England and Wales, individuals were asked: 'What is your religion?' They were not asked about religious practice or about religious belief.[4] In parenthesis it is important to note that the question in Scotland was worded differently and yielded rather different results.[5] In both cases, however, a profile of religious attachment emerges which can be correlated with a wide variety of other variables (age, gender, ethnicity, nationality and economic activity). It is also possible to discern geographical patterns (including marked regional differences). Third the data can be accessed at a variety of 'levels' (national, regional and local – right down to output area level).[6]

Much has been written about the profiles of religion that emerged from the 2001 Census. Most striking in this respect was the unexpectedly large number of individuals who self-identified as Christians (72%) – an apparent vindication for those who argued for the significance of passive as well as more active forms of religious identity. Such ideas, and the questions that they raise, will be pursued in detail in Chapter 4. Outline figures from the 2011 Census can be found in two summary documents published by the Office for National Statistics, which offer useful comparisons with the earlier enquiry (ONS 2012, 2013). Immediately apparent is the decline in 'Christian' self-identification, which fell from 72 per cent to 59 per cent – a shift of some significance (see Figure 3.1). Almost as striking is the growth in the percentage of people indicating that they have 'no religion'; this rose from 15 per cent to 25 per cent, provoking considerable public discussion. How should this shift be interpreted? Did it denote a significant generational mutation? Equally clear is the evident, but rather more modest growth in the other-faith communities. The combination encourages an understanding of British society which echoes the discussion in previous chapters. A historically Christian country is evolving fast. Significant sections of the population now think of themselves as secular rather than religious, and religion as such is increasingly diverse.

Two further figures provide more detail concerning the breakdown of religious affiliation in 2011. The first (Figure 3.2) fills in the overall picture and includes the relatively small number of people who declined to answer the question about religion.[7] The second gives more detail on the constituencies covered by the rubric 'minority religious groups' (Figure 3.3). Among the latter, the Muslims are by far the largest. Each of these groups will be described in more detail in the following section. At this stage the most important point to note is the relatively small size of this constituency in the overall picture: taken together the other-faith communities amount to less than 10 per cent of the population as a whole, bearing in mind that the proportions vary considerably in different parts of the country.

A fourth figure (Figure 3.4) deals with at least some of the geographical differences, noting that the statistics presented here mask important internal variations: regions of this size are rarely homogeneous. That said some interesting patterns emerge. London, for example, is distinctive. Unsurprisingly it is the most religiously diverse part of the country, containing the largest

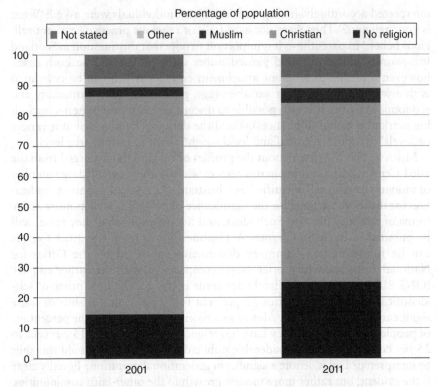

Figure 3.1   Change in religious affiliation, 2001–2011, England and Wales.
Source: Census 2011, Office for National Statistics licensed under the Open Government Licence v.2.0.

proportion of people who self-identify as Jews, Sikhs, Muslims, Hindus and Buddhists. Rather less predictably London has relatively modest numbers of people who declare that they have no religion. Indeed the case of London as a whole requires very careful thought: its religious profile is noticeably different from anywhere else, a fact that becomes even clearer when more detailed information is introduced (see below).

The north east and north west are the regions with the highest proportion of Christians overall, in contrast to Wales, which has the highest proportion of people reporting no religion. Neither is self-evident. The north east and north west contain a variety of post-industrial cities – locations considered particularly stony ground for religion in the post-war period. Even more strikingly, the national variations revealed in the 1994 edition of this book (drawing on information from Brierley and Hiscock 1993: 251) indicated the relative religiousness of Wales (indeed of the Celtic countries as a whole),

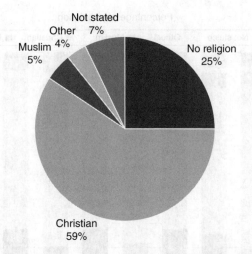

Figure 3.2 Religious affiliation, England and Wales, 2011.
Source: Census 2011, Office for National Statistics licensed under the Open Government Licence v.2.0.

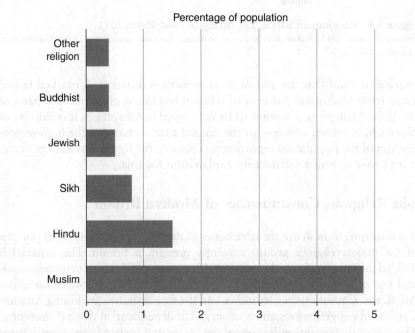

Figure 3.3 Minority religious groups, England and Wales, 2011.
Source: Census 2011, Office for National Statistics licensed under the Open Government Licence v.2.0.

Percentage of population

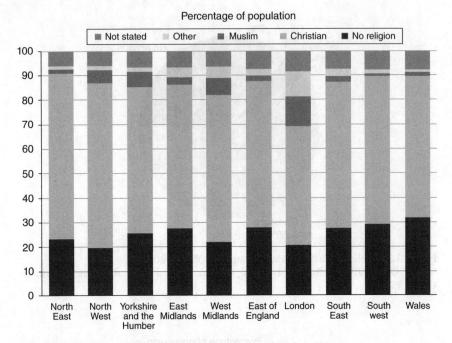

Figure 3.4 Religious affiliation, English regions and Wales, 2011.
Source: Census 2011, Office for National Statistics licensed under the Open Government Licence v.2.0.

bearing in mind that the unit of measurement is different. A marked falling away from traditional patterns of religion has taken place in these parts of the United Kingdom – a point to be developed in Chapter 5. It is the city of Norwich, however, which – for the second time – recorded the highest proportion of the population reporting no religion; the figure was 42.5 per cent. It isn't easy to find a satisfactory explanation for this.

The Religious Constituencies of Modern Britain

It is now time to flesh out the bare bones of these statistics with a brief portrait of the major religious groups currently present in Britain. The material is divided into two sections: the considerable variety of Christian denominations, and the other-faith communities. The first will include information about Anglicans, Catholics, the Orthodox and the free churches (including African-Caribbean congregations and a variety of 'independent' and 'new' churches). The second section will cover the principal other-faith populations (Jews, Sikhs, Muslims, Hindus and Buddhists). As was the case in the first edition, the portraits themselves are little more than outline sketches, which can be filled in with reference to a variety of complementary sources. They

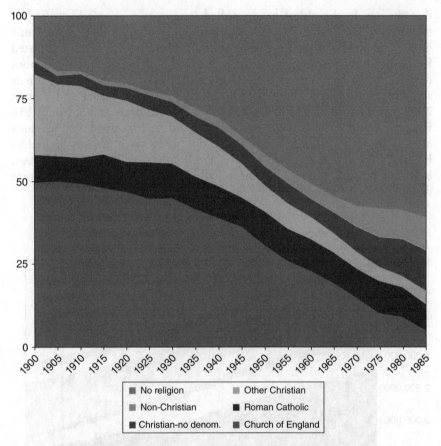

Figure 3.5 Religious affiliation by year of birth (five-year cohorts).
Source: British Social Attitudes surveys 1983–2011, pooled. Chart created by Siobhan McAndrew, British Religion in Numbers (http://www.brin.ac.uk/figures/). Creative Commons Attribution-Share Alike 2.0 England and Wales (CC BY-SA 2.0 UK).

should, moreover, be read as much in terms of their commonalities as their differences – that is with a particular eye to the cross-cutting themes which will be drawn together in a short conclusion. Important questions emerge from this discussion. Are the principal lines of demarcation beginning to lie across rather than between the various denominations – indeed the faith communities more generally? And how might these details fit with the factors set out in Chapter 1?

The portraits are prefaced by three figures, essentially pictorial representations of the changes that are taking place in the religious life of this country. Figure 3.5 depicts the shifts in religious affiliation by year of birth. It is easy to see that the Church of England has been disproportionately affected by this change. In the oldest group polled, one in two people identified as members of the Church of England; among the youngest that figure is one in 20. The middle ground is clearly shifting. These figures are not adjusted for gender, but a growing literature in this field both establishes the preponderance of women in every age category and seeks to explain why this is so (Walter and Davie 1998; Woodhead 2007; Aune, Sharma and Vincett 2008; Trzebiatowska and Bruce 2012; Voas, McAndrew and Storm 2013). Figures 3.6 and 3.7 have a different timeline and are concerned with religious attendance rather than religious affiliation. (They are moreover limited to England.) The decline is equally evident here, but the overall 'shape' is different. It is also possible to see adjustments, albeit small ones, between different denominations and faith communities.

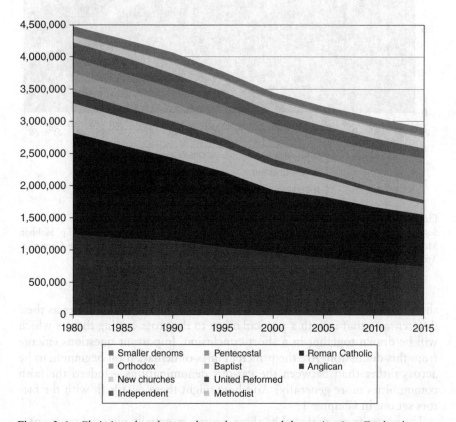

Figure 3.6   Christian church attendance by year and denomination, England.
Source: Peter Brierley 2014. *UK Church Statistics No 2, 2010–2020*, Tonbridge: ADBC Publishers.

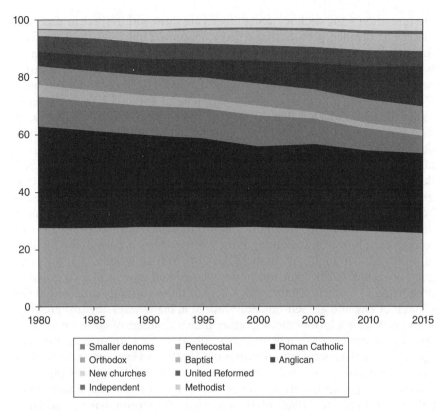

Figure 3.7 Christian church attendance by year and denomination, England (% of total).
Source: Peter Brierley 2014. *UK Church Statistics No 2, 2010–2020*, Tonbridge: ADBC Publishers.

Varieties of Christianity

Anglicans   In terms of the United Kingdom, the term 'Anglican' includes not only the Church of England but the Church in Wales, the Episcopal Church of Scotland and the Church of Ireland. Technically speaking the tiny Free Church of England, the Protestant Episcopal Reformed Church of England and one or two other similar bodies should also be mentioned if only in passing. The following section will look primarily at the Church of England; the non-English Anglican communities in the United Kingdom will be covered in Chapter 5.

Statistically there can be little doubt about the trends; they go downward.[8] Electoral roll figures, communicant numbers, baptisms per live births, confirmations, the proportion of marriages taking place in church and, up to a point, funerals tell a similar story. The overall figures need, however, careful interpretation – the decline occurs at varying rates with respect to time and place. The detailed profiles that emerge, moreover, quite clearly depend on the specific indicators selected. Figures for baptism, for example, an indicator which gives at least some idea of Anglican penetration into society at large, reveal a downward curve from 1950 on.[9] Baptisms per thousand births were 672 in 1950 (up a little since 1940), dropping to 466 in 1970. By the early 1980s the figure was less that 40 per cent and continued to fall thereafter: to 27.5 per cent in 1990, and 12 per cent in 2011.[10] Anglican confirmations demonstrate a rather different pattern. In the post-war period, they rose fairly steadily until 1960 but fell sharply thereafter. Between 1960 and 1982 the number of confirmations taking place each year dropped from 191 000 to 84 500, a fall of more than 50 per cent. There is little sign of this trend being reversed.[11] A rather similar shape of post-war rise and subsequent decline can be found for the number of ordinations (Hastings 1986: 535). In recent years, however, something rather different has occurred: the number of ordinands per annum is climbing back up, bearing in mind that the category 'ordinand' has become much more varied and now includes a growing proportion of women. Significantly many of those currently ordained in the Church of England are self-funded.[12] Indeed in many ways, the real problem in this respect is a lack of money, rather than a shortage of vocations.

Taking these statistics together, it is important to acknowledge the very sharp decline that occurred following the 1960s. As Hastings declares: 'It is not exaggerated to conclude that between 1960 and 1985 the Church of England as a going concern was effectively reduced to not much more than half its previous size' (1986: 603). Since then, the erosion has by and large continued, though less abruptly than before (Brierley 2011). The situation however is serious and becoming more so – an awareness that lies behind the Church Growth Research Programme initiated in 2012 (see note 8). That said three points are worth noting. First the effect of decline is uneven in the sense that some parts of the Church of England are noticeably more vulnerable than others. Second at least some of the trends noted above are the result of church policy rather than, or at least in addition to, changes in social practice. And third, in some parts of the country unexpected things have happened. Each of these points will be taken in turn.

In the first edition of this book, I evoked the diversity within the Church of England by quoting from a bishop's letter in a diocesan news-sheet. It was published in 1992 but is equally true of today. Indeed the range of possibilities is currently even wider – a fact that will become clear in Part III. The letter described – through the eyes of a visiting bishop – the liturgical unpredictability of modern Anglicanism:

> We come across every rite authorised for use in the Church of England, and
> occasionally liturgies which seem to have been borrowed from other sources

or simply originated in the mind of the incumbent; we move from places wreathed in incense to those in which the unwary production of a stole causes a sharp intake of breath; we lead services in which the congregational response barely amounts to a background murmur, and those in which there are so many participants it is difficult to find something to do; we change musical key from decorous Anglican chant to deafening enthusiastic chorus; we bellow to a handful of 20 scattered throughout a mini-cathedral, and we whisper through technological devices concealed in our garments to sardine-packed hundreds; we find ourselves in totally impracticable medieval buildings of great beauty, and in modern liturgically-efficient warehouses; we sing from more hymn books and hear the Bible read from more translations than Wesley or Wycliffe ever dreamed of; at the Peace we may give the congregation the most imperceptible half-smile before moving swiftly to the safety of the sanctuary, or we may be expected to greet every member of the congregation like a long-lost relative. (Davie 1994: 54)

At the same time the quotation revealed the disparities of Anglican attendance. The overall trends may have been downwards but certain parishes were undoubtedly flourishing; notably – in terms of numbers (and there are plenty of alternative criteria) – the eclectic parishes of suburbia, which gathered the like-minded, usually middle-class evangelicals, from a moderately large and well-populated geographical area. In the early 1990s, a second and rather different constituency was also beginning to emerge, a trend which has accelerated since. Cathedrals are attracting attention in a wide variety of ways: numbers are growing amongst worshippers, pilgrims, tourists and visitors. Commentators were slower to notice this trend but it is now increasingly remarked on (it is for example a thread in the Church Growth Research Programme). Understanding why these seemingly very different elements in the Church of England continue to prosper in twenty-first century Britain will constitute an important theme in this book.

The question of baptism is related. As indicated in Chapter 1, this rite is changing in nature as it becomes increasingly a sign of initiation into a voluntary community rather than a mark of Englishness. What might be termed 'contracting in' is beginning to replace 'contracting out'. The shift, moreover, is encouraged in a significant number of parishes – those which have strict criteria for baptism, and which limit availability to the children of regular churchgoers. Not everyone, however, has followed suit. Indeed the point to grasp is that there is huge variation in baptism policies across the country leading to an understandable confusion. Infant baptism can be encouraged and discouraged in neighbouring churches. Paradoxically, it tends to be the large, flourishing, usually evangelical parishes which restrict baptism to the children of churchgoers, to the disadvantage of 'parishioners' in the strict sense of the term. Precisely those congregations which produce disproportionate amounts of money and personnel for the Church may – at one and the same time – depress the figures for infant baptism in that area, meaning that the statistics must be interpreted with care.

That some parts of the Church of England were doing better than others was already clear in 1994. I did not, however, anticipate the significance of London in this story; nor, as far as I know, did anyone else. The overall profile of religion in London has already been identified (p. 43–4). It is clearly distinctive and becomes more so once the Anglican data has been added. These can be found in two reports (Jackson and Piggott 2003, 2011; see also Wolffe and Jackson 2012). The first report, entitled *A Capital Idea* and published in 2003, attempted to describe and explain the growth that has taken place in the Anglican Diocese of London since the early 1990s. The evidence is striking: in 1977, the electoral roll of the Diocese stood at 77 000; by 1990 it had fallen to 45 000; but by 2010 it had returned to the 1977 level. Why was this so? The second report, *Another Capital Idea* published in 2011, repeats the exercise and nuances the earlier findings. By this stage, attendance measures were falling slightly, but the membership measure continued to grow. Both, it is clear, need careful interpretation. More detail on the situation in London will be provided in Part II (pp. 107–09). The principal point to note here is that the unexpected can and does happen and not always in the places where it seemed most likely.

All that said, active Anglicans remain a tiny minority in the population as a whole. How small depends on the unit of measurement, but regular attendance hovers currently around the one million mark.[13] The Church of England remains, however, a parish church giving it a unique foothold in English society. The notion of a national church with comprehensive coverage makes more sense if the passive as well as active presence of Anglicanism is taken into account – a situation that is changing fast (see Figure 3.5). A 2013 poll suggests, however, that a third of the population continues to identify as Anglicans and their allegiance, though nominal, is not without meaning. Drawing on these data, Linda Woodhead describes the various sub-groups that emerge within Anglicanism and concludes by defending this identity with some vehemence:

> Many people write off the Church of England. But despite decline, Anglicans still make up a third of the population of Great Britain. Adherents of all the other faiths put together make up another third, and people who say they have 'no religion' the remainder. And the Anglicans are not merely nominal. They believe, they practise, and – because they still identify as Anglican even though there is no longer any social pressure to do so – they belong. There is every reason to take them more seriously. (Woodhead 2013a)

There is, finally, the question of establishment itself, which cannot be ignored in even the shortest discussion of the Church of England. Clearly the nature of establishment has altered considerably in the post-war period, but the essential link remains intact. It will be discussed in Chapter 5. The statistical framework constitutes an important element in the debate. The marked decline in Anglican activity militates against the privileged position of this church; the relatively large number of nominal members counteracts this argument at least in the short term. Whatever the case, a persistent (though diminishing) penumbra remains the distinguishing feature of the Church of England. And if baptism has declined markedly in popularity, it is still relatively rare for an English person to die without some form of religious ceremony.[14] At the end of their lives if not before, the Church of England will take responsibility for those who are not looked after by anyone else, a demanding, difficult and time-consuming ministry much of which takes place in crematoria. 'Contracting in' may well be edging into the organization of baptisms; so far the same phenomenon is less developed in the administration of funerals.

Catholics In the late twentieth century, we knew more sociologically about the Catholics in Britain (or at least in parts of Britain) than we did about almost any other religious denomination. This was very largely due to the work of Michael Hornsby-Smith, who established a solid body of empirical evidence concerning the Catholics in England and Wales. This material can be found in an impressive series of publications (a number of which have been re-issued), which should be consulted for a detailed picture of this community (see in particular Hornsby-Smith 1999, 2008 and 2009). The data reproduced here are selective.

The essence of Hornsby-Smith's thesis concerning post-war Catholicism in England and Wales is contained in the following extract:

> In sum, the evidence reviewed in this book points clearly to the conclusion that the transformations which have taken place in English Catholicism over the past three to four decades can best be interpreted as a process of dissolution of the boundaries which once defended a distinctive Catholic sub-culture from contamination in a basically secular society. It is too simplistic to regard such a process as one of decline. Rather it indicates that far-reaching changes have taken place in the relationships between the Church and British society since the Second World War. These have necessarily entailed radical changes in the nature of Catholic identity in England and Wales today. (Hornsby-Smith 1987: 214)

In that it looks primarily at the relationship between the Catholic community and the wider society, and attempts to assess the impact of changes in each of these upon the other, Hornsby-Smith's thesis fits well within the argument presented here.

The relevant data were obtained from a series of enquiries which took place in the middle and late 1970s and the early 1980s. The 'social portrait' that Hornsby-Smith depicts dates, therefore, from the third post-war decade.

As a community, Catholics emerged as relatively young and working class; tendencies which were also reflected in the lower home-ownership levels and higher than average Labour voting. Of the Catholics sampled, 25 per cent were first-generation immigrants, six times the proportion of the rest of the population. Around 40 per cent of the sample attended church weekly compared to 8 per cent of non-Catholics. Among the attenders there were more women than men; the age factor (more older people than young) was also significant. Social class differences were discernible, with professional and managerial Catholics attending church more often than manual workers. In the post-war period, there had been considerable geographical and social mobility – notably a persistent migration away from the north and west towards the south and east; away, that is, from the old, traditional, working-class and largely Irish parishes into the new suburban estates of all the major conurbations.

The portrait revealed that in many respects Catholics continued to display the characteristics expected of a largely immigrant group. Not least they retained norms of churchgoing which distinguished them sharply from the rest of the population. So, too, did the size of their congregations, which were far larger than in any other denomination. The emphasis in Hornsby-Smith's work, however, lay elsewhere. His purpose was to examine – with the aid of carefully collected empirical data – the extent to which Catholics could 'continue to be regarded as a distinctive sub-culture with a vital community life and identifiable religious belief and moral value-systems' (1987: 46). It was this that lay behind the stress on the increasing heterogeneity of English Catholics rather than the common characteristics of the community. What emerged from the data was considerable internal diversity, discernible with respect to origins, beliefs and practice and increasingly noticeable with each post-war decade that passed.

Hornsby-Smith shows us that the evolution in Catholicism was dominated by two interacting factors: first, the shifts in the English Catholic community occurring through increasing contact with the surrounding – and rapidly changing – society; and second the internal metamorphosis within the Catholic Church brought about by the Second Vatican Council. The overwhelming importance of the Council in the post-war period has already been mentioned (p. 31). It is hardly surprising that the outworking of its deliberations dominated the Catholic agenda in this country in the second half of the post-war period. Even more significantly, it altered the entire framework in which the relationships between the British churches took place.

What has happened since? The statistics can be updated from various sources: the work of Peter Brierley and Christian Research, the summaries on the BRIN website, the *Digest of Statistics of the Catholic Community in England and Wales, 1958–2005* (Spencer 2007),[15] and the series of surveys carried out by Linda Woodhead (2013b, 2013c). Three points emerge from these sources: that the Catholic population now constitutes about 8 per cent of the British population (rather smaller than the 11 per cent suggested by Hornsby-Smith in the 1980s), that attendance at mass is diminishing (see Figure 3.6), and that beliefs are drifting further and further from what might be termed Vatican style Catholicism.[16] In terms of community life, the arrival of a very significant Polish population has clearly made a difference. The influx began when Poland joined the European Union and the numbers grew steadily until 2008. Following the economic downturn, a number have left this country but by no means all. The 2011 Census revealed over half a million Polish-born people in the United Kingdom – a considerable increase from 2001.[17] That said it is important to appreciate that there is no one-to-one correlation between being Polish and being actively Catholic; it is quite possible, for example, that practice may cease on arrival in Britain. It is equally clear that Catholic immigration is very varied – it is certainly not limited to Poles. The situation, moreover, remains fluid: people are leaving as well as arriving and not all of them are captured in a single poll or snapshot. It seems none the less that the decline in Catholic activity may to some extent at least have been arrested by immigration, recognizing that the countries of provenance are now very different from those that predominated in the immediate post-war period.

The relative fortunes of the Catholic community extend beyond statistics. On the positive side, there have been a number of high profile conversions to Catholicism, the most prominent being Tony Blair following his retirement as Prime Minister. Huge attention, moreover, has been paid by the British press to Catholic events both in this country and beyond. The death of John Paul II in 2005 has already been mentioned – equal interest was shown in the election of his successor. Some eight years later, the unprecedented resignation of Benedict XVI received maximum exposure, as did the subsequent election of Francis I. The fact that Cardinal Keith O'Brien (the only British cardinal at the time) was unable to take part in the election of Francis I introduces a much more difficult question: the mounting evidence for inappropriate behaviour on the part of a significant, though numerically very small, group of Catholic priests.[18] The controversies concerning child abuse in particular have wracked the Catholic Church in this country as they have elsewhere. To a large extent they remain unresolved.

An interesting index of change regarding the Catholic community can be established by comparing the reactions of British people to the visits to this country of John Paul II (in 1982) with that of his successor Benedict XVI (in 2010). The 1982 visit was clearly iconic given that it was the first visit of a Pope to Britain since the Reformation, keeping in mind that John Paul II had already travelled widely by this stage in his career, attracting plane-loads of the world's media wherever he went. So why was a visit to Britain so special?

The trip was not without incident, however, given that it coincided with the outbreak of the Falklands War (cancellation was a real possibility). But once underway, the welcome was palpable: protests were limited to a small number of Northern Irish Protestants, notably the Reverend Ian Paisley. Equally positive was the boost given to ecumenical relations.

In 2010, the reactions were rather different, noting that this was a state rather than a pastoral visit. Residual Protestant displeasure could still be heard, but the bulk of the opposition came from increasingly prominent secularists, who objected amongst other things to the public funding committed to this occasion. A 'Protest the Pope' rally was held in London, where the arguments turned largely on moral issues, including child abuse, and questions of equality, notably gender and same-sex relations. The secular voices heard on these occasions were markedly more strident than before. The visit as a whole, however, was deemed a success and not only by the Catholic community. Interestingly, the media coverage was by and large critical before the Pope arrived, but became noticeably more affirming both during and after the visit itself. And as a postscript to this section, it is worth noting the markedly positive response to the initiatives undertaken by Pope Francis since his election in 2013.

The Orthodox   The brief paragraph on the Orthodox population that I wrote in 1994 contained the following sentences. 'The majority within the British Orthodox community have, up to now, come from the Greek tradition (mostly Greek Cypriots), but the dramatic events in East Europe in 1989 may well alter the religious map of West Europe in this respect. Increasing numbers are likely to arrive in the West – including Britain – from a variety of Orthodox traditions, a trend that cannot but enrich the religious life of this country' (Davie 1994: 60). Some 20 years later, it is clear the Orthodox population in Britain is now noticeably larger and more varied than it is was.[19] That said, the influx of a significant number of Russians in particular has brought with it serious tensions within the Orthodox community. Sadly, the Diocese of Sourozh in London has effectively split – a fissure brought about by the departure of Bishop Basil (in 2006), who saw no alternative to placing himself under the jurisdiction of the Ecumenical rather than the Russian Patriarchate. Scorer (2006) tells this very poignant story of schism in more detail. It turns on the nature of Orthodoxy and its sometimes dubious relationship with national identity, notably in Russia and parts of eastern Europe – a feature that has become increasingly prominent in recent decades.

The Free Churches   In many ways, the free churches constitute the most difficult category to deal with in this overview, in that the conclusions which emerge depend almost entirely on which denominations are included and which are not. The heading 'free churches' encompasses groups which are struggling badly but also some which are growing fast. To make matters more difficult, those which are flourishing are doing so for different reasons: on the whole the Afro-Caribbean churches serve an ethnically defined community; the wide variety of 'independent' or 'new' churches appeals to a rather different section of the population. A crucial question follows from this: what kinds of people are attracted by the latter? Are they effectively the disaffected members of existing churches, and, if so, which ones? Or are they 'new' people in the sense that significant numbers of them had no previous connections with a religious organization?

First, though, Old Dissent and the Methodists, remembering that the latter should, strictly speaking, be distinguished from the earlier Nonconformist traditions in this country. The Methodists are, in many ways, a unique denomination within Protestantism, a situation that becomes all the more significant with reference to Europe. Whereas the Presbyterians in Scotland, the United Reformed Church in England,[20] and the Baptists can make very obvious connections with the reformed tradition in Europe, the Methodists cannot. Their heritage – derivative of Anglicanism – looks in a different direction. Methodism shares, nonetheless, in the indisputable decline in membership that has afflicted the major Nonconformist churches in this country in the greater part of the twentieth century; a trend that accelerated in the post-war period. The following quotation puts this in perspective:

> The main Free Churches in England and Wales – Methodists, Congregationalists, Baptists and Presbyterians – reached their maximum membership in the years just before the First World War: the actual year is different for each denomination. Between 1914 and 1970 their total membership dropped by one third. . . This decline has been much sharper since the Second World War than it was before it: in the period between 1914 and 1939 the average decline in England and Wales was 6 per cent (in England alone it was slightly higher), but between 1939 and 1970 the average decline in England and Wales was 30 per cent (in England alone it was slightly less). (Thompson 1989: 100, using figures from Currie, Gilbert and Horsley 1977)

Post-1970, the downward trend continues, though more so for some denominations than others (see Figure 3.6). Specifically, the Baptists have been better able than most to resist. The Methodists and the United Reformed have not – in the last 20 years, their decline has been dramatic, bearing in mind that regional variations still matter. Quite apart from the presence of Presbyterianism in Scotland (see Chapter 5), Methodism retained at least until the end of the twentieth century a surprising degree of influence in some localities. In parts of the south west, for example, it was still possible in the mid-1980s to find a statistical correlation between the presence of Methodism and the Liberal vote (Davie and Hearl 1991).

In many ways it is not surprising that the Baptists provide a partial exception in terms of statistical trends, for they form something of a bridge between Old Dissent and newer forms of church life, notably those gathered together under a wide variety of headings, which include house churches, independent churches, new churches, Pentecostal churches and so on. In the first edition of this book, I engaged in this discussion by drawing on Andrew Walker's discussion of 'restorationism' and its relationship to the house church movement (Walker 1985); this was followed by a short introduction to the black-led churches found in the larger conurbations of Britain. In this edition, I have adopted the categories set out in Goodhew (2012a), whose analysis of church growth begins with the mainline churches (notably those in London) and moves through the minority and ethnic communities to a diverse group of 'new churches'. It is important to remember, however, that Goodhew's edited collection is about church growth, whereas my discussion is about a particular sector of denominational life. There is no necessary connection between the two. As Goodhew himself makes clear, growth and decline cut right across denominational boundaries. That said the statistical patterns found in the kinds of congregations covered in the following paragraphs are, on the whole, markedly different from those outlined so far.

Particularly significant is the presence of Pentecostalism, which to be properly understood needs to be set in a global context. World-wide, Pentecostalism is the fastest-growing section of the Christian church (for more information, see Pew Forum on Religion and Public Life 2006). The global figure is generally estimated at 250 million, recognizing that the vast majority of these people are located in the global south (Davie 2002). There are, however, important echoes in Europe, including Britain – notably in those churches with developed links overseas. The Afro-Caribbean churches constitute an excellent, though by no means the only example. Osgood's chapter in Goodhew's collection offers an overview of the Afro-Caribbean constituency and the ways in which it has evolved since 1980. The diversity is considerable: denominational churches exist alongside a multiplicity of independent churches, and non-locally minded mega-churches find their place alongside what might be termed community-conscious congregations (Osgood 2012: 110). The overall figures are difficult to estimate given the variety and the overlapping categories. That said Goodhew (2012b: 3) suggests half a million as a ballpark figure for the black majority churches in this country.[21]

The category 'new' churches is equally eclectic; it includes churches that derive from older traditions, churches that are grouped into umbrella organizations, congregations that are fiercely independent, gatherings of people who meet in homes, schools or warehouses, off-shoots of existing denominations and a growing group who describe themselves as 'emerging'. In his recent work, Peter Brierley (2011, 2014) deploys the following categories: 'independent churches', 'new churches', 'Pentecostal churches' and 'smaller denominations'.

Clearly the designation of churches or congregations to categories is somewhat arbitrary and can change over time, but – following Brierley's current analysis – the independent and new churches may have peaked, the smaller denominations fluctuate and the Pentecostals continue to grow strongly. Broadly speaking this is true across all three of Brierley's indicators: church members, church building and church leaders. Three further points should be noted. First that these are (for the most part) small churches, meaning that the percentage increases may be deceptive; the overall numbers remain modest. Second, they are 'gathered' churches – meaning that there is relatively little resonance with place and still less with territory. And third, the regional variations are very marked, a point that will resonate strongly in the discussions of London, Scotland, Wales and up to a point Northern Ireland.

Other-faith communities

The *existence* of religious diversity is widespread in an increasingly inter-connected and mobile world. In many places it is the norm rather than the exception. The *nature* of this phenomenon, however, varies markedly from country to country, a fact already noted in relation to the religious situation in different parts of Europe. Indeed in European terms, Britain is more rather than less diverse from a religious point of view: a wide variety of 'world religions' are present in this country, each of which has developed in a different way. These differences depend on many factors: distinctive theologies; countries of origin; dates of arrival; the ethnic, economic and social profiles of the communities in question; and external events. It follows that broad generalizations are unlikely to be helpful; indeed they almost always do more harm than good. The following paragraphs have been written with this in mind. In preparing them, Chapter 3 in Woodhead and Catto (2012) has proved a particularly useful resource; to facilitate cross-referencing I have ordered my list similarly. More recent data from the 2011 Census for England and Wales have permitted up-to-date statistics.

Jews The Jewish community – unlike most other religious minorities in this country – has experienced relatively little in-migration since the war (Waterman and Kosmin 1986). In this respect, the British situation differs markedly from the French, where arrivals from North Africa almost doubled the size of the French community in the post-war period. In Britain, the Jewish population peaked in the 1950s at just over 400 000. Subsequently it declined – for a variety of reasons (among them migration to Israel, marriage outside the community and reduced family size). Currently it is a little under 300 000 and constitutes 0.5 per cent of the overall population. On the whole it is a well-assimilated and largely ageing constituency concentrated in particular cities, notably London, Manchester, Leeds and Glasgow.

That, however, is not the whole story. There are indications that the decline in numbers may be slowing to the point possibly of reversing. This is due to the growth in the strictly Orthodox (*haredi*) section of the community, where unusually large families are the norm – reflecting a world-wide trend. A second point follows from this: the *haredim* are more likely than other sections of the Jewish population to resist assimilation, thus countering a second long-term tendency. The distinctive nature of the *haredim* is, moreover, illustrative of the fragmented nature of British Judaism overall. By no means all Jews practise, and those who do divide themselves into six identifiable strands which group themselves into two broad categories: the Orthodox and the non-Orthodox. Graham (2012: 91–92) covers these differences in detail, paying particular attention to the changing proportions of these strands since 1990. He also introduces the vexed question of who can speak for whom in this divided constituency, notably with respect to Israel – an increasingly delicate question. But whatever the case, one point remains clear: British Jews constitute the fifth largest Jewish community in the world, after the United States, Israel, France and Canada. Its significance should not be underestimated.

Sikhs   The Sikhs in Britain share with the Jews the fact they are an ethnic as well as a religious population. This fact has been important both in the self-identification of the Sikh community and in their recourse to law in the post-war period. With respect to the latter, ethnic minorities have been protected by the Race Relation Acts, a body of law that predated by several decades attention to discrimination on religious grounds. For this reason, Sikhs have frequently been seen as the pioneers of multiculturalism in this country as they campaigned to defend cultural (religious) as well as ethnic practices.

Settlement in Britain very largely occurred in the post-war decades in response to the need for labour prompted by economic recovery. Sikhs are of South Asian origin, noting that a significant number came to this country via East Africa, driven out of Kenya, Uganda and Tanzania by policies of Africanization. Interestingly, those arriving in Britain by this route have brought with them distinctive customs, not least the wearing of the outward symbols of Sikhism – habits that had ceased among those already living in Britain, but which invite immediate identification and require at times delicate negotiation.[22] The 2011 Census indicates a Sikh population of 400 000 plus – an increase of almost 100 000 since 2001. The majority (56.6 per cent in 2011) are British born. Sikh communities are heavily concentrated in London, the south east and the West Midlands. It is clear, moreover, that country of origin remains an important factor for this community. Sikhs come – directly or indirectly – from the Punjab, an area seriously damaged by the partition of India in 1947, which remains a disputed and at times violent region of the subcontinent. The Indian Army's entry into the Golden Temple in Amritsar in June 1984 had crucial repercussions for the British Sikh community, amongst other things propelling them into a leadership role in the Sikh diaspora (Singh 2012: 107).

Muslims Muslims form the largest non-Christian minority in this country and their numbers continue to grow. The 2011 Census established a figure of 2.7 million for England and Wales (i.e. 4.8 per cent of the population) – a significant increase since 2001.[23] British Muslims come from a variety of countries but the largest section of the community originates from the subcontinent, notably Pakistan and Bangladesh. In 1994, my remarks concerning this section of the British population reflected the attention to Islam provoked by Salman Rushdie's novel *The Satanic Verses* (1988) and by the first Gulf War. Much has happened since. It quickly became clear that the Rushdie controversy was but one of several episodes which took place in quick succession in different European societies, sparked by a mismatch in the assumptions between the host society and the Muslim community in that place. The reasons for these episodes and the difficulty in finding acceptable solutions to the issues that arise will constitute a central plank in the discussion in Part IV. The first Gulf War has been followed by further incursions by the west into the Muslim territory, not all of which have been considered legitimate. An obvious effect of these activities, together with the reactions that they have provoked, has been a heightened awareness of Muslim communities at home.

It is all the more important to establish the facts and figures with care. Gilliat-Ray's painstaking work (2010, 2012) offers an excellent guide. Mindful of the background against which she is writing, Gilliat-Ray takes a longer-term perspective than most commentators in order to consider the origins and patterns of settlement of the Muslim population in this country, its inherent diversity, and the institutions that provide a focus for community life. There is a welcome emphasis in her material on the everyday existence of British Muslims, as opposed to the crisis events that so often dominate the news. Chapter 5 of her *Muslims in Britain* profiles British Muslim communities in detail: in terms of size, geographical distribution, ethnicity, age and gender, country of origin and language use, household and residential patterns, employment, and health and well-being. It draws extensively on data from the 2001 Census, recognizing the importance of the Muslim constituency in promoting the question about religion in the first place.

What emerges is a relatively young population of which approximately half have been born in this country. It is, moreover, a minority characterized by social-economic disadvantage, for multiple and interlocking reasons. It is equally clear that Muslim communities vary noticeably from one part of the country to another, a fact which accounts for a considerable diversity in terms of 'schools of thought' and practice. There have, however, been moments of unity, not least the Rushdie controversy itself – a pivotal event in the self-understanding of British Muslims, which (quite rightly) has captured the attention of practitioners, antagonists, policy-makers and scholars. Among the latter, and at a very early stage in the controversy, Tariq Modood made the following very striking statement:

> 'the Rushdie affair' is not about the life of Salman Rushdie nor freedom of expression, let alone Islamic fundamentalism or book-burning or Iranian interference in British affairs. The issue is of the rights of non-European religious and cultural minorities in the context of a secular hegemony. Is the Enlightenment big enough to legitimise the existence of pre-Enlightenment religious enthusiasm or can it only exist by suffocating all who fail to be overawed by its intellectual brilliance and vision of man? (Modood 1990: 160)

And even earlier, Oliver Leaman (1989) put the same point in a different way: how do we (western commentators) accommodate 'that unusual phenomenon in our society, the person who takes religion seriously', and who is, in consequence, deeply offended by blasphemy? The question lies at the heart of what it means to live in a pluralist society. It raises complex and difficult issues that require the sustained attention of many different groups of people.

Hindus   The 2011 Census records a figure of 816 633 Hindus in England and Wales – a noticeable rise from 558 342 in 2001. Once again, the community originates overwhelmingly from South Asia, noting the significant proportion that came to Britain via East Africa, for the same reason as the Sikhs. The Hindu population is very largely urban and is concentrated in London and the Midlands (notably in Leicester). Relatively speaking, Hindus prosper from an economic point of view – they are well-educated and have made significant contributions in both business and the professions. One sign of this prosperity can be found in a gradual relocation to the suburbs.

Zavos (2012) charts the emergence of a distinctive Hindu identity in Britain underlining a shift towards a religious rather than an ethnic or national appellation (Hindu is preferred to Asian or South Asian). Important in this process have been the at times turbulent political developments in the sub-continent. Unsurprisingly, these have spilt over to Britain and include an undeniable degree of animosity between Hindus and Muslims – memories of partition die hard here as elsewhere. Rather more positive have been the establishment of Hindu organizations at local and national level and some notable building projects – not least 150 temples, including the well-known Swaminarayan Temple in Neasden and Bhaktivedanta Manor (the Hari Krishna Temple) in Letchmore Heath near Watford. The first publicly funded

Hindu schools are now beginning to emerge. Like other religious minorities, Hindus are sensitive to the image of their faith projected by the media and make strenuous efforts to correct inaccuracies.

Buddhists   Buddhists, like Muslims, are ethnically diverse but for a different reason. Of the 248 000 people who self-identified as Buddhists in the 2011 Census (an increase of a third since 2001), significant numbers are converts rather than immigrants. Almost 40 per cent of the Buddhist population is white. Converts and migrants, moreover, practise their Buddhism in different ways (Bluck 2012). Indeed an even more radical question must be posed at this point: that is to ask whether Buddhism should be considered a 'religion' at all? Given its emphasis on practice rather that belief and its essentially non-theistic nature, it is in some ways closer to the alternative spiritualities discussed in Chapter 8 than it is to a world religion.

Whatever the case, interest in Buddhism grew in the mid post-war decades, for internal and external reasons. New forms of spirituality, particularly those emanating from the east, were undoubtedly attractive to certain sorts of British people – mostly well-educated individuals with professional backgrounds. And at more or less the same time small, though significant groups of migrants arrived from Sri Lanka, Thailand, Burma and Tibet. Towards the end of the century further influxes came from East Asia (Japan and China) – the activities of Soka Gakkai (with its national headquarters at Taplow Court in Berkshire) are an important factor in this respect. Bluck captures the difference between western converts and newer arrivals as follows: 'Asian Buddhists value continuity with their religious and cultural roots, while converts are drawn by Buddhism's emphasis on personal responsibility' (2012: 141). For the latter group, Buddhism is chosen rather than inherited and is expressed in more individualistic ways.

An interim conclusion

The bare bones of this section are easily conveyed. With regard to the Christian constituency, it is clear that relatively few British people either belong to a church or attend religious services with any regularity, and those that do either of these things divide their attentions pretty evenly between the Anglican, Catholic and free church categories (assuming that the Afro-Caribbean churches and the 'new' churches are included in the last of these). And given this state of affairs, it must be argued, surely, that the religiously active of whatever Christian denomination have more in common with each other than any of them do with the majority of the population – a statement that should perhaps be extended to the other-faith populations as well. Here, in short, are the individuals in British society who take faith seriously. But taking faith seriously is becoming, increasingly, the exception rather than the norm, a situation exemplified not only by the data reviewed here but by the genuine incomprehension that is revealed day after day in the debate about religion in public life. What is to be done?

The relationship between these individuals and the majority of British people offers a possible starting point, recognizing that a noticeable shift has occurred. Some 20 years ago, the following statement remained valid: 'the considerable diversity both within Christianity and between faiths in this country overlays a more or less Christian nominalism, which (in England at least) tends to take Anglican form' (Davie 1994: 69). In contrast, secularism – at least in any developed sense – remained the creed of a relatively small minority. That is no longer the case. Christian nominalism still exists but is diminishing relatively fast – a point to be developed in Part II. Secularism, conversely, is on the rise, though it too should be carefully nuanced (see Chapter 9).

An additional point puts the religious constituencies into a broader perspective. Both religious membership and attendance continue to decline – there can be no doubt about that. Both, however, remain a relatively popular form of 'belonging' (in the sense of membership of a voluntary organization). Even a cursory glance at the information emanating from the long-running British Social Attitudes survey will reveal this fact, noting in particular the parallel decline of political parties, trades unions or even public houses. The same point emerges from Helen Cameron's careful work on different types of voluntary organizations, a field in which generalizations should be avoided (Cameron 2001; see also National Council of Voluntary Organizations (NCVO) 2011). In short, religious organizations of many different kinds continue, despite everything, to be a significant feature of contemporary British society. For this reason if no other, they merit careful investigation.

Media Portrayals of Religion

In the preceding paragraphs, I have introduced as clearly as possible the contours of religion in this country. In so doing I have used a variety of sources, all of which are freely available to commentators in this field. Why is it, therefore, that the portrayals of religion that appear in the press offer all too often a rather different impression: to the point at times of serious misrepresentation? At one level the answer is straightforward and relates to the factors set out in Chapter 1. The six factors introduced in this discussion push and pull in different directions. For this reason, they need to be considered alongside each other. If one of these is selected at the expense of others and is disproportionately foregrounded, the whole picture becomes distorted. The most obvious illustrations of this tendency can be found in either the over-emphasis of secularization or the inflated presence of Islam (related in turn to an exaggeration of immigration).

To answer this question in more detail, I will draw on a revealing piece of research conducted as part of the Religion and Society Research Programme. 'Media Portrayals of Religion and the Secular Sacred' is a particularly interesting project in that it replicated an earlier study that took place in 1982–1983.[24] Using similar methods to the earlier enquiry, it looked in detail at one month's content from three British newspapers (*The Sun*, *The Times* and *The Yorkshire Evening Post*) and at seven days' television from three channels (BBC1, BBC2 and ITV). In the second study, the researchers also included a broader variety of outputs: *The Guardian*, *The Daily Mail*, Channel 4 and Sky News. In addition, the team ran a series of focus groups with the wider public. Particular attention was paid to the media coverage of two episodes: the banning of Dutch MP Geert Wilders from entering the United Kingdom in 2009 and the visit of Pope Benedict to Britain in 2010. Interestingly, the first project had coincided with the visit of Pope John Paul II to Britain some 30 years earlier.

A number of points stand out in their results. The first confirms that the media coverage of religion has increased over the period. It is interesting to ask why given the facts and figures presented above. Predictably much, though not all, of this growth is accounted for by the attention paid to Islam, almost all of which is negative (an excellent example of disproportionate attention). Rather more surprising is the growth in coverage of Christianity, despite the fact that the Christian churches overall are clearly losing ground in British society. Most striking of all, however, is the juxtaposition of two statements. This first recognizes that the media thrive on controversy: '[n]ewspapers and television attract audiences by focusing on conflict, deviance and, of course, celebrity.'[25] Accounts of religion are constructed accordingly. At the same time, in a nation which is increasingly illiterate regarding religion (including Christianity), the media become a correspondingly important source of information about religious issues. The implications of this combination are disturbing and will be revisited more than once in the chapters that follow.

Notes

1 Peter Brierley is the prime mover in this respect. In 2007, he retired from Christian Research, but continues to be active in the field. For his current work, see http://www.brierleyconsultancy.com/index.html (accessed 5 August 2014).

2 See www.christian-research.org/ for more details (accessed 5 August 2014). An additional publication appeared in 2006 entitled *Pulling Out of the Nosedive: A Contemporary Picture of Churchgoing* (Brierley 2006). The title itself is revealing: Brierley emphasizes the urgency of the present situation indicating that unless something is done in the relatively near future, the churches will face inexorable decline.

3   See www.brin.ac.uk (accessed 5 August 2014). This website is a mine of information and repays careful study. The secondary reflections on the material initially published in *Religious Trends* can be found on http://www.brin.ac.uk/news/2011/church-attendance-in-england-1980-2005/ (accessed 5 August 2014).

4   For an introduction to this question see the short paragraph on measuring religion in the summary paper on 'Religion in England and Wales 2011' from which much of the material in this section is taken (ONS 2012). Further information about the implications of question wording and other methodological issues can be found on the BRIN website. See for example the post entitled '2011 Census – Searching for Explanations' at http://www.brin.ac.uk/news/2012/2011-census-searching-for-explanations/ (accessed 5 August 2014). Also helpful is David Perfect's briefing paper on 'Religion and Belief' prepared for the Equality and Human Rights Commission, which includes a list of sources regarding statistical data about religion and belief in Britain (Perfect 2011).

5   In Scotland, the question about religion was more specific than that in England and Wales. In the latter, the population was asked 'What is your religion?' In Scotland, the wording was as follows: 'What religion, religious denomination or body do you belong to?', which yielded a rather different result. The question about religious upbringing used in Scotland in 2001 was dropped in 2011.

6   Output areas (OAs) comprise circa 125 households. The term is explained at http://www.ons.gov.uk/ons/guide-method/geography/beginner-s-guide/census/output-area--oas-/index.html (accessed 5 August 2014).

7   The question on religion is the only optional question in the Census. This is so for legal reasons. See http://www.brin.ac.uk/news/2012/2011-census-searching-for-explanations/ (accessed 5 August 2014).

8   The following sources should be noted in this overview: *Statistics for Mission 2011* (2013), *Statistics for Mission 2012* (2014), and the material gathered together on the Church of England's Church Growth Research Programme website – see www.churchgrowthresearch.org.uk (accessed 5 August 2014). The findings from this programme merit careful attention.

9   David Voas (2003) argues that the slide has in fact been continuous since the late 1930s; the apparent uptick around 1950 is simply a statistical artefact.

10 See *Statistics for Mission 2012* (2014), Table 16 and Figure 32.

11 See *Statistics for Mission 2012* (2014), Table 22 and Figures 39 and 40, and the long-term data on the BRIN website assembled from a variety of sources: http://www.brin.ac.uk/news/wp-content/uploads/2011/04/Confirmations-1872-2009.jpg (accessed 5 August 2014).

12 See http://www.churchofengland.org/media/1370733/2010ordinationsreaderadmissions.pdf (accessed 5 August 2014). For additional material on ministry in the Church of England see *Statistics for Mission 2012: Ministry* (2013).

13 See *Statistics for Mission 2012* (2014) and http://www.brin.ac.uk/news/2011/church-attendance-in-england-1980-2005/ (accessed 5 August 2014). Quite a bit depends on frequency of attendance and whether or not weekday activities are included.

14 See *Statistics for Mission 2012* (2014), Table 19 and Figures 36 and 37.

15 For more recent figures, see www.prct.org.uk (accessed 5 August 2014).

16 This is the principal finding of Woodhead's surveys. Her summaries in *The Tablet* indicate that only 5 per cent overall and 2 per cent of the under-30s now conform to the model of 'faithful Catholics' according to the Church's *Magisterium*. The data tables for the Catholic sample can be found at: http://d25d2506sfb94s. cloudfront.net/cumulus_uploads/document/k0rbt8onjb/YG-Archive-050613-FaithMatters-UniversityofLancaster.pdf (accessed 5 August 2014).

17 See http://www.ons.gov.uk/ons/dcp171780_229910.pdf (accessed 5 August 2014).

18 See http://www.bbc.co.uk/news/uk-scotland-21580885 (accessed 5 August 2014).

19 This is true both in terms of community size and in terms of attendance (Brierley 2011; Perfect 2011).

20 An account of the union of the Presbyterian Church of England and the majority of churches in the Congregational Church in England and Wales to form the United Reformed Church is given in Orchard (2012).

21 David Voas (personal communication, 2014) thinks this an overestimate unless the figure includes sections of the mainstream churches in which Afro-Caribbeans predominate.

22 The most sensitive in this respect is the obligation for observant Sikhs to carry the 'kirpan' – a ceremonial sword or dagger that would otherwise be considered an unlawful weapon.

23 A useful comparative perspective can be found in the figures published by the Pew Forum on Religion and Public Life. See http://www.pewforum.org/future-of-the-global-muslim-population-regional-europe.aspx (accessed 5 August 2014).

24 See http://www.religionandsociety.org.uk/uploads/docs/2011_03/1301305944_Knott_Phase_1_Large_Grant_Block.pdf (accessed 5 August 2014). This website has links to further resources. See also Knott, Poole and Taira (2013) and Woodhead and Catto (2012), chapter 7. I have a personal interest in this project in that I remember its starting point very well: that is, the earlier study of media portrayals of religion which was carried out in 1982–1983 and which to an extent informed the first book that I wrote (Ahern and Davie 1987).

25 See note 24 for the source of these quotations.

Part II

Religious Legacies

4

Cultural Heritage, Believing without Belonging and Vicarious Religion

We live in a society that is changing fast, notably with respect to religion. Some things however are constant in the sense that they underpin our everyday lives and the assumptions that go with these. Our expectations about time fall into this category. We take for granted that the working week for most of us runs from Monday to Friday and that the weekends are primarily for leisure. An important focus for these changes can be found in the legislation relating to 'Sunday observance'. Step by step modifications in what we can and cannot do on Sundays are widely interpreted as indicators of secularization – rightly so in the sense that activities that were unthinkable in the immediate post-war period are now commonplace. They range from major sporting events to regular high street shopping, adjustments that discomfit those who prefer not to work on Sundays. The underlying point, however, lies elsewhere: to note that it is Sunday that has changed, rather than any other day, a framing that derives from our Christian past.

The rhythm of the working week can be approached from a different perspective. Economic activity from Monday to Friday, with time to do something different at the weekend, fits well with most of our lives, whether we practise our religion or not. For the most part, active Christians are free to attend their places of worship on (mostly) Sundays and those for whom religion is less important can do as they please. This is less easy for religious minorities, notably those whose schedules derive from a different cultural heritage. Orthodox Jews, for example, will begin the Sabbath at sunset on Friday, well before the end of the working day in winter months. The obligations of Friday (indeed daily) prayer for Muslims may require special arrangements in the workplace. And it is very unlikely that the major festivals of the many faith communities now present in this country will fit with

Religion in Britain: A Persistent Paradox, Second Edition. Grace Davie.
© 2015 Grace Davie. Published 2015 by John Wiley & Sons, Ltd.

what British people call 'holidays' – unaware for the most part of the religious etymology of this term. Unsurprisingly, managing diversity in the workplace has become a significant issue in British society and includes an important legal dimension (see Chapter 10).

Similar expectations pertain in terms of space. Taken-for-granted situations are disturbed when a new building is proposed – the more so if its shape and form are deemed exotic and if it is to become the place of worship of an unfamiliar faith. Protests are made and arguments recorded, which reveal – sometimes unwittingly – the underlying assumptions of the protagonists, many of which derive from a distinctive past. Planning applications and the local press are excellent sources of information in this respect. Rather the same is true in terms of sound. It is true that there are occasional complaints about church bells, but by and large these are part of a familiar soundscape. The Muslim call to prayer – essential to the rhythm of a Muslim culture – provokes a very different response.

That said controversies about space are hardly new. The siting of a sacred building is, and always has been, significant in that location denotes power – real as well as symbolic. Such buildings are often expensive, not to mention the land on which they are built. Learning to 'read' a city, or even a village, becomes therefore a crucial element in the understanding of religious history (Martin 2002). In terms of this chapter, two points in particular should be noted. The first is the overwhelming presence of Christian buildings in this country and the visual expectations that are created thereby; the second is the changing fortunes of different religious communities, both Christian and other, which can be discerned from their relative locations. In short, careful observation of the skyline can tell you a great deal about the presence of religion in the town or city in question, and how this has developed over time and continues to do so.

Equally revealing are the contents of these buildings and the activities that take place within them. Accumulations of religious art and artefacts, assorted liturgies and the music that accompanies them have been formative in European culture. They spill out into the wider society. Art galleries and concert halls are full of them though in different proportions in different parts of the continent. And given that this has been going on for centuries it is hardly surprising that Christian imagery permeates what we see, what we hear and what we read. Regarding the latter, particular translations of the Bible and definitive editions of liturgical texts have not only acquired iconic status, they are recognized as seminal in terms of language – cadences so deeply embedded in the way that we speak that we scarcely know that they are there. So much so that their origins are forgotten, meaning that the serious student of art, literature or music will often require a course in Christian theology in order to appreciate the significance of what they are learning. Paradoxes abound in this field. Art and artefacts that were created as prompts or reminders for populations who were well acquainted with the Christian story but who could not read or write, are now beyond the reach of a fully literate population which has lost touch with the narrative in question.

Such a statement introduces a central theme of this book: that is, the need to understand not only the historical legacy itself but the markedly ambiguous ways in which this influences the present situation. British people are both attached to this inheritance and suspicious of it: the physical and cultural presence of the historic churches may be one thing; a hands-on role in the everyday lives of British people quite another. How then can we explore this constantly fluctuating middle ground? This chapter approaches this question in two ways. The first locates the terrain in the sense that it identifies the relatively large number of people who acknowledge a residual attachment to Christianity but who rarely practise their faith. In this sense it adds to the facts and figures established in Chapter 2. The following sections introduce the conceptual tools that are helpful for a better understanding of this constituency. It looks first at the notion of 'believing without belonging' in a discussion that pays close attention to the debate provoked by the first edition of this book. An outline of 'vicarious religion' follows from this – an idea that both builds on to and questions the earlier approach. At this point the discussion makes maximum use of examples. The institutional dimensions of the same question (the continuing connections between church and state and their influence in different sectors of society) will be developed in Chapter 5.

The Evidence for Religious Belief

One point should be clarified before going further: the concept of 'belief' is in itself part of our engagement with history. It derives from our Christian past and is much less applicable to other faiths whether they are located in this country or elsewhere. But even in 'Christian' Britain belief is a tricky term: what should or should not be included in this amorphous category and how best can this be captured? The 1994 edition of this book drew on quantitative and qualitative data to elucidate this question and approached the topic from an individual and a collective point of view. This section updates the statistical material introducing a variety of sources.[1] It then recalls the particular enquiry that stimulated my interest in the field before turning to more recent work.

In broad terms, the patterns that emerge are relatively clear: between half and two-thirds of the population continue to believe in some sort of God or supernatural force, but within this category there is a continuing shift away from those who believe in a personal God towards those who prefer a less

Table 4.1   Belief in God, Great Britain, 1991, 1998 and 2008.

	Per cent		
	1991	*1998*	*2008*
Believe and always have	45.8	47.6	36.7
Believe, didn't before	5.9	4.2	5.1
Not believe, did before	12.1	11.6	15.2
Not believe, never have	11.6	13.2	19.9
Can't choose	22.7	21.7	21.7
Not answered	1.8	1.7	1.5
Total (%)	100.0	100.0	100.0
Base	1222	815	1975

Source: British Social Attitudes, 1991–2008. Table created by David Perfect 2011. *Religion or Belief*. Manchester: Equality and Human Rights Commission Briefing Paper. Table 11. http://www.equalityhumanrights.com/publication/briefing-paper-1-religion-or-belief. Used by permission of the Equality and Human Rights Commission (EHRC).

specific formulation. At the same time the number of unbelievers has grown. A similar drift is taking place in some but not all European societies.[2] Tables 4.1 and 4.2 and Figure 4.1 demonstrate these trends, which can be used to frame the discussion in this chapter; the same findings will be deployed in Chapter 8 on the proliferations of the spiritual, and in Chapter 9 on secular reactions.

Despite the fact that the unit of measurement varies from one enquiry to another, it is clear that these data capture a distinction already made: that is, the difference between hard and soft variables in the measurement of religion. The tighter the definitions of either 'belief' or 'belonging', the smaller the numbers involved. The trends, however, are clear: on the one hand towards greater heterogeneity and on the other towards greater secularity. Both, moreover, derive from the same process – that is a continuing shift away from anything that might be termed 'orthodoxy', itself reinforced by religious attendance.

This is clearly the case with respect to heterogeneity. At one end of the spectrum, beliefs have recognizable links to Christian teaching and are supported by occasional, if not very regular practice – more often than not at a major festival or one of the occasional offices. At the other they are enormously diverse and include (following the categories used in a very detailed 1980s enquiry) healing, the paranormal, fortune telling, fate and destiny, life after death, ghosts, spiritual experiences, prayer and meditation, luck and superstition.[3] More recent enquiries deploy a rather different vocabulary (see Chapter 8) but the essential point remains the same. Either way there is abundant evidence of the non-rational, but in forms that have little to do

Table 4.2 Reported beliefs, selected European countries, 2010.

	Percentages				
	Believe there is a God	Believe there is some sort of spirit or life force	Do not believe there is any sort of spirit, God or life force	Don't know	Base
Austria	44	38	12	6	1000
Belgium	37	31	27	5	1012
Cyprus	87	9	3	1	502
Denmark	28	47	24	1	1006
Finland	33	41	22	3	1001
France	27	26	40	6	1018
Germany (West)	52	27	17	4	1002
Great Britain	37	33	25	5	1009
Greece	79	16	4	1	1000
Iceland	31	49	18	2	501
Ireland	70	20	7	3	1007
Italy	74	20	6	0	1018
Malta	94	4	2	0	500
The Netherlands	28	39	30	3	1018
Northern Ireland	59	23	15	3	302
Norway	22	44	29	5	1037
Portugal	70	15	12	3	1027
Spain	59	20	19	2	1004
Sweden	18	45	34	3	1007
Switzerland	44	39	11	6	1026

Source: European Commission (2012): Eurobarometer 73.1 (January–February 2010). Table created by author from cross-tabulation provided by David Voas, Institute for Economic and Social Research, University of Essex.

with Christian teaching. So do they or don't they count as belief? Opinions differ. The line between orthodox and less orthodox believing, moreover, is distinctly porous.

Take the following as an example. Visitors to religious buildings are frequently prompted to offer or to ask for prayer.[4] If they so wish, they are invited to write their requests down and to leave them in a designated place; they are informed that their petitions will be gathered up on a regular basis and will be included in the corporate cycle of prayer associated with that building. Such provision is widely used and by very different types of people. Even the most casual scrutiny of these requests reveals, however, that their content is varied and not always in keeping with Christian teaching. Their

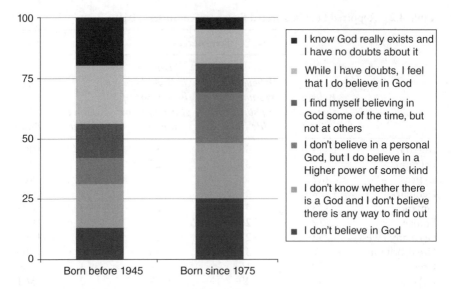

Figure 4.1   Belief in God among old and young (%).
Source: British Social Attitudes survey 2008. Chart created by David Voas, Institute for Economic and Social Research, University of Essex. Used by permission of David Voas.

articulation implies nonetheless a certain expectation: not only that this is an appropriate thing to do but that the efficacy of the prayer will be enhanced by the location in question.[5] It is equally clear that many of these petitions are for healing, once again a concept that crosses many boundaries: between science and religion; between conventional medicine and alternative therapies; between 'traditional' forms of religion and alternative world-views; and between individual aspiration and corporate faith. The institutional responses to these continual realignments will be discussed at a later stage. Here it is enough to indicate the complexity of religious belief and to recognize that a rigorous division between strictly Christian and other formulations is at times misleading.

Precisely this point emerged very clearly from a small study that took place in Islington in the late 1960s, which was formative in my thinking (Abercrombie *et al.* 1970). Though limited in scope and by now somewhat dated, the rigour with which this study was carried out has earned for it a high reputation. It also includes one of the best quotes in the literature. When respondents were probed about their belief in God, they were asked 'Do you believe in a God who can change the course of events on earth?' To which one respondent replied, 'No, just the ordinary one.' Answers such as these are worth pondering: they point up the paradox at the heart of this issue. What is the significance, sociological or otherwise, of an 'ordinary' God? Is this, or is this not, evidence of religious belief? If it is not belief, what kinds of categories are necessary to understand this persistent dimension of British life and how would these relate to more orthodox dimensions of religiosity, including practice? The conclusions to the Islington study contain some interesting observations:

> The analysis in the section above suggests the tentative conclusion that religious belief, when not associated with active membership of a church, tends to be associated with superstitious belief while church attendance tends to be antithetical to superstition. Moreover, we have some evidence that for those people who do not go to church yet say they are religious and pray often, religious belief has moved quite far from the orthodox church position and is really much closer to what would normally be called superstition. (Abercrombie *et al.* 1970: 124)

A second point follows from this: the patterns that emerge in this fascinating field derive from the cumulative effect of individual choices, many of which incorporate blurred distinctions and a somewhat approximate grasp of Christian doctrine. The observer may wish to separate out the orthodox from the less orthodox in these highly personal packages; the believer on the whole does not. Equally significant is the influence of social and cultural factors, reflecting once again the weight of history in the ways that we think. Conceptual categories do not drop from the sky; they are formed and reformed over long periods of time. It follows that what appear to be very personal packages of belief are not simply generated by the individual in question; they – just as much as 'official' bodies of religious teaching – reflect a distinctive cultural heritage.

Increasing heterodoxy is encouraged by the decline in religious practice. Increasing secularity runs parallel. But as Lois Lee (2015) shows us, unbelief can be as varied as belief and requires equally careful scrutiny if it is to be properly understood. In terms of context, Lee's work reflects a growing interest in the secular as a topic of study in its own right, as scholars in different parts of the western world reflect on the changing situation in their own countries – a body of literature to be foregrounded in Chapter 9. A central theme of Lee's work is nonetheless important at this stage. It concerns the distinction between absence and presence in the understanding of the secular, which she articulates as a discernible shift from the 'hollowly secular' to the 'substantively nonreligious'. In other words unbelief or non-religion becomes not simply the absence of religion but something that is actively expressed, more often than not in the company of others.

Lee also recognizes the complex interrelationships between the secular and the religious, noting that both are not only socially embedded but distinctively patterned. In short, cultural heritage impinges on the secular as it does on the religious, with the obvious corollary that those who do not believe are often acutely aware of the deity that they have rejected. Such rejections can be vehement as in the case of the group known as 'new atheists'; they can however be as understated as the beliefs which are put to one side. And as Lee convincingly reveals, these positions should not be seen simply as reasoned epistemologies; they emerge instead from the complexities of everyday living.

Believing without Belonging

The notion of believing without belonging has already been introduced. It derives from the evident disparity between hard and soft measurements of religiousness and the need to understand not only the phenomenon itself but the implications of this situation for theorists and practitioners alike. The first edition of this book used this disparity as an organizing theme, paying particular attention to the ways in which it was manifested in different parts of society – contrasts which remain significant. It is still true, for example, that belief and practice are better aligned amongst the more educated sections of the population; those who believe are more likely to practise, those who do not are more likely to lead consistently secular lives. Women, moreover, are different from men; they score higher on both variables. Equally predictable are the generational shifts as the young drift further from the inherited model. Echoes of all these features will be found throughout this book, as will the evidence for belief without belonging in different areas of the country, in urban and rural contexts and in different institutional settings.

The principal point to be pursued here, however, is other: it is to understand why an expression that was tucked in as an unofficial subtitle to the 1994 edition caught the imagination of so many people. Why was it that this catchy if rather imprecise phrase 'rapidly spread across the world and beyond the borders of scholarship'? (Voas and Crockett 2005: 11–12) The extent of this discussion can be found by typing 'believing without belonging' into an internet search engine. The expression appeared everywhere: in academic papers all over the world, in more popular writing about the churches in this country and in others, in the statements of religious leaders, in religious journalism, in A-level textbooks and in student exam papers. Quite clearly, believing without belonging resonated for many, very different, constituencies. Why?

Voas and Crockett provide a helpful categorization of this discussion into strong and weak versions of the 'theory', before embarking on a series of empirically based criticisms. Following the Voas and Crockett distinction, the strong version argues that with the exception of a relatively small number of atheists, Europeans (including the British) continue to believe in God and to have religious (or at least spiritual) sensibilities: the proportion of believers has changed little in recent years. In other words: 'belief in the supernatural is high and reasonably robust while religious practice is substantially lower and has declined more quickly' (2005: 12). The weak version allows for a much greater drift in the content of belief and very quickly becomes circular in that the thesis is proved if this, that or the other formulation of religious belief is included, and disproved if it is not. Insightfully, Voas and Crockett suggest that the strong version of the thesis is very often asserted based on evidence for the weaker interpretation. Generously they exempt me personally from many of their most trenchant criticisms.

I very much respect the careful empirical analyses of David Voas and others in this field,[6] and by and large I concur with the questions that they raise. That said, I return to the core idea that was, and to an extent still is, driving my thinking. In 1994 I expressed this as follows:

> The terms 'believing' and 'belonging' are not to be considered too rigidly. The disjunction between the variables is intended to capture a mood, to suggest an area of enquiry, a way of looking at the problem, not to describe a detailed set of characteristics. Operationalizing either or both of the variables too severely is bound to distort the picture... But the question very quickly becomes semantic, for it is clear that we need some way, if not this one, of describing the persistence of the sacred in contemporary society despite the undeniable decline in churchgoing. (Davie 1994: 93–94)

The key phrase in this paragraph is the following: 'operationalizing either or both of the variables too severely' and the distortions that emerge if this happens. Not everyone has heeded that advice. But whatever the case in terms of empirical enquiry, the underlying disparity persists. It is true that church-going has diminished, bringing with it a corresponding decline in anything approximating Christian orthodoxy. The middle ground, however, has not disappeared. Though smaller and more diverse than it was, it remains the largest section of the religious spectrum both in this country and in most parts of Europe and for this reason alone continues to demand sociological attention.[7] To pursue this further I have introduced a second analytic tool: that of vicarious religion. Before engaging the latter directly, however, it is worth reflecting on the reactions of two very different constituencies to the earlier conversation.

The first are a wide variety of church leaders. Understandably enough, significant numbers of individuals charged with the maintenance of religious organizations both in Britain and elsewhere have embraced the notion of believing without belonging, at least in part to justify their continued existence. Things are not as secular as they seem. As it happens, I do think that the churches have an important role in British society, and will have for the foreseeable future, but for reasons that require careful and detailed consideration. Specifically the churches' personnel need to appreciate that the situation described as believing without belonging is neither better nor worse than a more straightforwardly (if one may use that term) secular society. It is simply different. Those that minister to a half-believing, rather than unbelieving, society will find that there are advantages and disadvantages to this situation, as there are in any other. Working out appropriate ministerial strategies for this continually shifting and ill-defined context is the central and very demanding task of the religious professional. A firm and necessary grasp of the sociological realities is but the beginning.

A second constituency can be found in a particular cluster of sociological thinkers. For the most part these are American scholars who are known as rational choice theorists. Davie (2013) provides an outline of their approach, which can be summarized as follows. Religious organizations are more likely to flourish in a market which stimulates competition. In such a situation, each religious community has to compete for its existence and only the fittest survive: those, that is, who can attract sufficient members to cover their financial and other costs. It is generally agreed that the approach works relatively well in the United States where tens of thousands of free-standing congregations co-exist and where there is no dominant or historically privileged church. It is rather less applicable on this side of the Atlantic.

Applicable or not, rational choice theorists have used the data marshalled to support the believing without belonging thesis (i.e. the fact that many more people believe than practise) as confirmation of a central plank of their argument: that there is a relatively constant demand for religion in modern as well as less modern societies. That demand remains unmet in large parts of Europe – the reason residing in what these theorists perceive as a 'lazy monopoly' (i.e. the historically dominant church), which is unable either to stimulate or to fulfil the latent religious needs of the population for which it is responsible. If a free, or freer, market were allowed to develop, Europeans including ourselves would become as actively religious as their American counterparts; unattached believers would be captured and sustained by active and competitive religious organizations. I am not as convinced as the rational choice theorists that this would be the case for reasons that will become clear in due course, but the argument is worth bearing in mind as the religious economy evolves and as the range of choice increases. The rational choice approach is more pertinent now than it used to be.[8]

Abby Day (2011) has made a rather different and very useful contribution to the debate about belief in modern societies. In *Believing in Belonging: Belief and Social Identity in the Modern World*, she sets out to understand the nature and meaning of Christian nominalism in different parts of the western world. As her title indicates, she both builds on to and challenges the notion of believing without belonging. Her particular focus in Britain is the constituency which ticked the category Christian in the 2001 census. Why was it that so many British people chose this appellation? What was in their minds when they did this? Day responds to this question both theoretically and empirically. She draws on the resources of several disciplines (notably anthropology and sociology) to elucidate the meaning of belief. She also records the results of her own research in this field – a three-generational enquiry into the nature of nominalism in a small northern town. Most important among Day's well-argued conclusions, is her understanding of belief as a social rather than individual act – one moreover which is 'worked out' in practice and in different ways by different people.[9] Nominalism, it follows, is not simply a residual category, but contains within itself considerable variety: it can be 'natal', 'ethnic' or 'aspirational', the nuances of which need careful unpacking. The first is given by birth or baptism; the second is claimed, sometimes as a proxy for Englishness; and the third is aspirational in the sense that it confers respectability.[10]

Quite apart from this, the emphasis in Day's work on belonging as well as believing provides an ideal bridge to vicarious religion.

Vicarious Religion: Principles and Practice

The separating out of belief from belonging undoubtedly offered fruitful ways in which to understand and to organize the material about religion in modern Britain. Pertinent questions were asked and interesting things were discovered. On-going reflection, however, has encouraged me to think more deeply about these issues and in two ways. On the one hand was the recognition that both belief and belonging came in hard and soft versions (as explained in Chapter 1). On the other was the realization that the argument very largely turned on the relationship between the two – that is between the relatively restricted community of active believers who express their faith in more or less regular church-going, and the much larger penumbra who retain some sort of belief, and who wish from time to time to make contact with the institutions with which they identify.

The notion of vicarious religion emerged from these deliberations; it pivots on the idea that the smaller group is doing something on behalf of the larger one, who are aware (if only implicitly) of this relationship. It was defined in Chapter 1 (p. 6), in a discussion which outlined very briefly the four ways in which this notion operates. Churches and church leaders perform ritual on behalf of others; church leaders and churchgoers believe on behalf of others; church leaders and churchgoers embody moral codes on behalf of others; and churches can at times offer space for the 'vicarious' debate of unresolved issues in modern societies. It is worth noting that all of these functions have in common the perception of the church as a public utility: that is, an institution (or more accurately a cluster of institutions) which exists to make provision for a population living in a designated place, local or national, and which is found wanting if it fails to deliver.

Each of the four points will be examined in this light. The least controversial relates to the role of both churches and church leaders in conducting ritual on behalf of a wide variety of individuals and communities at critical points in their lives. The most obvious illustrations can be found in the continuing requests, even in a moderately secular society, for some sort of religious ritual at the time of a birth, a marriage and, most of all, a death. The facts and figures presented in the previous chapter indicate that the demand for the first two of these has diminished sharply in modern Britain but has by no means disappeared. The same data reveal that this is much less true at the time of a death.[11] It is at this point above all that significant sections of the population come into direct contact with their churches and would be deeply offended if their requests were met with rejection. A refusal to offer either a funeral service or appropriate pastoral care to the family or community in question would violate deeply held assumptions.

But churches and church leaders do more than conduct ritual: they also believe on behalf of others in the sense that they 'hold the faith' for society as a whole. For this reason their public statements are closely scrutinized. And the more senior or visible the church leader, the more closely their pronouncements are examined. An excellent example can be found in the furore that greeted the then Archbishop of Canterbury, Rowan Williams, in 2008, following a much misinterpreted remark concerning Shari'a law.[12] Clearly Dr Williams' intervention on this occasion did not concern Christian doctrine as such, but his attempt to think creatively about the place of religious minorities in the British legal system prompted a reaction so extreme that it is hard to explain. It is important to note, however, that the largely irrational outburst was provoked not so much by the very thoughtful lecture that Rowan Williams gave on 'Civil and Religious Law in England: A Religious Perspective' at the Royal Courts of Justice in February 2008, but by an unguarded comment on a news programme that trailed the event. Simply the phrase 'Shari'a law' uttered by the Archbishop on Radio 4 sent the media into a tailspin.

Similar pressures emerge with respect to behavioural codes: religious professionals, both local and national, are expected to uphold certain standards of behaviour. In Protestant cultures, including our own, these very often relate to more rather than less traditional representations of family life. And 'failure' in this respect – in the form of divorce or family breakdown – leads not only to accusations of hypocrisy, but to expressions of disappointment.

We demand more of religious professionals than we do of ourselves. Such expectations become at times unreasonable, particularly in relation to the partners and children of the individuals in question. The pressures in a Catholic culture are different but equally demanding: celibacy is hardly an easy option. Interestingly there is widespread sympathy for the celibate priest and the exacting nature of this role. Quite different, however, are the public's reactions to the abuse of children. Both the phenomenon itself and the failure to deal adequately with it are considered abhorrent. The reason is simple: at the heart of this debate lies an abuse of trust on the part of an individual (of whatever denomination) and of the institution of which he or she is part.

A final possibility with respect to vicarious religion is rather different. It is also more provocative. Could it be that the churches offer space for debate regarding particular, and often controversial topics, which are difficult to address elsewhere? In the early years of the twenty-first century, heated debates surrounding same-sex relationships were a case in point. At least some of these found expression in a series of painful controversies relating to senior appointments in the Church of England, a theme to be developed in Chapter 6. The point at issue here is not the rights and wrongs of the arguments, which – as far as the churches are concerned – remain largely unresolved. It is to ask once again why so much attention was paid to a supposedly marginal institution by the national and indeed international press. It is the unremitting attention that leads me to suggest that this is one way in which society as a whole comes to terms with profound shifts in the moral climate. The presenting issues may change over time, but the underlying questions endure.

Precisely this point was articulated by Rowan Williams, prompted this time by the Occupy London controversy in 2011, introduced at the end of Chapter 2:

> It has sometimes been said in recent years that the Church of England is still used by British society as a stage on which to conduct by proxy the arguments that society itself does not know how to handle. It certainly helps to explain the obsessional interest in what the Church has to say about issues of sex and gender. It may help to explain just what has been going on around St Paul's Cathedral in the past fortnight.[13]

And what the former Archbishop describes as the 'cataract of unintended consequences' that followed does not invalidate the basic point: namely that 'the Church of England is a place where the unspoken anxieties of society can often find a voice, for good and ill'. In this case these anxieties included the growing disparity between rich and poor and the apparent immunity of certain sections of the population to economic sanction.

The notion of vicarious religion has stimulated a continuing debate both in the churches and in academic discussion, though not quite on the same scale as believing without belonging. For the most part the reactions are positive – particularly among religious professionals on this side of Atlantic. Those responsible for ministry in the historic churches of Europe, including the different parts of the United Kingdom, identify immediately with this concept – unsurprisingly in that they encounter it on a daily basis. And in Europe as a whole, I have been struck by the number of people who respond to a presentation on this theme with pertinent examples from their own context. This is true even when I have worked through an interpreter who has to think carefully in order to find an equivalent term in his or her own language.[14]

Scholarly reactions are more varied. It is unwise to generalize, but on the whole those who resist the idea of vicarious religion fall into the same category as those who resist the notion of believing without belonging, and for the same reasons. By and large they do a similar thing. They take a concept that was intended to direct attention to the religious habits of a section of the population that remains loosely attached to the mainstream churches of Europe (and to find creative ways of thinking about their behaviour), and turn this into something far more rigorously defined that I intended. The next step is to 'test' this *reconfigured* notion in a way that is not always appropriate. Precisely this can be illustrated in a developed exchange with Steve Bruce and David Voas (2010; see also Davie 2010a). I welcome such debates but remain convinced that a notion that probes the implicit as well as explicit connections between a still significant body of people and the historic churches of Europe remains a useful contribution. Two points follow from this conviction. The first is methodological; the second relates to timescale. Each of them will be taken in turn.

It is already clear that vicarious religion as a sociological entity can be approached in different ways, one of which is statistical or quantitative and identifies the constituency in question. As we have seen, a wide variety of empirical enquiries point consistently to the middle ground: in this space can be found a cluster of individuals who call themselves Christian but who rarely practise. So much is straightforward. It is rather more difficult to understand this elusive phenomenon. Indeed to grasp the 'character' of vicarious religion, something more creative is required – a way of working that appreciates the subtle, many-layered and constantly evolving nature of human living. This means that the researcher must be sensitive not only to individuals, but to institutions, traditions, assumptions, emotions and dispositions – including unconscious ones. The approach may vary from place to place, but it requires above all a developed sociological imagination and an awareness of culture as well as religion.

One possibility is to describe the ways in which vicarious religion 'works' – hence the examples outlined above. A second is to observe societies at particular moments in their evolution when 'normal' ways of living are for one reason or another suspended and something far more instinctive comes to the fore. The reaction to Princess Diana's untimely death offers a much quoted example, already referred to in Chapter 1. A second illustration can be found in the unexpected and very poignant series of actions that took place at the end of Jade Goody's life (she died in 2009). Here was a young woman – a star of reality television – whose lifestyle was a million miles from the respectabilities of traditional Anglicanism.[15] But as the illness that was to kill her at the age of 28 took its toll, she turned to the church repeatedly – for the baptism of her children and for herself, for her somewhat unusual wedding to Jack Tweed, and finally for her much more traditional funeral. Quite rightly we know very little about the reasons for Jade Goody's decisions in this respect and how she chose to interpret these encounters. Somehow, however, she found her way to an institution, in this case the Church of England, which responded graciously to her requests.

A third example was brought to my attention by a priest in the north of England.[16] What follows, written in his words rather than mine, is a description of a very striking event which can be read in different ways – theologians for example will respond in one way, social scientists in another. Crucial in terms of the argument in this chapter, however, is the need to be attentive to moments, whether individual or collective, in or through which the implicit (or hidden) becomes explicit (manifest).

Awakenings

Ian Wallis

'We're carrying Kenny in!' ushered the arrival of four young alpha males emerging from a densely packed gathering of bereaved humanity. Creased black trousers, buffed shoes, freshly laundered white shirts, scrubbed flesh and gelled hair. Without another word being uttered, the manner of their appearance convinced the funeral director in an instant of their sincerity and resolve as the official pall bearers were instructed to stand down.

A slow, faltering pilgrimage wended its way into St Michael's. Pews rapidly filled and standing room was soon exhausted leaving a substantial residue outside. The community had gathered to honour one of its own and to express its grief. A palpable sense of kinship and solidarity pervaded drawing into an integrity people of various ages and outlooks who otherwise shared little in common. Family, friends and neighbours, teachers, social workers and those with a professional interest, partners in crime, members of warring factions, prisoners chaperoned by their wardens, uneasy individuals trying to look inconspicuous and remain undetected. Evidently, being present for some was a costly business and not without danger.

Such tensions seemed apt given that Kenny had been far from 'risk-adverse'. Last Saturday, an evening of TWOCing [car theft] ended with an high speed pursuit when, 'out of his skull' and pursued by the police, Kenny wrapped a recently purloined BMW around a lamppost, killing himself and injuring another. Not that this take on events was foremost in the minds of those present. For most, Kenny was a martyr – a passionate car fanatic who, denied the wherewithal to acquire his own set of wheels, died pursuing his cause in somebody else's. A conviction that reverberated through the lyrics of the joy-riders' anthem chosen for the service, 'racing 'cross the desert at a hundred miles an hour'.

Yet by whatever criteria one measured Kenny, there was no concealing the wealth of affection in which he was held. A loyal regard that showed no signs of being diminished by his moral ambivalence or recklessness, but seemed able to accommodate these characteristics and, through doing so, to invest his life with a dignity and worth that it did not obviously merit. This was never more apparent than at the commendation when those who carried Kenny into church gathered around his coffin once more and, gripping the timber shell as if it was his flesh, they shared in the priestly act of entrusting, 'Go forth on your journey...'

Of all those diminished by this young adult death, no one suffered the repercussions greater than his partner Cam who, it transpired, was carrying their child. A baby boy was safely delivered some months later. His name, of course, would be Kenny. Cam needed to mark the beginning of Kenny Junior's life as she had the end of his father's. Godparents had been selected from Kenny's closest pals, but none of them were baptized. 'Pete, Russie, Kev and Sam, how about it? To get you up to speed, there'll be some sessions. And given you're adults, it's not just Baptism we're looking at, but Confirmation as well.'

Their faces wore the same resolve as at our first encounter by the hearse. We arranged an all inclusive initiation service for Kenny and his supporters. Peter, Russ, Kev and Sam turned up in the same gear. They stood proudly before the Bishop and seemed comfortable to cloth their convictions with words of Christian commitment and belief. They seemed to know instinctively what was required of them as glory came to weigh on their shoulders once more. Before, they had been entrusted with bearing their mate on his final journey; now, with a stake in the nurture of his bairn. How things had changed for those four 'nobodies' who, through circumstances beyond their control, came to see themselves in a more forgiving light.

Years on, the flowers on Kenny's grave are never limp and his son is full of promise.

All three of the examples quoted above (Princess Diana, Jade Goody and Kenny) involve untimely deaths. These are moments when the 'secular' routines of life are suspended, when – to put the same point in a different way – the abnormal (the articulation of religion in words and actions) becomes at least for a short time normal. For this reason alone they merit careful sociological attention.

A rather different illustration was brought to my attention by an army chaplain.[17] It is drawn from a chapter which examines the nature and significance of liturgy in a recent operational context – that is Afghanistan (Ball 2013; see also King 2013). Some interesting statistics precede the discussion of liturgy per se. Well aware that the dominant demographic in the armed forces (relatively young men) is the one least associated with religious belief and religious practice in civilian life, Ball notes that the intensity of military operations sharpens very noticeably the focus of a soldier's thoughts regarding the purpose and potential of their lives. Specifically: '[W]hen compared with the UK Census statistics [2001], there is a much higher proportion of those who profess to be Christians within the military: in 2008, 93 per cent in the army were registered as Christian (as against less than 1 per cent other world faiths and 6 per cent declared atheists, agnostics or having no faith)' (Ball 2013: 118).[18] The reasons for this situation are various, but prominent among them is – once again – the proximity of death. This leads in turn to a greater ownership of liturgy amongst military personnel, even those who rarely practise, when they are on operations.

What follows is a fascinating account of the army's response (indeed that of all three services) to this situation and the effect that this has on the role of the chaplain who is – par excellence – the provider of liturgy. A second factor runs parallel. Since the Falklands War, military practice has changed in that the bodies of British soldiers are now repatriated rather than being buried in the country in which they fell. This shift has led to new rituals, which are distinct from a funeral as such given that the latter will take place in Britain or elsewhere in the Commonwealth. The nature of the conflict also has a bearing, sometimes preventing at least some of the comrades of the fallen soldier from accompanying their colleague to the airhead where the formal leave-taking takes place. For this reason simpler liturgies (vigil services) have also emerged for use in the outstations, with formats that allow an officer or senior soldier to preside in the absence of a chaplain.[19] Ball's chapter is full of examples of both formal and informal liturgies, many of them very moving, in which the crucial point is the following: military chaplains, whether in Afghanistan or elsewhere, endeavour to give meaning to whatever happens, 'be it victory, defeat, injury, death, or causing injury and death' (Ball 2013: 131). Ritual is a powerful tool in this process.

Enough has been said to substantiate the claim that a good deal of latent religiousness continues to exist in twenty-first century Britain and that the notion of vicarious religion offers one way (among others) to understand this elusive phenomenon better. But what of the future? Will what I have termed vicarious religion endure in the twenty-first century, and for how long? The question can be approached variously and must be placed in context, noting in particular that vicarious religion is only one among several factors that must be taken into account in grasping the complexities of religious life in this country. It addresses a certain way of being religious which derives from a particular historical heritage and which thrives in a particular kind of church, the nature of which will be addressed in the following chapter. It is not the sum total of religiousness in modern Britain.

That said, there is plenty of evidence to indicate that the idea resonates more in older generations than the young – a process that recalls the generational differences set out in Chapter 2.[20] Broadly speaking those born before World War II will respond most easily to vicarious religion – unsurprisingly given that significant numbers in this age group, especially women, have had extensive links with the churches. Day (2013, forthcoming). Those that follow – the baby-boomers – are less convinced. Generation X (born in the 1960s) reacts even more sharply against the inherited model, but retains at least some knowledge of what went before. Generation Y (their children) does not. The insightful work of Collins-Mayo, Mayo and Nash on *The Faith of Generation Y* (2010; see also Collins-Mayo and Dandelion 2010; Savage *et al.* 2011) is interesting in this respect in that the authors find some evidence of lingering affiliation and belief amongst the young and relate their findings to the idea of vicarious religion. For the most part their data are unequivocal: Generation Y has lost the rebellious hostility towards formal religion that was characteristic of earlier decades, for the obvious reason that there is nothing to rebel against. Religion, vicarious or otherwise, is very largely an irrelevance in their day to day lives.

This, however, is less the case for those who are facing difficult situations of whatever kind. Circumstances alter cases, as both Collins-Mayo *et al.* and the examples above have shown. All of them focused on individuals or constituencies dominated by Generation Y: nonetheless Jade Goody found solace in the occasional offices; Kenny's family and friends not only wanted a Christian funeral for their friend, but participated actively in it; and up to a point the young men serving in Afghanistan bucked the statistical trends. All three give pause for thought.

Notes

1   See for example the huge amount of material gathered on the BRIN website under the rubric 'Changing belief in Britain' available at http://www.brin.ac.uk/

figures/#ChangingBelief (accessed 5 August 2014). This is updated on a regular basis.

2   In the table, the European comparisons are limited to former west European countries. More extensive data are available in the Eurobarometer Report. See http://ec.europa.eu/public_opinion/archives/ebs/ebs_341_en.pdf (accessed 5 August 2014).

3   The project was entitled 'Conventional and Common Religion in Leeds' and took place in the early 1980s. It was funded by the (then) Social Science Research Council. The findings were published by the Department of Sociology at the University of Leeds in a series of occasional papers.

4   Interestingly the incidence of prayer as such remains surprisingly constant. See for example the data from Round 6 (2012) of the European Social Survey. Trend statistics (weighted) for the claimed frequency of private prayer (i.e. apart from during religious services) in the UK are assembled at http://www.brin.ac.uk/news/2013/prayer-and-other-news/ (accessed 5 August 2014).

5   The work of Tania ap Siôn (2009, 2010) is important in this respect. For more details see http://wrap.warwick.ac.uk/view/author_id/7801.html (accessed 5 August 2014)

6   Study after study has emerged. See for example Gill, Hadaway and Marler (1998), Bruce (2002), Gill (2002), Voas and Crockett (2005) and Glendinning and Bruce (2006).

7   See for example, David Voas's own work on 'fuzzy fidelity'. Voas (2009) uses this term to denote casual loyalty to the Christian tradition in much of Europe. He recognizes that residual involvement is considerable but argues that religion pays only a minor role in the lives of such people.

8   It is worth noting in this connection that the notion of believing without belonging is beginning to resonate in new ways in the United States (as indeed in Britain) as the number of 'nones' rises. The term 'nones' means no religious attachment, but it would be incorrect to assume that no religious attachment means no religious belief. See the Pew Forum on Religion and Public Life (2012).

9   The parallels between Abby Day and Lois Lee are very clear. Both see belief or unbelief (non-religion) as performative, i.e. as something that is worked out in daily living.

10 For more detail on natal, ethnic and aspirational identities, see Day (2011: 182 ff). On Christian identification in the Census, see also Voas and Bruce (2004).

11 To give but one example, in 2009 43 per cent of adults attended a church or place of worship for a memorial service for someone who had died. See http://www.churchofengland.org/about-us/facts-stats.aspx (accessed 5 August 2014)

12 For a full account of this episode and its aftermath, see http://www.archbishop ofcanterbury.org/articles.php/1135/sharia-law-what-did-the-archbishop-actually-say (accessed 5 August 2014). Interestingly Linda Woodhead (2013d) uses this episode as a take-off point for a discussion of the British situation more generally in a collection entitled *Contesting Secularism: Comparative Perspectives*. She argues that Britain is neither religious, nor secular, but a complex combination of both.

13 See 'Time for us to challenge the idols of high finance', http://www.archbishop ofcanterbury.org/articles.php/2236/time-for-us-to-challenge-the-idols-of-high-finance for the full text, published in *The Financial Times* on 1November 2011 (accessed 5 August 2014).
14 A number of these illustrations come from the Nordic countries, which are often thought to be some of the most secular in the world. The continuation of some form of church tax or voluntary contribution, however, ensures that the population as a whole continues to invest in the national church, even when the formal ties with the state have come to an end (as is the case in Sweden).
15 Wikipedia offers a full account of Jade Goody's colourful life. See http://en.wikipedia.org/wiki/Jade_Goody (accessed 5 August 2014).
16 This case study was presented at a meeting of the Littlemore Group in August 2005 and was included in Davie (2008). The Littlemore Group is a cluster of priest-theologians with experience of working in parishes, some of them demanding. I am grateful to Ian Wallis for allowing me to reproduce this extract. A protracted correspondence revealed that the copyright lay with the author, not with the publisher.
17 My informant was Padre Andrew Totten MBE, Assistant Chaplain-General.
18 Statistics released in 2013 indicate that the percentage of Christians has fallen since 2008; King (2013) makes the additional point that the indices of religious commitment diminish with age and rank. That said the overall figure remains noticeably higher than the population as a whole. See http://www.dasa.mod.uk/index.php/publications/personnel/combined/diversity-dashboard/2013-10-01 for more details (accessed 5 August 2014).
19 It is nonetheless interesting to discover in a passing reference that whatever the liturgy in question, more rather than less traditional formulations are preferred by the great majority of soldiers (Ball 2013: 128)
20 Tellingly, the decline in vicarious religion matches very closely the decline in Anglican identification by age group. See Figure 3.5 and the data presented in Woodhead (2013e).

5

Territory, Politics and Institutions

Chapter 4 dealt primarily with cultural legacies and their influences on belief and unbelief. This chapter covers similar ground but from a different starting point: it too is concerned with the legacies of the past but looks in particular at territory, politics and institutions. The key point has already been made (p. 21): that is, to recognize the tensions and partnerships between Caesar and God that exist all over Europe and the corresponding links between religion and national identity (Martin 1978: 100). How, then, do these long-term processes work themselves out in different parts of the United Kingdom? The plural nature of this question is important: England, Scotland, Wales and Northern Ireland are very different from each other in terms of history and political settlement and must be treated accordingly.

The English Case

A noteworthy fact about religious history in England is the absence of a political split which coincided with a major religious division. Instead the interactions between religious traditions and a wide variety of economic and political variables are multiple. This can be seen in what Beckford calls the great age of religious activity in England,[1] which opened in the mid sixteenth century and closed in the late eighteenth – a period which saw the emergence of Anglicanism, Quakerism, Congregationalism, Presbyterianism and Methodism. As a result, a relatively developed degree of religious diversity (mostly in the form of Dissent) existed at an early stage, unlike the situation in most of Europe. De facto toleration followed from this. Beckford

Religion in Britain: A Persistent Paradox, Second Edition. Grace Davie.
© 2015 Grace Davie. Published 2015 by John Wiley & Sons, Ltd.

notes the implications of this situation for political life: 'the very plurality
and diversity of religious groups prevented British politics from being dominated by a single, major confrontation between church and state, politics
and religion, or church and church' (Beckford 1991: 179).

Out of this situation emerged what is best described as a limited monopoly; a 'state church partially counterbalanced by a substantial bloc of dissent
dispersed in the population at large' (Martin 1978: 20). The church in question was a variant of the Protestant Reformation.[2] It was brought into being
by Henry VIII at the time of his marriage to Anne Boleyn. The bare bones of
the story are well known: Henry was determined to marry Anne; the Pope
refused to annul his previous marriage; Henry retaliated in a declaration of
independence. What became known as the 'break from Rome' became,
moreover, a defining moment in English history. It not only repudiated the
authority of the Pope, but established the monarch as the effective head of
the Church of England, which became exactly what its name implies. The
twists and turns of the subsequent decades are many, but the particular
nature of the church in question was gradually consolidated. Its essence was
captured by the Elizabethan Settlement, an arrangement which rejected
both servility to Rome and subservience to Geneva, giving rise to the
celebrated *via media*; a formula which embodied among other things an
essentially English church designed to meet the spiritual needs of the English
people (Moorman 1980: 213). In many ways this is still true: the Church of
England still does meet the spiritual needs of a sizeable, if declining, proportion of English people, despite their reluctance to attend its services.

In terms of theology – and indeed of ecclesiology – the Church of England
is distinct from its European neighbours, whether Catholic or Protestant. In
terms of territory, it is not. All of these churches have in common the fact
that their jurisdiction is bounded at national, regional and local level – an
arrangement with significant implications. The consequences for the nation
are clear: not only is the United Kingdom distinct from its European
neighbours, but England, Scotland, Wales and Northern Ireland are distinct
from each other. Such differences are increasingly finding political expression (see below). It is important to note, however, that confessional factors –
and the mindsets that go with these – predate these political movements by
several centuries. An interesting parenthesis follows from this. An increasing
stress on independence in Scotland and Wales has at times left the question
of Englishness in limbo: what precisely does this mean? Day's work on
believing in belonging, introduced in the previous chapter, is relevant to this
question. Those whom she terms 'natal' Christians are not, for the most
part, concerned with either belief or practice; they do however assume a
connection between their religious affiliation, expressed in Church of
England baptism, and Englishness (Day 2011: 55–56, 182). It was for this
reason that many of them checked the box 'Christian' in the 2001 Census.

Such connections are, of course, effected at local rather than national level. Baptisms take place in local, mostly parish churches, as indeed do marriages and funerals. Indeed the significance of the parish in the life of the historically dominant churches of Europe – including the Church of England – is hard to overestimate. It is central to their evolution over several centuries and brings both advantages and disadvantages. Taking the advantages first, the presence of a parish church in every part of England (north and south, urban and rural, rich and poor, expanding and contracting) is a definite plus. The parish system constitutes a comprehensive network that few can rival, which by its very nature denotes stability – it has been there for centuries, far longer that its political equivalents. Both presence and stability come, however, at a price: the former is costly in every sense of the term and the latter runs the risk of immobility. Each of these points requires expansion.

The debates surrounding *Faith in the City*, the report of the Archbishops' Commission on Urban Priority Areas, have already been noted (see Chapter 2). Crucially both the data that were brought to bear in this protracted discussion and the authority of the Commission's voice derived directly from the continuing presence of the Church of England, through its parish system, in some of the most troubled parts of urban Britain. The evidence was there for all to see, not least the parish priest, who encountered serious deprivation in the lives of both individuals and communities on a daily basis. The same was true in rural areas: *Faith in the Countryside* (1990), though less contentious than its urban counterpart, reported first-hand on the 'effects of economic, environmental and social change on the rural community' (see Terms of Reference). And more than two decades later the work continues in, for example, a recent discussion of credit unions. These are not a new invention. In the summer of 2013, however, the community-finance sector gained prominence as a viable alternative to payday loans. The point at issue was not a rival set of companies or indeed of credit unions but the provision of expertise and – even more importantly – outlets at grassroots level.[3]

All that said, the maintenance of the parish system and the circa 15 000 buildings associated with this, together with the wide variety of professionals (both lay and ordained) who sustain this enterprise, is a costly business and almost certainly beyond the means of the Church of England as we currently know it. Providing a universal service to be accessed according to need is expensive. It is all the more difficult if the constituency responsible for the service continues to diminish. So what is to be done? The Church of England has been ingenious in its use of unpaid as well as paid staff and there is an evident willingness on the part of communities up and down the land to sustain buildings that relatively few people use on a regular basis. Closures and mergers are, however, inevitable. Many have occurred already and more will follow. That this will happen is pretty much accepted; the argument turns on how such changes will be effected. Central in this respect is an awareness of history, both local and national, and the need to think deeply about what is at stake. What is good about the inherited system and should be preserved at all costs, and what is simply peripheral? It is very unlikely that the outcome will be the same in every case or that everyone will agree about what is proposed.[4]

It is worth noting that exactly the same question is demanding attention in many parts of Europe. *Portraits du catholicisme* (Pérez-Agote 2012) presents carefully gathered data on the Catholic Church in Belgium, France, Italy, Spain and Portugal. All five are Catholic countries in terms of history and culture and in all five the Church has been organized on a parish basis for more than a millennium. Can this continue as the statistical strains become increasingly acute – i.e. as the numbers of regular churchgoers fall, the resource base diminishes and the age profile of the priesthood rises? The answers vary.[5] In Italy and Portugal, the traditional pattern endures; Spain hovers uneasily on the cusp. In Belgium and France, however, the situation has reached crisis point. Specifically, the relationship with territory is being rethought: in France in the creation of 'new' parishes which are effectively amalgamations of older ones (counting more often than not in double figures); in Belgium, in 'fédérations' or 'unités pastorales'. In both cases different dioceses have resolved, or attempted to resolve, the problem in different ways, leading to a patchwork of solutions (Pérez-Agote 2012: 266). In short this is not only an English problem.

Stability is one thing, immobility quite another. Take for example the upheavals associated with the Industrial Revolution, at which point significant sections of the English population moved from the country to the city. Parish-based churches, locked into pre-industrial models of territory, were unable to follow suit. In the fullness of time, the system did adapt: it had to. New dioceses were established and impressive programmes of church building took place in towns and cities all over the country – to considerable effect. Churchgoing reached a high point at the end of the nineteenth century. All that said significant numbers of parish churches in England continue to exist in places where very few people live and the fact that they are often of considerable architectural value simply adds to the problem. Hence the dilemma: precisely the feature that ensured the continuing presence of a Church of England parish in the inner cities of late twentieth century England, and in the farming communities which have suffered badly in recent decades, prevents the Church from adapting quickly to economic change and to the population movements that go with this.

Classic statements of secularization derive from this. They argue that traditional forms of religion were unable to withstand either the dislocations of the Industrial Revolution or the philosophical challenges of the

Enlightenment that preceded them – and taken together these undoubtedly radical shifts constituted a shock from which the European churches have never fully recovered. There is truth in this, but all too often the wrong inference has been drawn: that is, to assume a *necessary* incompatibility between religion per se and modern, primarily urban life. This is simply not the case. Something quite different happened in the United States, for example, where territorial embedding had never taken place and where pluralism appears to have stimulated rather than inhibited religious activity, not least in urban areas. Equally distinctive are the global regions of the developing world, where some of the largest cities house some of the largest churches, not to mention tens of thousands of smaller ones.

More immediately, it is important to appreciate the new forms of religious life that emerged in the towns and cities of England, some of which grew almost as rapidly as the conurbations of which they were part. Both nonconformist and Catholic churches mushroomed in the nineteenth century, albeit for different reasons. The first filled the spaces left by the historic churches; the latter catered for new sources of labour coming in from Ireland. Either way, an already incipient market became increasingly visible. Two comments are important in this connection, noting first that the pros and cons of territorial embedding relate to absence as well as presence. It is true that the free churches were able to move quickly into the growing cities of urban Britain and to make contact with sections of society beyond the reach of Anglican parishes. That very mobility has however been found wanting in more recent decades as the free church presence, at least in its older forms, has ebbed away. The second point nuances this statement in the sense that new forms of 'free' church have emerged to take their place, not least among the newly arrived in this country. In the twenty-first century a bewildering variety of alternatives transcend (but do not replace) the parish system and – by and large – the bigger the city the more the alternatives. London, as we have seen, is the quintessential case. In terms of religion as in so much else, it has become a truly global city.

Thinking about 'establishment'

What then can be said about 'establishment' as such? Establishment does not mean that the Church of England is identified with the state. It does, however, signify a special relationship between that Church and the political order at least in its English forms.[6] But as in all relationships, there are two sides to consider. If on the one hand the established nature of the Church of England confers upon one and only one church within the United Kingdom certain 'rights and privileges', it is equally clear that these rights and privileges carry with them corresponding 'restrictions and limitations' (Welsby 1985: 45).

For example, 26 Church of England bishops currently have the right (at any one time) to sit in the House of Lords,[7] offering amongst other things a high-profile forum for debate. But is it a sensible use of a bishop's time to spend certain weeks in the year in attendance in the House regardless of the agenda, or in mastering a difficult brief for a crucial debate at the expense of a prior diocesan commitment? Not everyone would say yes. A second issue concerns not so much the existence per se of 'rights and privileges' but how these are implemented. On the plus side bishops and archbishops have used the House of Lords to make repeated, valuable and on the whole well-received interventions over several decades – on this the evidence is clear.[8] In June 2013, however, something rather different occurred. The bishops were seriously discomfited by the debate in the second chamber concerning the marriage of same-sex couples. Despite an unusually high turn-out, they were effectively sidelined.[9] Two days later Archbishop Justin Welby warned the General Synod of complacency in this respect. Society's attitudes to sexuality are changing radically rendering the Church – established or not – increasingly out of step with current realities.[10] The implications of this complex and continuing debate are revisited in Chapter 6.

In the meantime, there are alternative arguments to consider. A number of these are set out in Chapman (2011), which – among other things – considers the role of establishment in a religiously plural society. Interestingly this echoes a point introduced in the first edition of this book, which is best expressed by reversing the 'normal' question. Instead of arguing that current privileges should be restricted, might it be possible to extend them? If a seat in the Lords can be used by the bishops of the established Church to considerable effect (for the most part anyway), why not offer this opportunity to the senior members of other Christian denominations and to representatives of at least some other-faith communities? Their contributions to political debate especially on ethical or moral issues are not only helpful but necessary – and more (not less) so in a religiously plural society. Public discussion will be enriched if specific bodies of knowledge and opinion are brought to our (i.e. society's) attention, recognizing that disagreements are likely to remain – regarding, for example, the nature of marriage, the status of the embryo and what have become known as 'end-of-life issues'.

Since the early 1990s, Tariq Modood has talked persuasively in these terms, expanding the argument to support establishment as such. Take for instance his contribution to a discussion on moderate secularism, published in *Open Democracy* (Modood 2011a), in which he argues that it is quite possible in a country like Britain to affirm the claims of a wide variety of religions without abolishing the established status of the Church of England. And once launched, Modood pursues the argument to its logical conclusions: why not level up rather than level down? Might it, in other words, be possible to pluralize the state–religion link rather than sever it?

Such a statement is clearly provocative. It builds, however, on an idea that I find attractive and have considered myself: that is, the notion of a 'weak' rather than strong established church (Davie 2008, 2010b, 2014). It is abundantly clear that a strong state church runs the risk of being both excluding and exclusive, as indeed does a strong state. Examples of both can be found in different parts of modern Europe.[11] A weak state (or established) church, on the other hand, has the capacity to be more accommodating. Discerning its strengths from a distinctive past – that of a *partial monopoly* – it can use these imaginatively to welcome rather than exclude, and to encourage rather than to condemn. Such an approach counters the following oft-repeated assertion: that the present system (i.e. establishment) is no longer tenable, as it discriminates against minorities, both Christian and other, which are and will remain an essential part of British life. It is a tempting argument and skilfully deployed by Modood in an earlier text, which contains a careful review of the evidence *in favour* of the pluralist case for disestablishment (Modood 1994). The denouement, however, is unexpected:

> I have to state as a brute fact that I have not come across a single article or speech or statement by any minority faith in favour of disestablishment. This is quite extraordinary given that secular reformers make the desire to accommodate these minorities an important motive for reform. (1994: 61–62)

Modood has repeated this statement on a number of occasions since.[12] It derives from the logic that was brought into play at the time of the Rushdie controversy. The real danger to multi-faithism, he contends, does not come from a relatively powerless national church (not much comfort here for the Anglicans) but from 'a virtually unchallengeable and culturally insensitive secular centre which makes demands on all faiths, but especially on the least Westernised faiths at a time when the minority faiths are asserting themselves as a form of cultural defence' (Modood 1994: 66). In other words, disestablishing the Church of England may have unexpected consequences: not only would it marginalize the Church of England, it would at the same time sideline all those who choose to take faith seriously whatever their religious allegiance. It should not be undertaken lightly. Modood's approach underlines a further point: that the creation and sustaining of a tolerant and pluralist society requires creative rather than destructive thinking. What, in other words, do we need to *create* in order to ensure a healthy pluralism and to give this institutional recognition – a point to be developed in Chapter 9?

In the 1990s, a prescient approach to the issues at stake formed a dominant theme within Jonathan Sacks's celebrated Reith Lectures, subsequently published in *The Persistence of Faith* (Sacks 1991). At the time Lord Sacks was Chief Rabbi elect, a spokesperson for the oldest other-faith community in this country. In a plural society, he argued, we should indeed acknowledge our differences, but alongside the local language (or languages) of community it is equally important to seek a public language of citizenship in which to express shared values and to emphasize what we hold in common – a task traditionally fulfilled in England by, among other institutions, the established Church. But times have changed and current diversity within society 'makes many people, outside the Church and within, feel uneasy with that institution'. At this point, however, Sacks's argument – rather like Modood's – changed course, for rather than improving the situation, disestablishment would, he claims, do the reverse, for it would symbolize 'a significant retreat from the notion that we share any values and beliefs at all. And that would be a path to more, not fewer, tensions' (Sacks 1991: 68). Once again the presentation isn't all that reassuring from an Anglican point of view, for it implies that an established church is a lesser evil rather than a positive good. On the other hand, Sacks supplies yet another voice which counsels caution concerning the process of disestablishment.[13]

The role of the monarchy is part and parcel of the same discussion. Modood himself turns to this in the article cited above (Modood 2011a). Following Davie (2007a), he notes first that Prince Charles, the heir to the throne – and therefore to the office of Supreme Governor of the Church of England – has indicated that he would as monarch prefer the designation 'Defender of Faith' to the historic title 'Defender of the Faith' – a point that is frequently repeated by the media.[14] Modood also recalls the repeated affirmation by the present Queen that religious diversity is something which enriches society; it should therefore be seen as an asset, not as a threat.[15] This is even more the case in relation to the Commonwealth. Paradoxically, a bastion of privilege turns out to be a key and very positive opinion former in a persistent and at times delicate discussion.

Before closing this section, however, it is important to note that the relatively benign approach to establishment outlined so far is partial. It fits well within a chapter dealing with legacies of the past in terms of territory, politics and institutions. Sharper and more critical voices – both inside and outside the churches – will appear in due course. The insiders will be introduced in Chapter 7; the secularists in Chapter 9.

Stepping Westward

A persistent theme in David Martin's writing captures the 'stepping westward' of Northern European religion: from the overwhelmingly dominant state churches of Scandinavia, through the limited pluralism of Britain to the competing denominations of the United States. With reference to the Celtic fringes of Britain, the key point is the following:

> Even now England itself retains some elements of aristocratic hierarchy, and of the relationship of church to state, whilst its Protestant peripheries in Wales, Scotland and Ulster, as well as its overseas extensions in Canada, Australia and New Zealand, variously evolved towards something closer to the American pattern. (Martin 1990: 19)

In short, Scotland, Wales and Northern Ireland are one step out (or westward) in this process; all of them are noticeably more Protestant and more egalitarian than England. All three, moreover, have changed markedly since the first edition of this book went to press. In 1994 Scotland and Wales were visibly stronger in terms of religious membership than England (see Davie 1994: 50 for the relevant figures). This is no longer the case. The decline in membership (as indeed in affiliation) is pronounced in both cases. Northern Ireland remains an outlier in terms of overall statistics but here too significant changes have taken place – specifically, the political situation has reached a new stage with the Good Friday Agreement. Sectarianism has diminished, but has by no means disappeared. The devolution of political power in Scotland and Wales should also be noted; in the case of Scotland this has included the build-up to the 2014 referendum on independence.

In the first edition of this book, the evidence for the relative religiousness of Scotland, Wales and Northern Ireland was taken from Brierley and Hiscock (1993). It is interesting to look at this in the light of Brierley's more recent work. In the introductory chapter to *UK Church Statistics 2005–2015*, for example, Brierley (2011) records the denominations which are changing fastest in terms of decline and of growth.[16] Having established these lists, he adds the following observation: with one or two exceptions, it is clear that the denominations which have declined most over the period (2005–2015) are almost all located in Wales or Scotland. They are, moreover, small churches, except for the Church of Scotland. Put differently, almost all the decline in religious membership north of the border can be accounted for by a dramatic drop in membership in the Church of Scotland.[17] Church membership in England, conversely, is relatively stable – by and large decreases are offset by increases, many of which are due to immigration. The statistics relating to the number of churches, the number of denominations and the number of ministers display a largely similar pattern.[18]

With this in mind, the situation in Scotland and Wales might be described as late-onset secularization: the process was delayed for longer than it was in England but was particularly sharp when it came. Both the delay and the subsequent shift require careful thought. Statistical decline, moreover, is only one element in the overall picture and is experienced differently in different places.

Understanding religion in Scotland

In Scotland things were, and still are, very different from England (Morris 2009).[19] No Anglican *via media* here. For most, though not all, of Scotland has been straightforwardly Protestant for several centuries, and its Protestants remain overwhelmingly Presbyterian. They are distributed over a variety of denominations, among which the Church of Scotland, 'established yet free', is both the largest and most significant. It is 'established' in that it is in historical continuity with the Church of Scotland reformed in 1560 and whose liberties were protected within the Treaty of Union (1707). But the Church is also 'by law made free of the State' and for this reason is very different in nature from the established church south of the border. Brown's *Social History of Religion in Scotland* (1987) describes, but does not oversimplify, the historical connections between religion and national identity in this part of Britain.[20] Rather more than other commentators, Brown stresses the variety within Scotland's religion. He also points out the possibilities for disagreement about exactly which features of theology or ecclesiastical government have contributed to Scottish distinctiveness; the equations are not self-evident. Scotland, however, lacked its own resident head of state from 1603 and its own legislative assembly from 1707. For both these reasons the national church became, alongside the legal and the educational systems, a major carrier of national consciousness.

Indeed, until the constitutional changes of 1998, the General Assembly of the Church of Scotland was the only place where Scottish concerns could be scrutinized by Scottish people. Unsurprisingly its deliberations – especially those pertaining to the wider society – were closely covered by the national media. Distinguished visitors attended this body, not least Mrs Thatcher, who in 1988 chose this venue to deliver her 'Sermon on the Mound' (see pp. 34). Just over 10 years later (1999) the then Chancellor of the Exchequer, Gordon Brown, the son of a Presbyterian minister, used a General Assembly speech to outline his thinking on international debt; he returned in 2008 as Prime Minister. And in 2009, Desmond Tutu electrified the gathering. It is still the case that the deliberations of the Assembly are streamed live for those who wish to follow them, but the locus of debate in Scotland has shifted. It now takes place in the Scottish Parliament, whose functions and roles are governed by the Scotland Act (1998). Religion is vestigially present in this body in the form of a Time for Reflection (TFR), which provides a weekly opportunity for representatives of religions and other belief systems to address the assembled gathering.[21] The thrust however lies elsewhere.

A similar shift can be seen statistically. The Scottish Census – like its counterpart in England and Wales – contained a question on religion in 2001, a practice repeated in 2011. The question, however, was worded differently, meaning that comparisons with the rest of Britain are difficult.[22] Comparisons apart, these data tell us that 54 per cent of Scottish people indicate that they are Christian (a decrease of 11% since 2001), and 37 per cent declare that they have no religion (an increase of 9% since 2001).[23] Among Christians, the Church of Scotland remains the largest group (32% of the population, but with a fall of 10% since 2001), followed by Catholics at 16 per cent (no change). The presence of other faiths should also be noted, but it is relatively small; it now stands at just over 2 per cent of the population overall, of which 1.4 per cent are Muslims. As in England and Wales, the data can be broken down by a wide variety of socio-economic and geographical variables.

It is at this point that Brown's remarks about variety begin to resonate, bearing in mind that that denominational differences are compounded by regional variations – a factor reinforced not only by Scotland's geography but by the proximity of its west coast to Ireland. Irish immigration in the nineteenth century was a significant factor, a movement that brought appreciable, though never huge, numbers of Catholics to Scotland. These communities remain concentrated in a relatively small part of the south west and account for a history of sectarianism in that part of Scotland. The implications of regionalism continue to be felt in other ways as well. In the Western Hebrides, for example, the proportion of people declaring themselves to be Christian is noticeably higher than in most of the country, commitments that spill over into everyday life. Echoes of sabbatarianism – once commonplace in Scotland – persist. In this residually Calvinist enclave, the decision in 2006 to promote Sunday sailings to the Isle of Harris was controversial. That said attitudes differ on different islands. Further south where the Catholic influence endures, ferries were welcomed seven days a week (Seenan 2006). Old habits, it seems, die hard.

In conclusion, it is clear that the constitutional position of Scotland would have altered significantly had there been a 'yes' vote in September 2014. No change to the legal status of any religion or of Scotland's churches was proposed,[24] but the wider implications of a vote for independence were undoubtedly far-reaching. During the course of the debate, however, the Church of Scotland (to give but one example) took care to remain impartial on the issue itself. Active participation was encouraged but no steer was given.[25] The decision to host a service of reconciliation for all parties at St Giles' Cathedral in Edinburgh on the Sunday following the vote is also worth noting.

Nonconformity in Wales

In Wales, the situation is different again. As in Scotland there is a dissenting or Protestant culture but there is no national church. Indeed Dissent in Wales persists in splitting itself – both denominationally and linguistically – into a number of smaller groupings, each of which is numerically inferior to either the (disestablished) Church in Wales, with its English connotations, or to Catholicism. Historically, however, the chapels and chapel culture have had huge significance. They amounted to what Martin calls 'established dissidence', becoming thereby important carriers of Welsh identity. Specifically they provided the cultural background from which emerged a whole stream of political leaders in the twentieth century, mostly of Liberal and Labour persuasion, destined for Westminster (Martin 1990: 34–35). This is no longer the case.

Currently the Catholic and the Anglican Churches in Wales are indeed the largest Christian communities, but the overall numbers are not only modest but declining.[26] Membership of the Presbyterian Church of Wales and the Union of Welsh Independents hovers at around 1 per cent of the population; the Baptist Union of Wales is smaller still. All three, moreover, figure in Brierley's list of declining churches, as indeed do the Welsh Catholics.[27] The Census data tell a similar story though the overall numbers are much larger: in 2001 circa 70 per cent of the population considered themselves to be Christian, a figure that fell to 57.6 per cent in 2011. The drop, in other words, was greater than it was in either England or Scotland. Wales emerges, moreover, as the region in England and Wales with the highest number of people who have 'no religion' (see Figure 3.4). As in Scotland, there is an other-faith presence but a small one. Predictably, the Muslims constitute the largest other-faith community and are mostly located in Cardiff where Yemeni sailors arrived in the late nineteenth century. Interestingly the oldest mosque in Britain is in Cardiff and was established in 1860.

How should these figures be interpreted? In a continuing series of publications, Chambers offers a rather more nuanced account of religion in Wales.[28] His approach fits well into the overall framework of this chapter. In his discussion of secularization, for example, Chambers underlines the distinctiveness of the Welsh case, specifically that 'modernization and industrialization were the motors that led to an incremental growth in indigenous religious institutions' – thus reversing 'normal' assumptions (Chambers 2012: 221). The reason moreover is clear. These institutions were not parish churches locked into pre-industrial territory; they were free churches from different denominations that were able to move rapidly into the newly industrialized regions of Wales and competed for the privilege: the architectural evidence is there for all to see. The converse, however, is also true: these chapels and the impressive local culture that they sustained declined rapidly alongside the communities of which they were part. The dramatic collapse in both steel-making and mining in the 1980s had a devastating effect, from which neither the communities in South Wales nor the religious institutions associated with them have been able to recover. Tentatively Chambers suggests a more positive future for religious organizations in community-based social action, relating his findings to the changing political situation in

Wales. Devolution, he argues, affords new opportunities to the churches (see also Chambers and Thompson 2005). Time will tell.

Political change in Northern Ireland

In Northern Ireland, conservative Protestant values have occupied a pre-eminent place in the political arena for most of the twentieth century. Indeed it was the refusal of the Protestant population of Ulster to be assimilated into the Irish Free State on its formation in 1921 that lay behind the creation of Northern Ireland in the first place. It is unsurprising therefore that the identification of the interests of the Northern Irish state with those of its Protestant majority dominated political thinking in this part of the world for decades. The situation seemed, moreover, to be self-perpetuating, for each time a more ecumenical, more liberal or more secular set of assumptions suggested itself, the reaction set in. The lines were hardened and the support for Unionism – embodied in the uncompromising views of a politician such as Ian Paisley – strengthened.

That was certainly the case when the initial version of this chapter was drafted (i.e. in the early 1990s), at which point no one anticipated the political metamorphosis that was to take place in less than a decade. But in 1998, the period that had become known as the Northern Ireland 'Troubles' – one of the western world's most longstanding and intractable conflicts – was effectively brought to a close with the historic Good Friday/Belfast Agreement. The most visible outcomes of the Agreement have been the end of the violence (or most of it), the setting-up of power-sharing political arrangements, the decommissioning of weapons and the transformation of policing. The Irish Republic has dropped its constitutional claim to the six counties which form Northern Ireland. For all these reasons and more, it is hardly an exaggeration to say that the Good Friday Agreement marked a sea change in the Northern Ireland landscape – so much so that Northern Ireland has become a model for the resolution of ethno-religious conflict elsewhere. It is equally evident that the Agreement and its at times chequered aftermath (not everything has gone right) have generated a flood of comment and reflection.[29]

A full analysis of this pivotal moment lies beyond the scope of this chapter. It is important, however, to grasp the significance of religion both in the preceding conflict and in the decade and half that has followed, recognizing that in the Agreement itself, there is very little mention of religion as such. It would, however, be naïve in the extreme to imagine that religion was anything but a central factor in the division of Ireland that preceded this seismic shift and in the motivations of its major protagonists. Other factors are, of course, important, but the enduring and intractable quality of the conflict derived from fact that the competing populations in Ireland adhered to different religious traditions, which created in turn self-contained and seemingly impenetrable life-worlds (Bruce 1986: 249).

Nor have these differences disappeared. Politically the situation is very different but religion remains a crucially important identity marker in Northern Ireland. Mitchell (2005, 2012; see also Mitchell and Ganiel 2011) is clear on this point, refuting the assumption that the decline in conflict in Northern Ireland would lead necessarily to a decline in religious commitment. This is not the case. The statistical profiles are complex. Mitchell, supported by Brierley (2011), argues for persistence (on a wide range of religious indicators) in the Protestant population of Northern Ireland, but acknowledges a marked degree of secularization amongst Catholics. Mass attendance has decreased sharply and understandings of doctrine have become increasingly individualized (Mitchell 2012: 240; see also note 16). Statistics from the Census, however, tell a rather different story, bearing in mind that the unit of measurement is different – it is concerned with community size rather than with beliefs or practice.[30] The breakdown by religious denomination (in terms of numbers and percentage) for 1991, 2001 and 2011 is, nonetheless, revealing.[31] It displays a steady growth in the Catholic population. Overall however, the Protestants remain the slightly larger group: 48 per cent of the Northern Irish population are either Protestant or brought up Protestant (a drop of 5 per cent from the 2001 census), and 45 per cent of the resident population are either Catholic or brought up Catholic (an increase of 1%). Only 7 per cent fall outside these categories.

Even more important, however, is the distinctiveness of the Northern Irish population overall and not only in terms of religion. Questions of national identity (introduced in the 2011 Census) resonate differently in this corner of the United Kingdom. It would, moreover, be unwise to equate religious belonging with national identity in Northern Ireland – they measure different things. Birth rates, age profiles and patterns of migration are also significant in that they can alter the balance between Protestant and Catholic in a relatively short space of time, most obviously in the profiles for particular localities.[32] In recent decades, the south and west of Northern Ireland have become steadily more Catholic whilst Protestants are increasingly concentrated in the east. Perhaps the most telling difference of all, however, concerns the question on religion per se. The fact that this has been included in the Census in Northern Ireland since 1861 reveals in itself the long-term significance of religious identity for Northern Irish people.

The Importance of Locality

Local differences have already revealed themselves within the Celtic fringe. Welsh-speaking chapels have an obvious geographical base in the Welsh-speaking parts of the country. The Highlands and Islands of Scotland are noticeably different from the south east. And even within the relatively restricted area of Northern Ireland, profiles vary. The same is true in England but on a larger scale.

One way of approaching this question lies in relatively straightforward denominational mapping, though this, in many ways, begs the essential question: why was it that certain denominations took hold in some places rather than others? A second set of differences cuts across denominational divides, those for example which emerged from the 2001 and 2011 Censuses – an analysis that can be pursued at many levels. Precisely this point is made by David Voas concerning neighbourhood variation in the self-reporting of religion or non-religion in the 2011 census.[33] The statistics are extraordinarily varied between wards (i.e. small areas with an average population of about 6500). But why? Is this a question of composition or context or both? In other words, 'are religious and non-religious people geographically concentrated for reasons not directly related to religion (but rather because of personal characteristics that may not be obvious)? Or are local norms and religious environments sufficiently distinctive that individuals will think and behave differently depending on where they live?' Such questions merit further exploration.

In the first edition of this book, I used two contrasting parts of the country to explore the question of region more fully: the far south west and the north west of England, paying particular attention to the city of Liverpool. Up to a point they could be seen as mirror images of each other. In the south west, for example, the historic presence of Methodism pushed the established Church in one direction; in the north west, residual recusancy and Catholic immigration from Ireland pushed it in another. The consequences can still be felt. For this edition I have selected different examples: the first is York and relies considerably on the careful analyses of Robin Gill over many years. The second is London, noting once again that developments in the capital are of particular interest in the overall picture of religion in Britain.

Robin Gill's (2012) study of York fascinates for several reasons. It is long-term, empirically driven, comprehensive (at least of Christianity) and interestingly reflexive in the sense that Gill continues to revise his opinions as new material emerges. Regarding the latter, Mathew Guest's book-length study of St Michael-le-Belfrey (Guest 2007) and Goodhew's overview of new churches in York (Goodhew 2012c) are important. To understand Gill's approach fully, it is necessary to place the York study within his broader analyses of church decline in Britain (Gill 1993). A major thread in this work concerns the overbuilding of churches and chapels in mid to late nineteenth-century Britain, which led over and over again to an all-too-predictable scenario: overprovision, empty seats, financial strains, growing demoralization and eventual decline. Both Anglicans and nonconformists were guilty of this, but especially the latter. In York, as elsewhere, the architectural evidence is manifest. Interestingly the Catholic Church avoided this problem at least to some extent. Instead of increasing their seating as numbers rose, York's Catholics adopted a policy of repeated celebrations of the mass in a single building – a cheaper and more flexible alternative.

A walk through York with Gill's 2012 chapter in hand would bring a great deal of *this* chapter to life – both in general and in relation to the city itself. It also anticipates the discussion in Part III. The first point to note, however, is that York like everywhere else is distinctive. First and foremost, it is a major centre of Christianity in this country – the seat of the Archbishop of York and the hub of the Church of England's Northern Province. The long-term Quaker presence is also significant, partly for the making of chocolate (developed as a beneficial alternative to alcohol), but also for Seebohm Rowntree's much-quoted reports on the social conditions discovered in the city in the first half of the twentieth century. Amongst other things these documents contain detailed data on adult church attendance in the same period – an important source of information for Gill's analyses.

The take-off point for his account can be found in the 24 Anglican parishes that dominated York in the mid eighteenth century. These parishes co-existed in a relatively small space meaning that churchgoers were able to pick and choose from an early stage (Gill 2012: 121). There is plenty of evidence that precisely this happened. The fortunes of the different parishes rose and fell accordingly, noting however that the population as a whole was growing relatively fast, which partially offset the problem of overcapacity. The peak in church attendance comes in the mid nineteenth century (i.e. some 100 years later), by which time there was a measurable Catholic presence and a rapidly growing number of free churches. Indeed by this stage, chapel-building was proceeding apace especially among different groups of Methodists. Notable among the new constructions was the Centenary Chapel, built in 1840 to accommodate 1469 people. This ambitious undertaking was but one of many. By 1935 York possessed 22 Methodist and six Congregationalist chapels, three Salvation Army Halls and five other free-church buildings (Gill 2012: 143).

Overprovision on this scale was unsustainable. Decline however took place differently for different denominations. Unsurprisingly, 'traditional' nonconformity was the worst hit and began to diminish almost as soon as it had reached its peak – Methodists, moreover, keep careful records providing unequivocal data. Catholics and Anglicans were more resilient (for different reasons) but here as well the numbers shrink, though not quite so fast as the free churches. And in both cases, an additional factor is increasingly noticeable: that is, the relative vitality of some, if not all, city centre congregations. This feature can be seen to this day. In 2011, for example, Gill estimates that that three such churches, two Anglican (the Minster and

St Michael-le Belfrey) and one Catholic (St Wilfred's), attract between them circa 2000 people on most Sundays – a figure large enough to alter the profile of churchgoing in York. The reasons why these types of churches are currently thriving will be addressed in Chapter 7.

In the meantime, it is important to record the presence in York of a wide variety of 'new' churches, many of which have emerged to serve a particular and identifiable community, including a growing student population. Goodhew (2012c) documents this trend in detail, listing 27 churches that have originated in the last 30 years. Not everyone would agree with his categorizations,[34] but a survey of religious activity in York that failed to take these innovative congregations into account would be seriously incomplete. These findings must, however, be set against the data from the 2011 Census. Clearly some churches in York are thriving, but the proportion of the population who declare themselves Christian has fallen noticeably in the last 10 years – from 74 to 59.5 per cent. It is also clear that the number of those professing no religion (30%) is higher than the national average.[35] As ever a number of contradictory trends exist alongside each other. Taken together, however, they indicate significant and continuing shifts in the religious economy of a particular city.

The distinctiveness of London has already been mentioned: the profile that emerges from the 2011 Census provokes reflection (p. 43–4) as does the relative success of the Anglican Diocese of London (p. 52). A similar trend can also be seen in 'The London Church Census', a comprehensive survey carried out in 2012 and published a year later (Brierley 2013). The opening sentences of the summary report catch the eye:

> Church attendance has grown from just over 620,000 in 2005 to just over 720,000 in the 7 years to 2012, a 16% increase. Nowhere else in the UK has attendance grown so dramatically. While these numbers are across all denominations, the growth is especially seen in the Black Majority Churches (Pentecostals) and the various Immigrant Churches (Smaller Denominations).[36]

These remarks, however, need to be carefully nuanced: the growth may or may not continue and the increase in attendance is almost entirely due to relatively high levels of immigration in the capital. Rising levels of religious activity need moreover to be set against a decline in the proportion of London's population declaring itself Christian, from 58 per cent in 2001 to 48 per cent in 2011 – that fall however was the smallest of any region in the country.

These caveats are important. Nonetheless the detail in Brierley's report and the work that lies behind this makes startling reading for those accustomed to a narrative of decline. For example, two new churches opened every week in London between 2005 and 2012, noting that two thirds of these were Pentecostal black-majority churches (BMC) and one third were catering for a particular language or ethnic group (the diversity is endless). Putting the same point in a different way, 300 existing churches in London closed in the seven years following 2005, whereas some 1000 new ones were set up. Of these new churches, 93 per cent were still in existence after 5 years, against a 76 per cent survival rate elsewhere. The information that Brierley provides regarding gender and age profiles repays equally careful attention: the growth is disproportionately female (heavily so), but the age distribution is more balanced in London than it is in most places. Congregation size is significant in this respect: larger churches grow faster than smaller ones and attract more young people. Pentecostal churches multiply fastest of all and now account for 32 per cent of London's churchgoers.

So much for the Christians. London, however, is religiously diverse and becoming more so. Between 2001 and 2011, the percentages of Londoners identifying with the major other-faith communities grew (or not) as follows: Muslims from 8.5 to 12.4 per cent, Hindus from 4 to 5 per cent, Buddhists from 0.8 to 1.0 per cent and others from 0.5 to 0.6 per cent. The percentage of Jews fell from 2 to 1.8 per cent, and the Sikhs remain unchanged at 1.5 per cent. Residential patterns are highly significant: different faith communities live in different parts of the capital. Detailed information about these clusters can be gleaned from the Census, tracked over time and mapped against a multitude of other variables.[37] Nowhere however is the diversity more noticeable than in London's east end, an area that has attracted attention from a wide range of scholars. Two projects can be used as illustrations. The first concerns the careful mapping of this part of London by a group of geographers from University College London.[38] Among their publications is Kershen's and Vaughan's (2013) analysis of patterns of immigrant settlement in relation to religious practice over the past 350 years, reminding us that immigration (and thus religious diversity, both Christian and other faiths) is hardly new in this area. The second example forms part of the Oxford Diasporas Programme; it too has an historical dimension. The project title: 'Religious faith, space and diasporic communities in East London: 1880–present' reveals the major emphases within this work, which aims to tease out the complexity of the diasporic experience.[39] The focus lies on Christianity, Judaism and Islam in the 'long' twentieth century.

More examples could easily be found. And taken together these projects denote a renewed interest in religion in the city, in this case London. The active participation of geographers and the emphasis on space is particularly interesting and fits well within a chapter concerned with territory, politics and institutions, bearing in mind that the discussion has moved some way from its starting point in the territorial patterns of the established church. That said even the east end of London is divided into parishes, and here too the parochial model offers advantages and disadvantages. Most significant of all, however, is the willingness to discover new ways of 'imagining' the city, bearing in mind the traditional assumptions of secularization theory: namely a necessary incompatibility between religion and the urban environment. Manifestly the latter is not the case – we need to understand why.

Notes

1   It is important to note that Beckford includes Wales at this stage in the argument.
2   A clear and authoritative account of the evolution, structure and organization of the Church of England can be found in M. Davie (2008). To avoid any possible confusion, I am not related to Martin Davie.
3   This question was extensively covered in the press in July and August 2013. See for example the *Church Times*, 2 August 2013. The company in question was Wonga, a British payday loan company offering short-term, high-cost credit.
4   Precisely this point is central to the Church Growth Research Programme. An interesting finding emerges from their work. It seems that single church units under one leader are more likely to grow than churches that are grouped together. This does not preclude amalgamations, team ministries or group benefices, but it does indicate the need for care in the way in which these accommodations take place. A local focus is essential. See 'Summary Report: From Anecdote to Evidence', p. 28, available at: http://www.churchgrowthresearch.org.uk/report (accessed 6 August 2014).
5   It is important to note that organizational changes of this nature are more often than not driven by finance, or rather the lack of it. It is equally clear that European churches are very differently placed in this respect (Robbers 2005).
6   An excellent discussion of the constitutional aspects of establishment in the twenty-first century can be found in Morris (2009).
7   The reform of the House of Lords ebbs and flows in political discussion. The future is still uncertain. Reform – if it happened – would almost certainly include some adjustment to the place of bishops in the House.
8   The data can be found in Hansard. In addition the interventions of recent Archbishops are listed on their respective websites. See http://www.archbishopofcanterbury.org/articles.php?action=search&tag_id=6 and http://rowanwilliams.archbishopofcanterbury.org/articles.php?action=search&tag_id=6 (both accessed 6 August 2014).
9   Fourteen diocesan bishops were present on 4 June 2013 at the vote on a wrecking amendment to the Marriage (Same Sex Couples) Bill in the House of Lords. Of the 14, nine voted for Lord Dear's amendment to deny the Bill a Second Reading and five abstained. The amendment was rejected by 390 votes to 148. The full debate in the House of Lords can be followed in Hansard. See http://www.publications.parliament.uk/pa/ld201314/ldhansrd/text/130604-0001.htm (accessed 6 August 2014).

10   For more details about this intervention, see http://www.theguardian.com/uk-news/2013/jul/06/archbishop-canterbury-welby-sexuality-revolution (accessed 6 August 2014).

11   The Orthodox churches of eastern Europe are noticeably dominant institutions; France has a strong, centralized and ideologically secular state.

12   Tariq Modood continues to write extensively in this field. See the bibliography on his personal website: www.tariqmodood.com/ (accessed 6 August 2014). Modood has emerged as a leading advocate of multiculturalism (see Chapter 9).

13   Jonathan Sacks retired as Chief Rabbi in the summer of 2013; his departure more or less coincided with the retirement of Rowan Williams as Archbishop of Canterbury. In many ways their careers run parallel; both are recognized as public intellectuals and both have seats (as Life Peers) in the House of Lords. It is also true that both (at times) have been sharply criticized by the communities that they have been called to represent.

14   See, for example, the carefully prepared statements on the Prince of Wales' official website: http://www.princeofwales.gov.uk/the-prince-of-wales/promoting-and-protecting/faith (accessed 6 August 2014).

15   The evidence can be found on the official website of the British Monarchy: http://www.royal.gov.uk/MonarchUK/QueenandChurch/Queenandotherfaiths.aspx (accessed 6 August 2013). See also Chapter 9, p. 181.

16   The details can be found in http://www.brierleyconsultancy.com/images/csintro.pdf (accessed 6 August 2014)

17   In terms of membership the relatively large Catholic Church in Northern Ireland also shows a marked decline.

18   It is worth reading Brierley's analysis in detail in order to appreciate the significance of congregational size. As ever, impressive growth in small congregations does little to change the overall picture; it is the larger churches that count.

19   Morris (2009) provides an up-to-date review of establishment in Scotland including the place of the Monarchy within this. It is worth noting in passing not only that this is different from the situation further south, but that the Scottish model is periodically invoked as a possible way of working for the Church of England. A greater degree of autonomy from the state is the principal attraction.

20   A new and substantially reworked edition appeared in 1997, under the title *Religion and Society in Scotland since 1707*. I am grateful to Callum Brown for supplementary information on the Scottish case.

21   For more details see http://www.scottish.parliament.uk/PublicInformation documents/TimeForReflectionGuidance111011.pdf (accessed 20 August 2014).

22   For the wording of the Scottish question, see Chapter 3, note 5, p. 66.

23   These data were published in September 2013 and can be found on http://www.scotlandscensus.gov.uk/en/censusresults/. For a more detailed breakdown see http://www.scotlandscensus.gov.uk/documents/censusresults/release2a/rel2A_Religion_detailed_Scotland.pdf (both websites accessed 6 August 2014).

24   See Question 590 in the Q&A section of 'Scotland's Future': http://www.scotland.gov.uk/Publications/2013/11/9348/15 (accessed 6 August 2014).

25 See 'Imagining Scotland's Future: Our Vision' (2014) and the material gathered together on http://www.churchofscotland.org.uk/speak_out/politics_and_government/articles/imagining_scotlands_future (accessed 6 August 2014).

26 For the Anglican Church in Wales, see the summary on BRIN: http://www.brin.ac.uk/news/2010/church-in-wales-statistics/ and http://www.churchinwales.org.uk/wp-content/uploads/2013/08/Members-Finance-English-on-line.pdf. For the Catholic Church in Wales, see http://www.brierleyconsultancy.com/images/csintro.pdf and www.prct.org.uk. All websites accessed 6 August 2014.

27 See http://www.brierleyconsultancy.com/images/csintro.pdf (accessed 6 August 2013).

28 Chambers (2012) includes extensive references.

29 A good example can be found in the British Academy discussion held at the University of Liverpool marking the anniversary of the Good Friday Agreement. See http://www.britac.ac.uk/events/2008/gfa/index.cfm (accessed 6 August 2014).

30 In 2011, the question in Northern Ireland was similar to that used in Scotland.

31 See http://cain.ulst.ac.uk/ni/popul.htm. The notes to these tables are worth perusing in detail. For more information about CAIN (Conflict Archive on the Internet) as such, see cain.ulst.ac.uk. Both websites accessed 6 August 2014.

32 Migration takes place at a number of levels: both in and out of Northern Ireland as such and between different parts of the province.

33 For more information, see http://www.brin.ac.uk/news/2013/local-variation-in-levels-of-religious-affiliation/ (accessed 6 August 2014).

34 Goodhew includes four Orthodox churches in his list. They may indeed be new to York, which is interesting in itself, but they are hardly 'new' churches in the generally accepted use of the term.

35 To complete the picture it is worth noting that the other-faith presence is low in the city of York, but relatively high in the surrounding region.

36 See 'London's Churches are Growing', available at http://brierleyconsultancy.com/images/londonchurches.pdf, p. 3 (accessed 6 August 2014).

37 For more detail about the Census results for London, see http://www.ons.gov.uk/ons/dcp29904_291554.pdf (accessed 6 August 2014).

38 More information about the wider ramifications of this work can be found at http://www.bartlett.ucl.ac.uk/graduate/research/space/research/mapping-the-east-end-labyrinth (accessed 6 August 2014).

39 The project website can be found at http://www.migration.ox.ac.uk/odp/religion-separation-exclusion.shtml (accessed 6 August 2014).

6
Presence: Who Can Do What For Whom?

This chapter is divided into three parts. It starts with a discussion of chaplaincy, paying particular attention to 'presence'. The key question follows from this: who can do what for whom in a religiously plural society, in which large sections of the population prefer to live outside the sphere of religion for most of their lives? Four illustrations of chaplaincy follow: in health care, in the prison service, in the armed forces and in higher education. None of these accounts is comprehensive; indeed each of them emphasizes a rather different point. Taken together, however, they evoke an interesting range of issues. The final case study provides a bridge to the following section, which is in some ways an excursus. It looks at the connections between religion and education more generally, and in so doing addresses a specific issue: the decline in religious literacy that is becoming increasingly evident in British society.

The final section returns to the churches as such, and re-poses the question of who can do what for whom, looking this time at senior appointments and paying particular attention to gender and sexualities. A string of issues follows from this, including the manner in which the relevant decisions are effected, the possibility of splits and defections, the influence of co-religionists in the global south and – perhaps most important of all – the relationship with society as whole. Why does it matter to significant numbers of people that the church runs counter to modern cultural trends? And where might the logic of this argument take us? Is a church that is in step with society desirable or does this almost by definition compromise the distinctive qualities of a religious institution?

Religion in Britain: A Persistent Paradox, Second Edition. Grace Davie.
© 2015 Grace Davie. Published 2015 by John Wiley & Sons, Ltd.

Chaplaincy

Historically, chaplains have been attached to a wide variety of institutions, both public (e.g. hospitals, prisons and the armed forces) and private (e.g. royalty, noble families, sports clubs and businesses), recognizing that the distinction between the two is somewhat arbitrary. Traditionally chaplains in this country have been Christian, but they now include personnel from many different faiths – and in some cases individuals with secular world views. The role, moreover, has evolved to embrace increasing numbers of lay people, who in most cases receive appropriate training for their task alongside their ordained colleagues.[1] Remunerated chaplains are frequently assisted by volunteers.

The day-to-day life of a chaplain is extraordinarily varied and is best illustrated by means of examples (see below). Broadly speaking, however, chaplains exist to represent, or more accurately to embody, a religious tradition in what is often a very secular location; they also exist to 'look after' those who find themselves in the institution or environment in question. In other words the role is both prophetic and pastoral; it concerns values as well as care. Controversies over funding are central to both dimensions. In a society in which a dominant religion can no longer be taken for granted, who should pay for the chaplain and how far should his or her ministry extend? One point however is abundantly clear: the funding mechanisms involved are as varied as chaplaincy itself and – like so much else in the institutions in question – are frequently under strain.

Chaplains in health care[2]

The relationship between religion and health care is historically rooted. Simply the nomenclature of hospitals in this country denotes their religious origins. Institutions such as St Thomas's or St Bartholomew's in London are now at the cutting edge of medicine; their beginnings lie however in the monastic orders and their obligations to care for the poor and the sick. Traditional understandings of secularization emphasize the separating out of these functions – specifically the development of medical care as a secular profession, financed by the state (in Britain by taxation), and underpinned by its own professional codes. This process is seldom disputed and lies behind the creation of the National Health Service (NHS), definitively established in 1948 – an iconic date for many British people. Chaplains have been part of this service since its inception.

Interestingly late modern understandings of health care pay more rather than less attention to religion in its broadest sense (see Chapter 10). Care is increasingly seen as holistic – a word which implies that religious and spiritual needs should be met alongside other aspects of treatment and should be delivered with the same professionalism. For this reason, NHS hospitals not only employ chaplains but produce policy statements indicating how they will meet the physical, mental, social, spiritual and religious needs of their very varied patients. These documents are carefully written and open to public scrutiny. They relate moreover to widely differing institutions: acute hospitals, long-stay hospitals, specialist units and hospices, each of which has particular needs. The work of the chaplain has to be modified accordingly.

Paradoxically, the constituency which might be expected to demand most of chaplains – the religiously committed – is very often looked after by representatives, both lay and ordained, from the faith communities of which these individuals are part. Care in this case is an extension of parish or congregational life, bearing in mind that distance makes a difference – the institution in question may or may not be local. There is also a sizeable number who want no contact with religion whatsoever, whether in hospital or not. In between is a wide spectrum of people characterized by the various kinds of nominal attachment outlined in previous chapters. Admission to hospital, moreover, is likely to focus attention on issues that may be set to one side in 'normal' circumstances. At best there is a heightened vulnerability; at worst the unexpected or the tragic can and does occur. In such cases the chaplain's work is reactive, urgent and stressful – a call to intensive care or to the neo-natal unit in the middle of the night is never easy. More routinely, the chaplain will be involved in the care of staff at every level of the hospital, in the maintenance of worship and sacred spaces, in the organization of a multi-faith team and in the training and support of volunteers.

Equally important, however, is a 'critical' presence in an institution which is required on a daily basis to think through issues of major ethical importance and their implications for care. Difficult decisions must be made. Confidentiality moreover is central, recognizing that religious affiliation is classed under the 1998 Data Protection Act as 'sensitive personal data'. Such sensitivities must be respected. One point, however, is undisputed: almost all of us will require specialist medical care at some point in our lives and may well be admitted to hospital. For this reason we are for the most part affirming of those who will contribute to our care. Whether or not this should include a chaplain is a different matter – one moreover that is likely to become more rather than less controversial in a service which is increasingly conscious of costs. The National Secular Society (NSS) has already offered an opinion in this respect: public money that is currently invested in hospital chaplaincy could be better spent.[3] Not everyone will agree.

The prison service

Rather fewer of us will be directly involved in the prison service. In March 2013 the prison population of England and Wales was 83 842 – a figure that has risen sharply in the post-war period, peaking in 2011 (Berman and

Dar 2013).[4] The number is high by west European standards but represents a small percentage of the population overall. The prison population moreover is untypical: it is overwhelmingly male and distinctive in terms of nationality, ethnicity and religion. Foreign nationals are disproportionately present as are minority ethnic groups. In terms of religion, the percentage of Christians in prison is relatively low (50%) and the percentage of Muslims relatively high (13%), as is the number of prisoners with no faith (almost 30%) (Berman and Dar 2013: 11).

Sociologically we know more about religion in prisons than we do about many institutions. This is very largely due to the path-breaking work of James Beckford and Sophie Gilliat, who published *Religion in Prison: 'Equal Rites' in a Multi-Faith Society* in 1998. The argument of their book echoes very precisely the question that underpins this chapter: who can do what for whom? Specifically what should be the role of the Anglican chaplain in a service that now accommodates prisoners from all faiths and none, mindful of the fact that the established church has been heavily involved in the development of the prison service since the nineteenth century? Empirically driven, Beckford's and Gilliat's work considers the increasingly controversial nature of traditional ways of working. Their conclusion, however, is interesting. Clearly the 'leading representatives of some faith traditions would like the opportunity to speak for themselves and to be heard in the corridors of power', but (my insertion) 'without wishing to appear ungrateful for all offers of Anglican support or mediation' (Beckford and Gilliat 1998: 218). Such a sentiment reflects in turn the generally positive view of establishment held by many representatives of other faith communities noted in Chapter 5.

In his subsequent writing, Beckford has pursued his interest in religion and prisons, both in general and with reference to the prison chaplain in particular.[5] Gilliat (now Gilliat-Ray) has been equally industrious, working on religion (notably chaplaincy) in higher education (see below), on Islam in general (Gilliat-Ray 2010) and most recently on Muslim chaplaincy (Gilliat-Ray, Pattison and Ali 2013). In Beckford's case, much of this work has been comparative, emphasizing the very different developments that have taken place in France where religion in prisons has received scant attention – a stance that derives from the unitary and secular (*laïque*) nature of the French state.[6] In Britain, activity in this area is longstanding: the religious (and ethnic) identity of prisoners is officially recorded and the law requires not only the appointment of chaplains in all establishments but also the provision of facilities for religious practice (of different faiths). Chaplains are fully integrated into the management structure of prisons and, revealingly, the functioning of chaplaincies is carefully monitored alongside other aspects of prison life.

Diversity, moreover, is increasingly acknowledged as the representatives of other faiths find their place alongside Christian ministers, both as members of the Chaplaincy Council and as individual faith advisers. But here, as elsewhere, lines are drawn somewhat arbitrarily in terms of who is, or is not, included – some new religious movements are accepted, others are not. Beckford is also aware that the heterogeneous nature of faith is often (perhaps necessarily) reduced to a standard set of practices; there is little room for minority views within a tradition. All that said, he applauds the Prison Service Chaplaincy of England and Wales, which has been in the vanguard in terms of the official recognition of faiths other than Christian. The appointment in 1999 of the first Muslim Adviser to the Prison Service constituted a significant marker in the development of policies that are both mindful of and responsive to those of other faiths.

In the armed forces[7]

The religious constituencies in the armed forces are different again (see pp. 87). Here the level of Christian affiliation is higher than it is in the wider society and the other faith populations are largely conspicuous by their absence. The military chaplain has also been introduced, albeit briefly – largely with reference to the need for innovative forms of liturgy when on active service. This section probes more deeply the ambiguities of the military chaplain's role. It draws considerably on the collection of papers brought together in Todd (2013) and the empirical data assembled by King (2013).[8]

The role of a military chaplain is ambiguous almost by definition. For a start, military chaplains serve a section of society which is under review in terms of its future, despite being committed – sometimes simultaneously – to a series of overseas conflicts in recent decades: in the Balkans (from 1992), in Sierra Leone (from 1999), in Afghanistan (from 2001), in Iraq (from 2003) and in Libya (2011). Iraq and Afghanistan in particular have been costly in every sense of the term, a situation in which the presence, profile and appreciation of military chaplains have risen. That said British combat operations in Afghanistan concluded in 2014, and the army is returning from the bases it has held in Germany since World War II. Public war weariness and economic austerity are both at play. Downsizing, however, is a complex process, in which the balance is shifting from full-time personnel to reservists, and the nature of life for those who remain is changing. Many soldiers and their dependants, for example, no longer live on army bases, and much firmer links are envisaged between the military and civil society in the United Kingdom. This will have a corresponding effect on the way in which chaplains go about their tasks.

Much more radical, however, is the ambiguity that lies behind the role as such: a military chaplain serves two rather different institutions. Is this necessarily a contradiction in terms? In terms of pastoral care, probably not: chaplains are there to serve people in the circumstances in which they are caught up, including armed conflict. Their work is much appreciated (King

2013). Andrew Totten (2013), however, raises the more significant and more intractable question of 'morale' (itself related to 'moral'). If chaplains are enjoined or feel called to sustain the morale of the army, are they effectively participating in the military effort – in the sense that they are enhancing the capacity of a unit that sooner or later will be involved in the use of lethal force? This question, moreover, leads inexorably to another: when is the use of such force justified and when is it not? A full exposition of the arguments that have been brought to bear on this timeless issue lies well beyond the limits of this chapter. One point, however, must be noted: the 'sending churches' of the chaplains in question may well have different views on these questions from the institution in which they are called to work on a daily basis.

David Martin (1997, 2011) uses the phrase 'an angle of eschatological tension' to express the strain that emerges – inevitably – between the exigencies of the gospel and the specificities of any given situation. Documenting and explaining the sharpness of this angle are sociological tasks. The role of the military chaplain offers a particularly clear illustration of this tension in that the individual in question is exposed at one and the same time to a gospel of peace and to the realities of the world at their most brutal. Working out the implications of this statement in a rapidly changing economic, political and religious context requires sustained theological reflection. The papers in Todd (2013) have been compiled with this in mind.

In higher education

Higher education has expanded dramatically in the post-war period, becoming effectively a mass rather than an elite system, with far-reaching implications for finance, governance and teaching. The student body is not only hugely bigger, but much more varied with a significant influx of overseas students. The same is true of the institutions they attend: they are considerably more numerous, more diverse and more competitive (market-driven) than they were in the mid post-war decades. They range from the ancient and collegiate to the recent and technical; some are very large, others quite small. Arrangements for chaplaincy are equally varied. These were carefully mapped by Sophie Gilliat-Ray (2000) in her prescient study of the multi-faith campus. Appreciating that the university campus is, if anything, even more religiously diverse than the society at large, Gilliat-Ray sought to gather information about how the institutions under review were responding to a series of practical issues – such as worship space, dietary needs and timetabling – but more profoundly to discover how universities (or their equivalents) were accommodating a growing variety of religious identities. Paradoxically, in what are often avowedly secular institutions, a partial and at times uneven process of de-secularization was clearly taking place in the sense that there was an increasing awareness of religion on campus.

As part of this process, Gilliat-Ray sought to determine which forms of chaplaincy worked best and how the historically Christian role of chaplain can be taken up by the representatives of other faiths. She calls the latter process 'approximation', meaning by this the ways in which roles change in a faith community when it comes into contact with the dominant tradition. 'Professional roles that already exist in the "host" context have a determining influence on how other faiths without such roles engage in public institutions' (Gilliat-Ray 2000: 80). In short the increasing presence of other-faith 'chaplains' is not quite as simple as it sounds. There is rather a mutual learning process as communities of different faiths adapt themselves to British ways of working. Gilliat-Ray's subsequent work on Muslim chaplains develops this very interesting point further (Gilliat-Ray, Pattison and Ali 2013).

The nature of the university campus and the place of religion within this has been the focus of two further pieces of work. One of these is the Religious Literacy Leadership in Higher Education Programme (RLLP),[9] which exists to assist leaders in higher education both to engage positively with faith of all kinds, and to promote universities as places that shape informed responses to faith in the wider society. Regarding the former the RLLP is concerned with specific policy issues (including very practical advice). Regarding the latter it is engaged in a more searching enquiry regarding the place of universities in modern societies. The point to appreciate is that the goals of the RLLP reflect the core (not the peripheral) business of universities: namely provision for equality and diversity, widening participation, the student experience and good campus relations. The focus on religious literacy is nonetheless telling. It is by no means self-evident that universities and their personnel have the knowledge and understanding of this area that they will need in order to meet the expectations of leadership thrust upon them.

The final piece of research formed part of the Religion and Society Programme. Entitled *Christianity and the University Experience*, it sets out to discover the nature of student faith, and the ways that this does or doesn't change in the course of university life (Guest *et al.* 2013). The data are interesting. Given the age group in question, a surprisingly high number (just over 50 per cent of undergraduate students) self-identified as Christian, recognizing that the category 'Christian' is itself blurred. More specifically of the sample as a whole (over 4000 students in very different types of institution), 55.7 per cent think of themselves as religious or spiritual, 33.1 per cent are neither and 11.2 per cent don't know. The proportions are somewhat different for those who identify as Christians: namely 71.6 per cent, 15.4 per cent and 13.0 per cent. The authors then develop a typology of Christians, which draws on a range of variables including patterns of church involvement and moral/doctrinal values. The following categories emerge: active affirmers, lapsed engagers, established occasionals, emerging nominals and unchurched Christians.

The focus of this study is on the experience of Christian students. There is, however, a short but interesting section on chaplaincy, stressing the changing nature of the university context. In order to survive at all chaplaincies have had to reinvent themselves. The following options are noted: chaplaincies can be places of spiritual exploration; centres of ecumenical endeavour; embodiments of social cohesion (paying particular attention to international students); safe havens for students of many faiths and none; leading exponents of multi-faith awareness; and servants of the whole community (Guest *et al.* 2013: 142). Interestingly, these authors connect chaplaincy with the notion of vicarious religion, but for a limited number of people only. It seems that contact with a chaplaincy is frequently positive, but relatively few students (even those who call themselves Christian) avail themselves of it.

Religion and Education

British students entering higher education have been through the school system – a formative process in itself. A full discussion of post-war education cannot be attempted here, but two points deserve attention: the place of denominational or faith schools in a late-modern society and the teaching of religion in the classroom. Both are controversial. The latter relates immediately to the question of religious literacy in that the vast majority of children in twenty-first century Britain will glean their knowledge of religion from school rather than from a religious organization. The former raises a different point. Unlike the case of health care, which became almost totally secularized in the post-war settlement, education did not.

In England, approximately one third of all schools are faith schools of one kind or another – a significant institutional presence. Their development, together with that of religious education per se, takes place within a shifting framework of legislation, most obviously the Educational Acts of 1944 and 1988, each of which responded to the changing nature of society. Since 2000 the most significant organizational change has been the gradual emergence of 'academies' – that is, schools that are directly funded by central government and which are therefore free from the control of the local educational authority. So far this shift has affected secondary rather more than primary schools, though that may change. Interestingly Church of England schools have been markedly more inclined to make the move to academy status than Catholic schools. The legislative framework and its significance for the issues raised in this section are helpfully outlined in Jackson (2013).

Most of what follows concerns the English case. That said it is important to note – if only in passing – the distinctiveness of Scotland, Wales and Northern Ireland. In Scotland, both denominational and non-denominational schools are funded by the state, but with one exception (a Jewish school), the denominational sector is entirely Catholic. Religious education varies between sectors. The situation is Wales is closer to that in England, but following devolution approaches to the teaching of religion in schools are drifting apart. Wales, moreover, has resisted at least some of the more radical policies introduced in England, not least the shift towards academies. In Northern Ireland, the system is shaped by the specificities of history in this part of the United Kingdom. Religious education, unsurprisingly, continues to be more influenced by Christianity than it is elsewhere. A more detailed discussion of each of these cases can be found in Rothgangel, Jackson and Jäggle (2014).

Denominational or faith schools[10]

Paradoxically, or perhaps not, comprehensive and up to date data on the numbers and types of faith schools in England are meticulously maintained by the British Humanist Association (BHA).[11] The data are broken down by numbers, types and size of school, by denomination and faith community, and by numbers of pupils. Gains and losses are carefully noted. These tables tell us that more than 30 per cent of schools in England are of 'a religious character' (of these 23% are Church of England and 10% are Catholic), and that over 20 per cent of pupils are educated in such schools (of which 13% are in Church of England establishments and 10% are in the Catholic equivalent). There are in addition a limited number of schools belonging to smaller Christian denominations and to other faith communities. This is a sizeable section of the educational system. It is however very varied. The proportion of denominational schools is considerably higher in the primary sector than it is among secondary schools. There is, moreover, little in common between a Church of England school in a village which is effectively the sole provider of primary education in that place and always has been, and a sought-after Church of England or Catholic secondary school in a city where the competition for places is fierce. It is equally clear that the relatively new and very distinctive 'Christian' schools and those which belong to minority faith communities are different again.

Why do such schools persist in a society that is increasingly secular in character? And, even more pertinently, why do these schools remains disproportionately popular with parents? This is hardly a new question. Mairi Levitt's small-scale study of religion and education in the west of England in the early 1990s includes a quote from a realistic Diocesan Director of Education, who declares that substantial numbers of parents opt for a church school for the following reasons: 'uniform, discipline, traditional education, manners' (see Levitt 1992, 1996), not, it would seem, for religious reasons at all. Though why church schools have come to be associated with this particular formula requires in itself an explanation. Some 20 years later, Linda Woodhead – using the very different methodology of a YouGov poll – discovered that little had changed. In the (hypothetical) choices of parents regarding church schools, academic standards (77%), location (58%) and discipline (41%) rank well above ethical values (23%), prestige (19%), the grounding of pupils in a faith tradition (5%) and the transmission of belief about God (3%).[12]

Woodhead's poll also reveals the controversial nature of faith schools. Almost half of the population actively disapproves of the public funding of faith schools. Interestingly however younger generations are less opposed than older ones. It is equally clear that traditionally Christian (notably Church of England) schools receive a higher level of public support than other schools with a religious character (notably the very few 'other faith' institutions), but – once again – there is greater generosity towards the latter amongst younger people. Unsurprisingly resistance to faith schools is a central plank of both the BHA's and the NSS's policy-making – hence the motivation for the careful collection of data by the former. The logic of their views is abundantly clear. Attitudes to schools of a religious character are part and parcel of their broader campaigns for a truly secular state, free from any form of discrimination on grounds of faith or belief. This implies an inclusive, secular school system: the admissions, employment and curriculum policies of church schools are challenged on these terms.

They endure nonetheless, recalling the more searching question intimated above. Why is it that large numbers of denominational schools conform to the kind of school preferred by parents even if the motivations of the latter are rarely concerned with religion per se? It is clear that academic standards, location and discipline rank above ethos or any kind of religious transmission, but to what extent can these attributes be separated in practice? Might it be the case that ethos, commitment, parental support, and the motivations that surround these, drive up standards? Or is it something quite different? There is a vociferous lobby that argues that high (or higher) academic attainment is simply the result of a skewed intake. In other word church schools attract disproportionate numbers of middle-class pupils who prosper in a competitive environment. It is true that some such parents become 'church-goers' to meet the necessary criteria for selection. It is equally true that middle-class parents will move house to meet criteria of location or hire tutors to meet exacting entry standards. The reason is clear: these parents are in search of 'good' schools – no more, no less – and large numbers of church schools meet their requirements. A virtuous (or if you prefer vicious) circle ensues. It would, it follows, be unwise for a politician – local or national – to campaign for their demise.

Are faith schools divisive? Antony Grayling, a leading secularist, clearly thinks so, basing his argument largely on the Northern Irish case.[13] The association is revealing. It is true that the education system in this corner of the United Kingdom is organized on sectarian grounds – for historical reasons that relate to the evolution of Northern Ireland itself. The corollary, however, is clear: the educational system is the result of such divisions not the cause of them. To argue from this starting point that denominational or faith schooling is necessarily divisive is to miss the point. Faith schools, just like any other schools, have the capacity to be excluding and exclusive. Some are. For the most part, however, they are not, a fact that reflects the arguments set out above: most parents choose these schools for educational rather than religious reasons.[14] It is also the case that families from other faith communities frequently opt for a Church of England school rather than a secular equivalent on the grounds that faith as such is valued rather than a particular expression of this. They will, moreover, participate fully.

Religious education

The developments in religious education in the second half of the twentieth century reflect very clearly the changing nature of society. These are well exemplified in the assumptions underpinning the two Education Acts already referred to. The 1944 Act introduced the Agreed Syllabus of Religious Instruction. This was a non-denominational form of teaching just about acceptable to Anglicans and nonconformists (Catholics had their own syllabus), but with no anticipation that this situation might change – in other words with no anticipation that there might sooner rather than later be significant other-faith communities in many British cities. The 1988 Act evolved in a different atmosphere. In its early drafts, religious education (as a compulsory subject but not part of the core curriculum) occupied but a few lines of the Bill – a situation which prompted vigorous protests, led for the most part by lay politicians, notably Baroness Cox and a group of supporters in the House of Lords. As a result the clauses on religious education occupied 15 pages of the Act, including an explicit reference to the Christian content of religious teaching – in itself a marker that Christianity could no longer be taken for granted. It was true that schools where significant number of children came from other-faith families could follow a different path, but only by contracting out of what was to be considered normative. Interestingly the same obligation – to 'reflect the broad traditions of Christian belief' – should also characterize religious worship in county schools. (In parenthesis it is worth noting that a great deal of discussion in this area confuses religious education and provision for worship. It is not uncommon to see headlines concerning religious education alongside a picture of a school assembly.)

What is the situation some 25 years later? One point is abundantly clear: the ambiguities in the teaching of religion in schools remain very largely unchanged. In many ways this is hardly surprising in that they derive from a series of unresolved questions. What is religious education for? How should it be resourced? What is its place in the curriculum? Who should teach it and how should these people be trained? These were the questions interrogated by two projects that took place under the auspices of the Religion and Society Programme. The first was led by Robert Jackson and was based in the Warwick Religions and Education Research Unit – an important centre for research in this field.[15] The project aimed to elucidate young people's attitudes to religious diversity and the place of the classroom in their formation. In so doing, the work was responding to a growing recognition that religion can no longer be relegated to the private sphere and that religious education and citizenship lessons have an important role in fostering social cohesion – the policy implications are immediate.

Speaking of these goals and more specifically of the team's findings regarding the state of religious education, Jackson (2012) notes the following: that students by and large appreciate the classroom as a 'safe place' in which to discover knowledge about one another and about mutual interests, but that some religious students cannot identify with the portrayal of their own religion as it is presented by the media, by some teachers, and by certain books and electronic resources. With this in mind, Jackson makes a number of suggestions. First that religion – or more accurately religions – must be presented with considerable care, not least with respect to their internal diversity; second that the geographical and social context of the school must be taken into account in the planning and presentation of religious education; and third that competences (capacity for dialogue for example) are important as well as knowledge, bearing in mind that accurate information is crucial. In short we need better provision regarding the place of religious education in the curriculum, the training of teachers and the delivery of resources.

The second project comes to similar conclusions. It is entitled 'Does religious education work?' and was directed by James Conroy at the School of Education in the University of Glasgow.[16] Professor Conroy is passionate about his subject. In the course of their research he and his team discovered superb examples of religious education, but were forced to conclude that such success was achieved against the odds. By and large, religious education in Britain is under-resourced, over-burdened (in terms of the extras that it is required to deliver) and marginalized (it is a compulsory subject but excluded from the core curriculum).[17] Does this matter? The answer is an emphatic 'yes'. Examples of good practice 'reveal [...] that good RE is about something absolutely fundamental: a space for serious, critical exploration of the meanings and values by which we live. To live good lives, individually and together, we need to be able to make sense of our world and ourselves – and RE offers the only place in the curriculum where that can still be done systematically' (Conroy 2012: 1).

So what does good religious education look like? The first point to note is that good teaching in this field can be found in very different types of schools, but those that do it well necessarily engage with the local community, paying close attention to its religious composition. It is also the case that good teachers explore with their students the meanings which underlie the ritual, social and personal practices that they observe or learn about. In other words, their teaching has depth. It follows that religion is seen as an essential part of life, at home as well as abroad, but is also something which should be approached critically – a process that demands intellectual rigour. Conroy ends this short piece with a powerful statement: 'Religious education matters as never before. We cannot understand our own culture without religious knowledge, let alone that of others. As religious and secular diversity increases, students need to be able to articulate their own beliefs, and engage seriously with those of others, as never before. Respect and social harmony depend upon it' (Conroy 2012: 3).

Strikingly the organizations that represent the secular by and large agree, asking at the same time for a degree of rebalancing. Specifically, the BHA campaigns for an extension of religious education to include non-religious beliefs such as humanism. Religious education should, moreover, be fully recognized in the curriculum as a national entitlement and should be as inclusive, impartial, objective and fair as possible. Members of the BHA are enjoined to be pro-active in their local SACRE to this end.[18] The view of the NSS is broadly similar though the perspective is a little sharper. Religious education should be replaced with 'a new programme of study that allows pupils to take a more objective and religiously neutral approach to the consideration of moral and ethical issues'. Importantly, religious and belief groups should have no privileged input into the syllabus, which should be established at national rather than local level.[19]

Whatever the starting point, an underlying theme emerges strongly. In a society which is both religiously plural and increasingly secular, religious education matters more, not less. It is here that students will discover not only the information but the critical faculties that they will need to become effective citizens. For this reason if no other, schools of all kinds must overcome their inhibitions about dealing with faith in the classroom. They will find it easier if the Department of Education gives a clear and effective lead.

Religious Leadership

Specialists in religious education have a daunting task. They are, however, members of the teaching profession and are (or should be) trained accordingly.[20] Quite different are the demands placed on church leaders – a role which invokes particular pressures. Not only are church leaders called to sustain ancient institutions in a rapidly changing society, they are at the same time answerable – or so it seems – to a wider public. Two separate, but nonetheless related, matters exemplify these tensions with particular clarity: the ordination of women to the episcopate of the Church of England and the controversies concerning same-sex relationships. The question of presence or who can do what for whom is central to both debates, which concern the Anglican Church in particular – for reasons which will become clear as the discussion unfolds.

All churches – indeed all religious organizations – have had to consider the changing role of women in western societies. They have come to different conclusions. On the whole Protestant churches have embraced the change and include women at all stages of seniority in their ministries. So far the Catholic and Orthodox churches have resisted, at least in formal appointments. On both sides of the debate, the reasoning rests on different understandings of ecclesiology – that is the branch of theology that is concerned with the nature, constitution and functions of a church, and the ministries that take place within this. The Anglican Church is distinctive in this respect in that it is both Catholic and Reformed and is therefore caught in the crossfire of different ways of thinking. It is also a global church, in which each Anglican Province has considerable autonomy in deciding who can and cannot be a priest or a bishop.

As the first edition of this book went to press, the first women priests were ordained in the Church of England – hence the need in that volume to explain a complex process of change and the sometimes very sharp reactions to this. This involved a certain amount of detail about the decision-making structures of the church. Since 1994, impressive cohorts of women have constituted a growing proportion of the ordained ministry, and have proved themselves more than capable of the priestly role. Without doubt their 'presence' has made a difference. It would be unwise, however, to assume parity between genders in the Church of England. Although the proportions of men and women who are currently recommended for training are becoming more equal, far more women find themselves in non-stipendiary (unpaid) ministries than men and levels of seniority remain uneven.[21] Some of this imbalance may correct over time; there remain nonetheless some formidable barriers. One of these has concerned the ordination of women to the episcopate, which for many people (both inside and outside the church) is a logical next step. It raises, however, noticeably different understandings about who is able to do what within the Anglican Church.

The argument turns on the extent to which those who reject the ordination of women to the priesthood (at any level) should be 'protected' from their influence within the church. The question arose in the early 1990s,[22] leading to a certain number of defections from the Church of England and a complicated system of 'opting out', whereby certain parishes could remove themselves from the jurisdiction of a diocese and place themselves under the authority of a different bishop. A very small number of parishes (3% of the total) chose to do this and to maintain what is effectively a parallel existence, isolated and insulated from the influence of women priests.[23] For the most part they include a certain kind of Anglo-Catholic and more extreme evangelicals, the reasoning being different in each case.[24] The possibility that women might become bishops complicates the situation, given that a bishop has authority over the whole diocese and will herself ordain priests. On the one hand are those who wish for at least some level of 'protection' to continue; on the other are those who argue that any kind of ring-fencing would compromise, necessarily, the authority of the new bishop. Much of the ensuing debate has circled round these issues.

The first vote on Final Approval for the 'women bishops' legislation took place in the General Synod in November 2012. To pass the measure required a two thirds majority in each house of the Synod voting separately – as indeed had been the case in 1992 with respect to women priests. In 1992 the measure was passed – narrowly. In 2012, the required majority fell short – once again narrowly. In both cases, the crucial vote was in the House of Laity; the majorities in the House of Bishops and the House of Clergy were more secure. More importantly for the argument here, the public response in 2012 was not only sharp but angry. Both the vote itself and its wider implications received overwhelmingly negative coverage in the national press, which depicted a Church that had shot itself in the foot. Disappointment, which is not the same thing as indifference, was widespread. Strenuous efforts within the Church to find a new and rather simpler way forward have accompanied the writing of this edition. An accelerated process was initiated, culminating in a second vote in July 2014. This time – to considerable relief – the revised motion was endorsed by a decisive majority in all three houses.[25]

In this connection, it is important to note that there are already 27 women bishops in active ministry in the Anglican Communion. Most of these are located in the western world, but the situation is changing. For example, in September 2013 Eggoni Pushpalalitha became Bishop of Nandyal, a diocese of the Church of South India, joining colleagues in Cuba, Swaziland and South Africa as well as those in Australia and New Zealand, Canada and the United States. And nearer home both the Episcopal Church in Scotland and the Anglican Church in Wales have endorsed the role of women in the episcopate, and the Church of Ireland has ordained its first female bishop.[26] Quite clearly this was a question of when, not if, for the Church of England. The change will be welcomed in most parts of the church and in the wider society. It will, however, be difficult for a small number of committed people, both lay and ordained, many of whom have served the church faithfully over many years.

What, fundamentally, is the reason for the change? It lies without doubt in the shifting nature of western society and the increasing attention paid to equalities within this. This places the church – indeed all religious organizations – in a difficult position. On which issues should the religiously committed follow suit and on which should they resist? The answers are far from clear. The at-first gradual and then much more rapid acceptance of same-sex relations offers a further example. In some ways similar to the evolving role of women, it raises distinctive and in many ways more intractable issues.

The shift itself has already been described with reference to the debate regarding the marriage of same-sex couples (see pp. 27–8). Particularly interesting from this point of view is the speed with which public opinion has altered. A telling way of capturing this change is to note the presentation of same-sex relationships in popular television series. In a very short space of time, it has become almost *de rigueur* for the 'soaps' not only to include a gay element in their story lines, but to portray this in a positive light. Same-sex relationships have become mainstream. Regarding the question of appointments in the Anglican Church, two episodes brought this issue to public attention. Both happened in 2003 and both involved senior churchmen who were known to be gay. In England, Jeffrey John was nominated as the Suffragan Bishop of Reading in August; under considerable pressure he subsequently withdrew his candidature. Shortly afterwards, Gene Robinson was elected and consecrated as Bishop of New Hampshire in the Episcopal Church of America. The repercussions of this appointment were immediate, revealing serious differences of opinion in the Anglican Communion. These took (unofficial) institutional form in the establishment of the Global Anglican Futures Conference (GAFCON), held in Jerusalem in June 2008 – a gesture that challenged the integrity of the Anglican Communion as a whole. The timing was important; this was one month before the 2008 Lambeth Conference, itself one of Anglicanism's 'Instruments of Communion'. A rather more constructive response can be found in what has become known as the Windsor Process.[27]

Picking apart the threads (indeed the knots) that constitute the essence of this debate would require a book in its own right. The following points, however, are central to the argument of this chapter. First: how should a church in a modern western society position itself when the society in question shifts noticeably in ways which challenge 'traditional' understandings of sexual relationships and family life? And who within the church has the authority to decide a change in policy? Second: should this, or should this not make a difference to who can and cannot be appointed to senior (or indeed any other) office in the church? And once again who is to decide? And with this in mind, is it acceptable to treat ordained people differently from the laity? Third: how should such a church understand itself if it is part of a larger (in this case global) entity in which different kinds of societies hold very different opinions on the questions under review? Is it necessary for all parts (Provinces) of the church to move at the same pace? If so, when should the change occur?

And if not, what does this imply for 'Communion' as this is commonly understood? Fourth: how is it possible to manage the tension between the exigencies of 'truth' (variously understood) on the one hand, and the untidiness of pastoral care on the other? Is it possible to be rigorous in terms of the former and generous in terms of the latter without ending in confusion? Fifth: is it legitimate to think in terms of exceptions to the rule? And, with this in mind, is it hypocritical to turn a blind eye, or simply judicious?

Questions of this import are hard enough to manage even if they are approached with goodwill. Manifestly that has not always been the case. Integrities have been challenged, borders crossed, jurisdictions compromised and authorities questioned – repeatedly. But one fact is abundantly clear: the Church of England has already shifted its ground and is likely to shift further. For example, any kind of discrimination regarding lesbian, gay, bisexual and transgender (LGBT) individuals is now roundly condemned and Civil Partnerships have become the answer rather than a problem. These are recent changes. The more searching question concerns the consequences for the Anglican Communion as it is presently constituted, bearing in mind that a large majority of Anglicans live in the global south and – relatively speaking – remain conservative in their attitudes to same-sex activity. But not entirely: exceptions exist. And given the speed of change in the more developed parts of the world, it is not impossible that something similar may be set in train elsewhere. I remain convinced that the unimaginable can happen, just as it has in Britain. And two, or even three, generations is not that long in the big scheme of things. I am equally aware, however, that even one generation is too long (much too long) for those caught at the sharp end of these intractable questions.[28]

As a postscript to this section, it is interesting to note the reactions of other churches to this taxing question. Unsurprisingly 'traditional' Catholic teaching is opposed to same-sex relationships, but makes a distinction between homosexual acts and homosexual desires: the former are deemed to be sinful, the latter not necessarily so. It is equally clear that certain lobbies within the Catholic Church and a sizeable section of the laity at least in the west hold different (more accepting) views. There is also change over time – a trend that is likely to continue under the current papacy. More than once in the summer of 2013, Pope Francis indicated a more forgiving and more tolerant attitude to 'gays' – a term that he uses in public pronouncements. In itself this implies recognition.[29] Much of this is similar to the shifting positions of the Anglican Church, but the question resonates differently for the Catholics in terms of clerical appointments, given the celibate nature of their priesthood. Celibacy implies chastity, in other words abstinence from all sexual activity, gay or straight – a distinctively Catholic position.

Also in the summer of 2013, the Presbyterian Church of Scotland took a decisive step with regard to its own ministry. After a lengthy process of deliberation,[30] the General Assembly voted in favour of a proposal that allows liberal parishes who are so minded to opt out of the church's policy on homosexuality and to appoint men or women who are living openly in same-sex relationships. This was not an easy decision, and recognizing its potentially divisive nature, the General Assembly took great care to minimize the impact. Traditional teaching – namely that sex should take place only within heterosexual marriage – was strongly affirmed. There are moreover further legal steps to be taken before the shift is fully acknowledged. That said, a very significant step has been taken – yet another sign of change in this controversial field.

Further examples could easily be found, each of which raises a particular facet of this complex issue. It is time however to turn the question round and to take note of the number of parishes and/or congregations in a wide variety of denominations who style themselves as 'inclusive', meaning that they welcome individuals to their churches regardless of their gender, race, sexual orientation, abilities or position in life. Some of them 'specialize' more than others. In short they appeal to different segments of a market, a concept that must now be explored in more detail.

Notes

1 See for example the qualifications in chaplaincy studies offered by Cardiff University: http://courses.cardiff.ac.uk/postgraduate/course/detail/p306.html (accessed 6 August 2014)

2 More information about health care chaplaincy is available on the following websites: http://www.nhs-chaplaincy-spiritualcare.org.uk/index.html; http://www.churchofengland.org/our-views/medical-ethics-health-social-care-policy/healthcare-chaplaincy.aspx; http://www.mfghc.com/index.htm (all accessed 6 August 2014).

3 See http://www.secularism.org.uk/nhs-chaplaincy-funding.html for more detail (accessed 6 August 2014). Note in particular, the specially commissioned 'Costing the heavens: Chaplaincy services in English NHS provider Trusts 2009/10' (2011).

4 The number of people in Scottish prisons passed 8000 for the first time in August 2008 and reached its record level of 8420 in March 2012.

5 See – out of an extensive list – Beckford (2005, 2007, 2012a, 2013). See also Beckford, Joly and Khosrokhavar (2005).

6 That said a markedly more positive approach can be found in Béraud, de Galembert and Rostaing (2013).

7 The following websites offer interesting information about the nature and development of army chaplains: www.army.mod.uk/chaplains/ and http://www.bbc.co.uk/religion/religions/christianity/priests/armychaplains_1.shtml. Facts and figures regarding chaplains in all three services can be found in the following briefing paper: http://www.churchofengland.org/media/39111/gs1776.pdf (all websites accessed on 6 August 2014). I am also grateful to Padre Andrew Totten for his help in understanding the complex and changing role of the army chaplain.

8   This collection grew out of a series of research workshops, supported by the British Academy, and convened by the Cardiff Centre for Chaplaincy Studies.

9   For more information about the Religious Literacy Leadership Programme and its work, see http://religiousliteracyhe.org (accessed 6 August 2014). See also Dinham and Francis (forthcoming).

10 An excellent overview of faith schools and the debates that they provoke can be found in Theos (2013b). A rejoinder was published by the British Humanist Association, to which the Theos team provided a further response. Details of all three reports can be found on the Theos website: http://www.theosthinktank. co.uk/research/society/education (accessed 3 October 2013). I fully endorse the Theos conclusion that the debate about faith schools has become a proxy for an at-times heated and heavily ideological exchange regarding the place of religion in public life.

11 See https://humanism.org.uk/campaigns/schools-and-education/faith-schools/ for more details (accessed 6 August 2014).

12 More information about the poll can be found at http://www.religionandsociety. org.uk/news/show/new_poll_reveals_what_people_really_think_about_faith_ schools (accessed 1 October 2013).

13 See http://www.heraldscotland.com/politics/political-news/argument-against-faith-schools-summed-up-in-two-words-northern-ireland-or-one-glasgow.12345 (accessed 6 August 2014).

14 Paradoxically schools which insist on denominational allegiance can be markedly more inclusive in terms of socio-economic indicators than schools which draw from a designated catchment area.

15 See http://www2.warwick.ac.uk/fac/soc/ces/research/wreru/aboutus/ for more information about the Unit, and http://www2.warwick.ac.uk/fac/soc/ces/ research/wreru/research/current/ahrc/ for more information about the project as such (both websites accessed 6 August 2014). See also Arweck and Jackson (2013) and Arweck (forthcoming).

16 For a short summary see http://www.gla.ac.uk/research/infocus/researchers/head line_281437_en.html (accessed 6 August 2014); see also Conroy *et al.* (2013).

17 Precisely these points were reiterated in an Ofsted report entitled 'Religious education – releasing the potential' published in October 2013, available at http://www.ofsted.gov.uk/resources/religious-education-realising-potential (accessed 6 August 2014).

18 See https://humanism.org.uk/campaigns/schools-and-education/school-curricu lum/religious-education/ (accessed 6 August 2014). SACRE stands for Standing Advisory Council for Religious Education. Every Local Education Authority (LEA) is required by law to have a SACRE.

19 See http://www.secularism.org.uk/religious-education.html for the full statement (accessed 6 August 2014).

20 Changes in the funding arrangements for postgraduate training dampened recruitment in this field very noticeably. For example applications to RE Postgraduate Certificate in Education (PGCE) providers (mostly university departments) via the Graduate Teacher Training Register (GTTR) in 2012– 2013 dropped by 25 per cent compared with the previous year.

21   Detailed information about types and categories of ministry broken down by gender (and indeed many other variables) can be found at http://www.churchofengland.org/about-us/facts-stats/research-statistics/licensed-ministry.aspx (accessed 6 August 2014).

22   An excellent time-line of the whole debate from the 1970s onwards is provided by the Church of England. See http://www.churchofengland.org/our-views/women-bishops.aspx (accessed 6 August 2014).

23   Exact figures are available in *Statistics for Mission 2012: Ministry* (2013), Table 15.

24   In many ways this is a marriage of convenience. Anglo-Catholics are particularly concerned about relationships with the Roman Catholic Church, and reject the possibility that the Anglican priesthood can be altered without reference to Roman Catholic teaching on the matter. Evangelicals take their cue from a conservative reading of scripture paying particular attention to male headship.

25   The breakdown of the vote can be found at https://www.churchofengland.org/media-centre/news/2014/07/church-of-england-to-have-women-bishops.aspx (accessed 21 August 2014).

26   This happened in November 2013. See http://www.bbc.co.uk/news/uk-northern-ireland-25159579 (accessed 6 August 2014).

27   More information about the structures of the Anglican Communion, the role of the Lambeth Conference and the Windsor Process within this can be found at http://www.anglicancommunion.org/communion/index.cfm and http://www.anglicancommunion.org/commission/process/index.cfm (both accessed 6 August 2014).

28   The attention paid to the Pilling Report illustrates the point perfectly. This report was compiled by the House of Bishops Working Group on Human Sexuality, which was chaired by Sir Joseph Pilling. It was published in November 2013 and attracted considerable publicity. It itself contained strongly held and divergent views.

29   See for example the account of Pope Francis' interview with an Italian Jesuit journal: http://www.theguardian.com/world/2013/sep/19/pope-francis-vision-new-catholic-church (accessed 6 August 2014).

30   Both the process and the arguments that lie behind this historic vote are set out in the report of the Church of Scotland's Theological Commission on Same-sex Relationships and the Ministry, available at http://www.churchofscotland.org.uk/__data/assets/pdf_file/0014/13811/20_THEOLOGICAL_2013.pdf (accessed October 5 2013). The following paragraph in the Preface is worth pondering. 'The Report of the Theological Commission does not offer a definitive recommendation in favour of one Case, or the other. Rather, it invites the General Assembly to weigh carefully all of the matters before it conscious of the extent to which the decision to be made will shape the identity of the Church of Scotland within the communion of the "One Holy Catholic and Apostolic Church".'

Part III

Shifting Priorities: From Obligation to Consumption

7

An Emerging Market: Gainers and Losers

The notion of a market in religion is hardly new; it has dominated discussion in the United States for several decades and is increasingly present in analyses of religion in Europe. The two cases, however, are very different. In America, the market is made up of tens of thousands of free-standing congregations that aggregate themselves into denominations, none of which has, or has had, a legally privileged position in the federal state. In Europe, an increasing range of choices is undoubtedly emerging but over the top of a historically dominant church which maintains (more or less) a comprehensive network of parishes across the country. This is also true in Britain bearing in mind that the historic churches are for the most part less dominant in this corner of Europe than they are elsewhere, meaning that significant minorities have flourished for centuries rather than decades. But here too there has been a degree of rebalancing as the concept of choice begins to outweigh a sense of obligation in the religious lives of most British people.

The current situation can be described as follows. De facto there are two religious economies which run side by side. The first is a market of active churchgoers who choose their preferred form of religious activity and join the religious organization which expresses this most effectively. This may, of course, be a parish within the established church. The second retains the features of a public utility and exists, for the most part, for those who prefer not to choose, but who are nonetheless grateful for a form of religion which they can access as the need arises. For historical reasons, the two economies are weighted differently in the different parts of the United Kingdom. In every case, however, they are in partial tension but also overlap.

Religion in Britain: A Persistent Paradox, Second Edition. Grace Davie.
© 2015 Grace Davie. Published 2015 by John Wiley & Sons, Ltd.

In the late 1990s, Danièle Hervieu-Léger – a French sociologist of religion – recognized the changes taking place in Europe and reflected conceptually about them (Hervieu-Léger 1999). Specifically, she appreciated that analyses of religion in this part of the world were not helped by divisions of the population into two groups: those who practise their religion (whether frequently or not) and those who do not.[1] It was more profitable to think in terms of movement, bearing in mind the fluidity of modern living. Hence the title of her book: *Le pèlerin et le converti: La religion en mouvement*,[2] which introduces two ideal types (in the sociological sense of the term):[3] that is two ways of being religious, both of which capture the mobilities of late modern society in a continent with a distinctive religious past. The 'pilgrim' denotes the seeker who explores different forms of religiousness within, across and beyond denominations; the 'convert' makes a choice, frequently a definitive one. More often than not he or she is discovered in a congregation of like-minded people, who feel more at ease within relatively firm boundaries. Both types, whether consciously or unconsciously, have broken away from the taken-for-grantedness characteristic of previous generations.

The following sections will explore the implications of these ideal types, relating them to particular forms of Christian activity: namely the cathedral and the charismatic evangelical church, both of which thrive in the current market. The converse is also important (i.e. the relative 'failures') – a discussion which recalls earlier debates in the sociology of religion in so far as many of the predictions made in the 1960s and 1970s turned out to be wrong. A short note follows which introduces what might be termed hybrid cases: evangelical festivals. The third section looks at the market from a different angle. It starts by emphasizing the sheer diversity of religion in Britain, recognizing that boundaries are crossed and re-crossed all the time: evangelical churches exist inside and outside the established church, and the notion of 'fresh expressions' indicates new ways of doing old things. It continues with a brief introduction to 'new' churches in a different sense: those which have emerged in response to demographic or lifestyle change, paying particular attention to migration.

One further clarification is important. A great deal of what is normally understood by the term 'religion' has little or no institutional focus – at least not in the sense understood so far. This is even more the case in relation to spirituality, which is the starting point for Chapter 8. This is one form of pluralism or fragmentation. It should be not be confused with a second understanding of the term, which concerns the co-existence of different world faiths and the reactions this provokes. These will be dealt with in Part IV.

Cathedrals and their 'Customers'[4]

To place cathedrals in a chapter concerned with the notion of a market in religion, and to refer to the many different groups of people who frequent them as 'customers' is doubly perverse in that cathedrals are obvious exemplars of vicarious religion – a term associated with 'old' rather than 'new' models of religion. It is clear that these instantly recognizable and in many cases iconic buildings act as repositories of religious memory on a grand scale, and that the worship which takes place within them is offered on behalf of ever-widening groups of people. The latter include regular worshippers, irregular worshippers, pilgrims and tourists, noting that the lines between these categories are manifestly porous. Muskett (forthcoming) starts from this point to address the vicarious nature of cathedral life, arguing that these institutions are an important means (she introduces the term 'mechanism') by which the passive majority becomes acquainted with the forms of religion performed by the active minority.[5] The location of cathedrals on the border between the religious and the secular enhances this capacity.

Muskett's insightful article explores this approach in some detail; it begins with the notion of cathedrals as the 'shop-window of the Church of England' – a metaphor which has found 'a comfortable niche' in reports and scholarship on many different aspects of cathedral life. The metaphor is helpful given the evident ability of the cathedral to attract those on the edges of formal religion and to draw them in. A recent report published by Theos provides chapter and verse for this statement. It presents the key findings of a carefully planned research project (Theos 2012a).[6] The data indicate that cathedrals have a particular role to play with 'peripheral' groups – those, in other words, who are distant from, and at times, hostile to formal religion. For example, a 'sixth of people (15%) who never attend a religious service as a worshipper [...] visited a cathedral in the last 12 months, as did the same proportion of confirmed atheists, and a quarter of those who once believed in God but no longer do so' (Theos 2012a: 11). All that said, Muskett correctly reminds us that the notion of a shop window necessarily denotes a language of consumption and an element of choice. Choices, however, operate differently among different groups of people. The paragraphs that follow will consider these motivations in more detail. They will work from the inside out: starting with the regular and less regular worshippers before moving on to the 'visitors', dividing the latter into pilgrims and tourists.

The question of regular worshippers raises very directly what it means to co-exist, or more strongly, to compete in a market. If significant numbers of Anglicans choose to worship in the cathedral rather than in their parish church, what are the consequences for the latter, bearing in mind that in most parts of the country the pool of churchgoers continues to diminish? As ever, there are two possibilities: push and pull. The 'push' factors are often constructed negatively: they include a 'bad' experience in a parish, personality clashes, antipathy to change, natural reticence and fear of over-commitment. Much more positive are the attractions: notable here are the beauty of the cathedral building, traditional (or at least predictable) liturgy, excellence in preaching and world-class music. The Theos report deals sensitively with the issue of competition (Theos 2012a: 50). It also underscores what is clearly the most important pull factor of all: the desire for anonymity – meaning the option to come and go without an explanation, or even a greeting, and to move gradually from one stage of commitment to another. It would be a mistake, however, to look for hostility between cathedral and parish where there is none. Dual allegiance is perfectly possible.

Irregular worshippers are attracted by the same things as their more regular counterparts: the combination of aesthetic pleasure, good preaching and absence of pressure. Access is easy and the problem of loyalty is by and large avoided given that the cathedral is often the only religious organization that irregular worshippers attend. In the fullness of time some may attach themselves more firmly to the regular congregation or to one or other of the associated volunteer groups and some may not. Once again the Theos researchers provide ample evidence for such statements, often in the form of case studies – pen portraits of individuals who found themselves in a cathedral for one reason or another (chance, the weather, a friend, an invitation, a concert) and decided to return. At least some of these people were 'visitors' in the first instance, in the sense that their motives were clearly other than religious.

Visitors, however, come in many shapes and sizes and range from the self-consciously 'secular' tourist to the 'committed' pilgrim. There is plenty to attract the former: heritage, architecture, sculpture, painting, stained glass, books, manuscripts and music – in short a museum of the first order. Important questions arise in this connection. The first concerns the capacity of the visitor to interpret what is displayed. The following quotation illustrates the point perfectly. It is taken from the publicity of a French organization – Communautés d'Accueil dans les Sites Artistiques (CASA) – which exists to welcome visitors to a cathedral or similar building in such a way that they move beyond its architectural or artistic qualities and are able to discover its spiritual dimension.[7] The need for such help is expressed as follows:

> [T]he churches and monasteries of Europe are open to all, often without payment; these buildings are frequently visited. They stand as a witness to the faith and *savoir-faire* of those who built them and contain images and symbols which were eloquent for their contemporaries, but which require rediscovery today.[8]

That is certainly true, and in this respect visitors in Britain are no different from those in France (see note 7). It should not be assumed, however, that the supposedly secular tourist is without sensitivity to the building as a whole, even if he or she is unable to interpret the details of the art and artefacts contained therein. On the contrary, 'the distinction between being a tourist and being a pilgrim may be overstated', and those who appear to be secular are often well aware of the spiritual and religious role of cathedrals (Theos 2012a:17). In short, a cathedral is indeed a museum, but it is something else as well. Interestingly, the same ambiguity is experienced by those responsible for their maintenance. How is it possible to 'manage' the very large numbers of people who visit and at the same time maintain an appropriate sense of calm, not to mention a regular cycle of worship? Refusing entry to the choir as evensong is about to begin is not always as straightforward as it sounds.

It is clear that the categories of tourist and the pilgrim overlap; it is also clear that individuals can move from one to the other, sometimes consciously, sometimes less so. The motivations of the pilgrim are nonetheless distinct: for the pilgrim there is a sense of purpose in coming to the cathedral, which is seen as a significant marker within, and sometimes the culmination of, a spiritual journey. This is hardly surprising given the close connections between pilgrimage and place, which have existed for centuries. Among other things, these derive from the links between particular English cathedrals and the veneration of certain saints whose relics were deposited in these buildings (Thomas Becket in Canterbury and Cuthbert and Bede in Durham are obvious examples). More noteworthy for the argument presented here, is the popularity – one could almost say revival – of pilgrimage in the late twentieth and twenty-first centuries, across continents and across faiths. This is as true in Europe as it is elsewhere. Examples proliferate: in renewed attention to medieval routes, notably to Santiago de Compostela in Spain; in the Marian shrines of southern Europe (Fatima in Portugal, Lourdes in France or Medjugorje in Bosnia Herzogovina); and in more recent manifestations such as Taizé in eastern France. The trend has been creeping northward and now includes Protestant as well as Catholic sites (Trondheim in Norway or Iona in Scotland come to mind). Equally buoyant is the academic study of pilgrimage and the late modern motivations for this.[9]

The shrine, or more accurately shrines, at Walsingham (in Norfolk) should be seen in this light. They offer a distinctive English example. The early history is common to both Catholics and Anglicans; it is of medieval origin and associated with Richeldis de Faverches, whose vision in the eleventh century led to the establishment of a perpetual memorial to the Annunciation. Walsingham was considered one of the greatest shrines of medieval Christendom, but along with many others was destroyed at the time of the Reformation. The Catholic shrine was restored at the end of the nineteenth century since when the practice of pilgrimage has grown steadily; its focus is the Slipper Chapel (the last of the remaining wayside chapels en-route to Walsingham). Currently it attracts significant numbers of pilgrims from many sections of the Catholic Church.[10] The Anglican story begins in the 1920s and led to its own (extensive) buildings and place of veneration: the Church and the Holy House, which contains the statue of Our Lady of Walsingham. Here too the numbers are impressive and include the National Pilgrimage, which takes place on the Spring Bank Holiday each year.[11] Many of these visitors, both Catholic and Anglican, will arrive as part of a parish group, a link considered by Coleman (forthcoming).

A full discussion of the modern phenomenon of pilgrimage cannot be engaged in here. That said it is worth recalling Hervieu-Léger's distinction between the 'pratiquant' and the pilgrim. Not only is the former associated with stasis and the latter with movement, it is also the case that the notion of pilgrim reinvents itself in different periods of church history (Hervieu-Léger 1999: 96–97). Marian shrines, for example, responded to particular developments in the Catholic Church in the nineteenth century. Such reinvention is equally true today. In late modernity, the pilgrim is seen as autonomous, flexible and individually motivated; he or she is free from the obligations of an inherited faith and of the norms prescribed by the institution. Religious practice is episodic rather than regular, individual rather than communal, and finds expression in the exceptional rather than the everyday. Paradoxically or not, one outlet for this 'type' can be found in the cathedrals of modern Britain. Others, secular as well as religious, will appear in later chapters. They include a widespread tendency to gather, but on specified occasions rather than week by week.

A short note concludes this discussion. The definition of cathedral should not be considered too rigidly. England, Scotland, Wales and Northern Ireland house a wide variety of iconic buildings which belong to different sections of the Christian church. Some of these are cathedrals. There are in addition the 'greater churches', a category which includes abbeys or minsters together with a cluster of 'civic' or city-centre churches, many of which fulfil similar roles to cathedrals but on a smaller scale.[12] Unsurprisingly, they attract similar types of people.

Conservative Enclaves

Chapter 5 included a portrait of churchgoing in York which noted the relative success of three city-centre buildings. One of these was York Minster, which despite its name is a cathedral; another was St Michael-le Belfrey, a classic example of a successful evangelical church. Their close proximity in the middle of the city nicely exemplifies the ideal-types set out in this chapter.

Helpfully St Michael-le Belfrey has also been the focus of a book-length study which not only describes the congregation as such, but sets this into a broader context: it examines the growth of evangelicalism both in this country and worldwide, noting the many different currents that are found within this (Guest 2007). A central theme emerges: that is the dual nature of evangelicalism, which in many ways shields itself from cultural change but at the same time incorporates much of its essence. It is a thoroughly modern phenomenon.[13]

The St Michael's story begins in the 1960s, when David Watson arrived in York to become in the first instance the curate at St Cuthbert's, which was transformed within half a decade from a moribund community to a 'thriving evangelical stronghold' (Guest 2007: 57). In 1973, the congregation moved lock, stock and barrel to St Michael-le-Belfrey, where David Watson presided over an innovative, varied and by any standards hugely successful enterprise, becoming himself an increasingly prominent member of the evangelical elite. He left York in 1982 and died only two years later, aged 50. Guest continues the story of St Michael's as one new incumbent followed another, bringing with them new ways of doing things. Quite apart from their various personalities, each exemplifies a different aspect of evangelicalism. These include the initial charismatic thrust, followed by a more liberal, social agenda before the reaction sets in with a period of doctrinal conservatism. This in turn morphs into a greater emphasis on diversity and renewed evangelism. In Guest's account, the numbers peak in the 1980s, bringing to an end a period of exponential growth. Robin Gill (2012: 137) notes a further rise in the statistics following the publication of Guest's book.

Who were these people and where did they come from? At the time of Guest's study, the congregation of St Michael's was relatively young, middle class and well-educated; it embraced disproportionate numbers of students. Notably, it included relatively large numbers of 'elective parochials' (Guest 2007: 69): that is, a group of people who are self-consciously aware of the mobilities of modern living and who make corresponding efforts to compensate for this. They do so by forging temporary connections with an institution in the locality in which they find themselves – in this case the church, which responds accordingly. This is one reason why the turnover in membership is high. The next question cannot be avoided. To what extent did the obvious success of St Michael's deplete other churches in York? That a degree of transfer took place especially in the early stages is undeniable, but other interpretations are possible. In partial agreement with Robin Gill (1993, 2012), Guest acknowledges that the growing numbers at St Michael's add to the overall numbers of churchgoers in York. Or, more accurately, they mitigate the decline that might otherwise have taken place.

Chapter 8 of Guest's book looks at 'The Bigger Picture'. It is widely referenced but draws significantly on the work of Christian Smith, an American sociologist who has coined the phrase 'engaged orthodoxy' to capture the lives of American evangelicals (Smith 1998).[14] The crucial point is the following. Positive engagements with the wider society do not lead necessarily to secularization; it is equally possible that these encounters – edgy though they may be – contribute to greater vitality in the communities in question. That said the different currents within evangelicalism need careful management. Some, such as charismatic renewal, fit well with recent cultural trends, notably the shift that has become known as the 'subjective turn'. Late modern tendencies such as expressivism, acceptance, self-awareness and reflexivity are seen as aids rather than barriers to evangelism. Not everyone in the evangelical world concurs, however. A conservative backlash is always possible; one, moreover, which is determinedly resistant to social change – and nowhere more so than in issues to do with marriage, the family and human sexuality. Endorsements of male headship do not fit well with twenty-first century understandings of gender.

A degree of tension between the two approaches is a healthy sign and a characteristic of an evangelical community which is in Smith's terms is 'embattled but thriving' (Smith 1998). Left to fester, however, such tensions can all too easily mutate into destructive hostilities, which are difficult to handle in any circumstances, but even more so in a segment of the market which is notoriously prone to schism. This is one reason why the evangelical churches in this country are so many and so varied: some are inside the historic churches and some are not; some are self-governing and some are not; some build themselves into federations and some do not; some embrace the charismatic movement and some do not; some accept the means if not always the message of modern culture; and some accept neither. Whatever the case, in the religious economy of almost every locality in this country, there will be at least one, if not several, evangelical churches which are holding their own (sometimes more than) in the market.

It is these congregations that exemplify Hervieu-Léger's second ideal-type. The convert is in many ways the mirror image of the pilgrim: whilst the latter thrives on the fluidities of modern living and transfers these to his or her religious existence, the former seeks a resolution in the form of a definitive identity. The possibilities vary: converts can move from one religion to another; they can come to faith from an entirely secular background; or they can re-attach themselves to an existing religion in new ways. All three, however, have in common a rejection of the status quo and share with the pilgrim an awareness that the regulatory power of traditional forms of religion has largely eroded. These are not enforced conversions; they are freely made choices taken by individuals who have considered different alternatives. They take place within a market in which the notion of opting in has replaced opting out.

A second point follows from this. More people opt in to conservative churches than to liberal ones, a pattern which reflects a global trend. It is the conservative forms of religion that flourish in the twenty-first century, and not only in western Christianity. Simply a glance at the global south, or at the Middle East, or at the Muslim world in all its variety will attest to this fact. But why is this so? And why, more specifically, did an earlier generation of commentators fail to anticipate this trend? The establishment of the World Council of Churches (WCC) immediately following World War II offers an instructive case study. The instigators of the ecumenical movement worked on two assumptions: that the world would become an increasingly secular place and that the forms of religion most likely to survive in these circumstances would be those that resembled the 'world' most closely – an analysis that favoured liberal forms of Protestantism (those, in other words, that came together in the WCC). Some 65 years later, the picture looks very different: the world is by no means a secular place and the forms of religion that thrive in the twenty-first century are not only more rather than less conservative, but are hesitant about ecumenism. That is also true in Britain.

An additional observation concludes this discussion. Two ideal-types of religion have been identified which are distinct from each other. They share however a common feature: both go beyond the purely cerebral. As so many who pass through the doors of a cathedral declare, the sacred is 'experienced' in a multitude of ways. The aesthetic pleasure of the building itself is enhanced by the liturgy and music that take place within it. The evangelical sector is not only different but diverse. Increasingly to the fore, however, are the charismatic versions of this, which deliver once again something all-embracing. Putting the same point in Durkheimian terms, both the cathedral and the charismatic service embody religion in the sense of the sacred or 'set-apart'. It seems that late modern populations respond warmly to this feature. Fewer people go to church than was the case in previous decades, but those who do want something distinctive. What happens on Sundays should be different from, rather than an extension of, the everyday.[15]

In parenthesis, it is worth noting that this approach is less applicable in Scotland that it is in England – or so I was told when presenting these ideas to a gathering of specialists on the religious situation north of the border. Here a rather different, biblically based and markedly more cerebral religious culture remains more resistant to experiential appeal in whatever form. That said Iona has become a notable place of pilgrimage in the twentieth century – the Abbey is of interest to pilgrims and visitors alike. It is quite clear, moreover that that there are successful evangelical churches in most, if not all, of Scotland's larger towns. The rather more varied case studies from Edinburgh, established by Roxburgh (2012), should also be read in this light.

Hybrid cases

A notable feature of evangelical life in recent decades has been a series of summer festivals which are in effect a hybrid of the two types set out

above: namely evangelically inspired gatherings which exist outside the routines of week by week churchgoing. By and large they represent a similar style
of worship to their congregational counterparts, but on a grander scale.
Indeed taken together these events attract tens of thousands of individuals of
all ages and stages in life. Among others, and with start dates in brackets, they
include Greenbelt (1974), Spring Harvest (1979), New Wine (1989) and its
offshoot for young people, Soul Survivor (1993).[16] Undoubtedly innovative,
these festivals follow a developed tradition. Tent or revival meetings have been
a feature of evangelical life since the nineteenth century, and the notion of a holiday week as a supplement to congregational life is admirably exemplified in the
Keswick Convention, an assembly which has met continuously since 1875.[17]

Modern festivals are nonetheless distinctive. Greenbelt will be taken as an
example of the (relatively) recent initiatives. Initially a Christian music festival, Greenbelt has met annually since its inception, usually over the August
Bank Holiday, and celebrated its 40th anniversary in 2013. For the previous
decade and a half, it has used Cheltenham Racecourse as its base, but in 2014
moved to a new venue in Northamptonshire. In terms of numbers its fortunes
have ebbed and flowed. Attendance was high in the 1980s (circa 20 000), but
for a variety of reason numbers dipped in the following decade; they are now
back to their peak. Greenbelt has an interesting history. It grew out of the
evangelical wing of the Christian tradition, but describes itself as progressive
and as an arts, faith and justice festival. Strikingly multi-disciplinary, it reaches
outwards. Performers are invited not because they are Christians, but because
their vision overlaps with the biblical idea of justice, or because they stand for
or are engaged in political issues that reflect the priorities of the organizers.
The visual and performing arts test the limits of acceptability and at times
transgress them. Significant numbers of mainstream musicians compete with
Christian bands for attention.

The emphasis is firmly on inclusion – the festival is family-friendly and
'accepting of all, regardless of ethnicity, gender, sexuality, background or
belief'.[18] Regarding the vexed question of same-sex relationships, there is no
doubt where Greenbelt stands. Bishop Gene Robinson was invited in 2009
and Peter Tatchell in 2010 and 2012. A much-appreciated safe space for
lesbian, gay, bisexual and transgender (LGBT) people is an integral part of
the facilities. Political stances are equally distinctive, captured in phrases
such as 'working for justice', 'challenging oppression' and 'using our
resources wisely'. Following from this, but rather more surprising given
Greenbelt's origins, is the attention given to the Palestinian question. The
relevant section of the website puts it thus:

> We know that our audience – whether in their churches or through their
> exposure to mainstream media – get plenty of input and coverage on the situ-
> ation in Israel-Palestine. But they don't necessarily hear from the voices of

those working for peace and justice and human rights on the ground in the region – outside of state and government structures, at a grassroots level, within civil society.[19]

Unsurprisingly the Palestinian debate has provoked comment. Indeed there are a number of issues within Greenbelt on which conservative Christians have expressed concern – to the extent that some have withdrawn their custom and gone elsewhere, illustrating once again the fissiparous nature of this type of Christianity. By and large, however, the result is impressive: Greenbelt displays a heady mix of views in an event which offers a unique opportunity to speakers and audience alike. Few (including myself) can resist the invitation to take part and those who listen will for the most part be exposed to 'honest debate' over a wide range of issues.

An Ever-Changing Kaleidoscope

The success stories of religion in modern Britain are many and varied, noting from the outset that growth and decline operate across denominations rather than between them. Of course the overall fortunes of different denominations vary, but a closer look reveals that all (or almost all) of them offer a mixed bag of success and failure. Indeed, it is quite possible to have more than one outlook within a congregation, particularly in rural areas. Here the potential for tension between a settled company of 'parishioners' and a newly arrived group of activists, flushed with the success of an urban initiative, is real. The former represent maintenance (more accurately gradual attrition), while the latter attempt new things. Both are important, but relationships between the two can at times be less than cordial.

Three 'categories' of innovation will be considered in this section: first the activities known as Fresh Expressions, then a range of churches that cater for new arrivals in this country, and third a rather smaller group of lifestyle churches. Goodhew (2012a) offers useful background for all of them.[20] Fresh Expressions – an Anglican initiative but with ecumenical partners – are many and varied. Taken together, however, they constitute 'a form of church for our changing culture, established primarily for the benefit of people who are not yet members of any church'.[21] The implication is clear: the emphasis lies on 'go to them' rather than 'come to us', recognizing that the latter – the underlying principle of the parish system – no longer resonates for the majority of people in this country. Society has changed and the church must adapt accordingly. Lings (2012) provides a concise history of the movement which contextualizes the current debate. This is important: Fresh Expressions did not emerge from a vacuum – a whole series of initiatives predate the present efforts to reach beyond the parish. The nomenclature is varied and at times confusing but the overall thrust is clear: it lies in the need to overcome the limitations of the 'inherited model'.

The term 'fresh expressions' found its place in print in the widely read *Mission-shaped Church: Church Planting and Fresh Expressions of Church in a Changing Context*, published in 2004. This Church of England report reviewed the initiatives that had taken place since the publication of its predecessor, *Breaking New Ground*, in 1994. The earlier report had set out to recommend good practices for church-planting and deployed the term 'supplementary' to understand the relationship between old and new forms of ministry. Some 10 years later, this vocabulary was no longer considered adequate, so much so that the notion of 'supplement' morphed into 'complement'. The shift was significant: to supplement is to add on; '[t]o complement is about two different realities needing each other to mutual benefit' (Lings 2012: 173). This distinction noted, 12 kinds of 'fresh expression' are then described in the *Mission-shaped Church*, paying attention to how these engage with the wide variety of cultures present in British society. Interestingly the introduction to the report addressed very directly the question of consumerism. It accepts that choice is the dominant mode of operation in a late modern society and that it will penetrate the ways in which individuals conduct their religious lives; at the same time it rejects the ideology of consumerism, going so far as to name this 'idolatry'. Whatever the case, a mixed economy of provision should be considered the norm.

The easiest way to grasp the scope and scale of the enterprise is to peruse not only the Fresh Expressions report created as part of the Church Growth Research Programme (see note 21), but the relevant sections of the Fresh Expressions website. The section on 'Stories', for example, can be searched by topic or location; at the time of writing there were just under 200 search tags for topics.[22] Even more interesting is the page entitled 'Networks of Fresh Expressions', which reveals the very different activities covered by the rubric. These include (selectively) networks concerned with new monasticism, café churches, activities for families including 'messy church', new spiritualities, and rural and urban initiatives.[23] The resource page covers reading lists, research and statistics, from which some idea of the size of the enterprise can be gleaned. The data are broken down by denomination and by diocese for the Church of England.[24] A degree of care is necessary when picking your way through the different sources of data given the widely differing methods employed, but some broad conclusions can be drawn. This is an extensive and continually evolving enterprise which reaches beyond conventional churchgoing circles, and includes significant numbers of young people. A forthcoming doctoral thesis suggests that the most popular categories are café church, cell and network churches, youth churches, new monastic communities and new traditional services. Messy church is particularly prominent among Methodists.[25]

So far, so good. It is clear that the Church of England, among others, not only accepts but welcomes these initiatives.[26] Not everyone, however, is so sure, and for a variety of reasons. Hull (2006), for example, raises questions about key theological concepts (kingdom, church, gospel and mission), which, he claims, are insufficiently distinguished in the *Mission-shaped Church*. Two years later Percy and Nelstrop (2008) brought together a series of essays which reflect on the Fresh Expressions initiative from different points of view. Martyn Percy's own contribution to this volume examines the tension between *intensive* and *extensive* models of church. Intensive models focus on individuals who have made a conscious decision to join in; extensive models focus on everyone unless they have chosen to opt out. The contrast raises important – and at times unresolved – questions of religious identity. Considerably more trenchant are the criticisms of Davison and Milbank in *For the Parish* (2010). Recognizing the growing significance of the Fresh Expressions movement, they stoutly defend the 'inherited' model. Theological traditions, they argue, are more important than cultural trends and work themselves out in distinctive ecclesiological forms, notably the parish (and by implication establishment). Form and content are inherently connected. The Church of England is called upon to serve the population as a whole, not simply those who sign up to special interest groups – too much attention to the latter denotes a capitulation to market values when resistance is the appropriate response.

Immigration is a 'hot' topic in this country. The discussion is wide-ranging, touching amongst other things on work, welfare, housing and education, revealing a strong and largely unfounded assumption that the newly arrived are here to take rather than give. Links are also made to the growing diversity within British religion, in which the excessive attention paid to Muslims should be noted. The influx of Christians is less remarked on; it is, however, a crucially important factor in the religious profile of this country, particularly in cities. As the 2012 London Church Census tells us, almost half of Inner London's churchgoers are black.[27]

The beginnings of this story are familiar enough. Afro-Caribbeans came to Britain in considerable numbers in the early post-war decades, responding to a call for labour as the economy expanded. Many of these people were active members of the historic (missionary) churches. Their rejection by the very same churches in this country is also well known, as indeed is its sequel: the formation of independent Afro-Caribbean congregations which collectively became one of the most vibrant sectors of the religious economy. It is these churches that provide the subject matter for an important series of chapters in Goodhew's collection.[28] A narrative that began in the 1950s continues to this day. New communities of Christians constantly emerge as the newly arrived from different parts of the world search for somewhere to put down roots. More appreciated now than at the beginning, however, is the significance of religion and religious networks in the migration process per se – quite rightly this has become an important focus for research in both Europe and North America (see, for example, Connor 2014).

Looking at this process from the receiving end, it is clear that a rapid turnover in population in the communities in question stimulates growth as well as decline. Congregations become adept at integrating newcomers – simply because they have to. Whether this capacity should be considered a service to the newcomer or a strategy for success is a moot point. Either way, a pertinent example can be found in what Brierley calls 'speciality' churches, meaning those which cater for different linguistic groups. He estimates that 14 per cent of church services in London across a wide variety of denominations are translated into languages other than English.[29] Ethnicity is equally significant, a fact revealed in the following percentages. Overall 9 per cent of London's population goes to church on an average Sunday: 4 per cent of Indians, Pakistanis and Bangladeshis; 8 per cent of the white population; 16 per cent of the Chinese, Koreans and Japanese; and 19 per cent of the black population. The significance of London as a 'super-diverse' global city is a central factor in this story, but it is not the only example. Marsh's (2012) and Stringer's (2013) descriptions of Birmingham – one of the most diverse cities in Europe never mind Britain – are equally instructive.

Not all of these churches are new churches, at least not in the conventional sense of the term. Harris (2012), for example, looks in detail at a Catholic parish in Canning Town, noting from the outset that the majority of Catholics in this country are of immigrant origin (see pp. 53–6). Predictably enough, the church that forms the focus of Harris' study was founded in the mid nineteenth century as a hub for Irish immigrants seeking work in the east end – an entirely familiar story. In the early twenty-first century, the building is still there but the congregation is changing in nature. It is also thriving: approximately 1200 people gather on a Sunday morning from more than 40 migrant backgrounds (Harris 2012: 45). The detail that follows makes fascinating reading, documenting the very specific contributions that Catholics from the Philippines, the West Indies and different parts of Africa make to this parish. The wheel moreover is turning full circle: these enterprising people are bringing back to this country practices originally exported by missionaries, thus re-animating aspects of devotion that have waned in Britain. It is equally clear that these practices respond to material as well as spiritual needs.

The idea of 'reverse mission' resonates in this context. This tricky but important notion was examined in detail in a doctoral thesis (Catto 2008). In a more recent chapter, Catto (2012) summarizes this work referencing a wide range of illustrations: these include the 2005 mission to Britain of the (Anglican) Melanesian Brothers and Sisters, individual (evangelical) missionaries from Latin America and a congregation of Koreans in a relatively small city in the south west, who are linked to a Methodist church. Illustrations such as these indicate the shifting parameters of global Christianity, as assumptions about flows from the west to the rest give way to a much more complex picture. Christians arrive in this country for many different reasons; some are motivated by religion and some are not. But taken together these individuals make a significant difference to the varieties of Christianity on offer, both inside and outside the mainstream churches. A crucial aspect of this shift concerns the continuing links between recently arrived Christians and the churches from which these people come: contacts take place on a daily basis and give substance to the notion of transnationalism in religious life. They are greatly facilitated by new forms of communication.

How should this vibrant, growing and diverse section of the Christian market be assessed? In terms of overall figures, it would be wrong to suggest that these inflows compensate for losses elsewhere (see below). All too often, however, the vitality of religion in London is attributed simply to 'immigrants', with the strong implication that a whole category of churches, and the activities that they foster, need not be taken into to account in the big picture. This is incorrect. The point to grasp is that the big picture itself is changing. Movement and mobility, and thus immigration, are central to modern living and will continue to be so. The flows and counter-flows of religion are part and parcel of this changing situation, and operate in a wide variety of ways. It follows that an overview of religion in this country must pay close attention to these resourceful people, noting their presence, their churches and their influence both within and beyond the communities that they serve.

The third form of innovation – that of lifestyle churches – offers a different response to the following observation: that any church or congregation which relies on obligation or habit to bring people to worship is likely to struggle; conversely those which make it worth the while of people to attend have a much greater chance of success. It is at this point, moreover, that an important difference between Britain and the United States should be noted. It is displayed in the work of a distinguished group of American scholars engaged in congregational studies. Take for example the collections brought together by Nancy Ammerman (1997, 2005). These reveal not only the variety but the sheer resilience of religious congregations in American life, despite the multiple vicissitudes that some of them face. It is true that many of these congregations confront decline, whether in the long or short term (Ammerman 1997: 44), but even the contents pages of these volumes gives an impression of persistence, relocation, adaptation and innovation in combinations that would be hard to match in Britain.[30]

Such evidence leads inexorably to the advantages of a system based on voluntarism (the very essence of the congregations that Ammerman describes) over a relatively immobile established church. Indeed the *raison d'être* of 'Fresh Expressions' lies here – they exist to overcome the limitations of the 'inherited model'. This is very different from the American situation where the inherited model itself embodies flexibility. All that said it is possible to find congregations all over Britain (both inside and outside the historic churches) that serve distinctive communities: that is, particular categories of people, however defined. Examples abound. They include churches that cater for the arts and for artists, for actors (St Paul's Covent Garden), for particular styles of music, for families, for single people, for the elderly, for the disabled, for specified professions, for those with a passion for social justice, for fair trade, for the environment and so on. Rarely are these interests the sole concern of the church in question. They become nonetheless places where the like-minded can gather in order to reflect on their ideas in the light of Christian teaching. Unsurprisingly networks develop between similar congregations in different parts of the country. It is worth noting finally that inclusivity as well as exclusivity can become a niche.

A developed example offers a bridge to the next chapter on 'Proliferations of the Spiritual': it can be found in the very many activities associated with St James Piccadilly, a parish church in the west end of London. St James 'welcomes and celebrates human diversity' – a position made clear in its Mission Statement.[31] There is, moreover, a reference to pilgrimage, and indeed to another St James, in the form of the 'Camino course' designed for those who are exploring the journey of faith in relation to contemporary life and work. The list of activities associated with the church makes interesting reading in itself:[32] quite clearly it evolves, but in 2013 it included a Julian group (for silent, contemplative prayer); a meeting of mainly Christian spiritual enquirers; an additional group dedicated to exploring creative spiritual alternatives; a cluster interested in the Sanbo Kyodan tradition of Zen; those involved in danced liturgies and different kinds of music (the lay singers and Taizé chants); an LGBT group; a drop-in counselling service; hospitality for the homeless and concern for refugees; a fair-trade stall; and the Piccadilly Market. It is important to note that not all of these are officially linked to St James as such. But either way the crucial point remains the same: namely that seeking and searching, commitment and gathering extend beyond the Christian tradition – a point to be explored in due course. The boundaries, moreover, are porous.

Who is Right and Who is Wrong?

The emergence of a market in religion raises important questions – for scholars of religion and for those with responsibility for the churches. Two will be raised as a conclusion to this chapter. To what extent does the idea of a market challenge the status quo? And to what extent do the associated initiatives compensate for the overall decline in religious activity? The answer to the first question must be placed in context: there has always been a market in religion in the sense that significant minorities have existed in this country for centuries rather than decades. Not everyone moreover observed conventional orthodoxies; variety existed within as well as between traditions. That said, a step change is clearly underway as the notion of obligation recedes and the possibilities of choice develop. Protagonists of the latter, moreover, desire more rather than less room for manoeuvre and for this reason alone are frustrated by the restrictions of the territorial model, the attitudes that go with this, and at times the constitutional structures that underpin these arrangements. Traditionalists have reacted accordingly, defending the status quo. A fight to the death isn't helpful. Both models – public utility and market – are varied, and both can be used constructively or less so. They also overlap. Deploying the good points of each in a genuinely mixed economy is a more sensible policy than protracted mutual hostility.

The second question has provoked a lively debate between Steve Bruce, the leading defender of the secularization thesis in this country, and David Goodhew, the editor of *Church Growth in Britain*. An initial exchange on the BRIN website has been expanded into a series of articles, published in the *Journal of Religion in Europe*.[33] These take the form of an extended review of Goodhew's collection by Bruce, a response by Goodhew and a further rejoinder by Bruce. Bruce argues that examples or pockets of church growth, as documented by Goodhew and his colleagues, do not refute the secularization thesis as he understands it; nor do they compensate in any significant way for the persistent decline in indices of religious activity. Goodhew responds by repeating his claims about the changing position in London, especially amongst black, Asian and minority ethnic communities, and certain kinds of new churches– a claim that is strengthened by the data emerging (after the drafting of this response) from the London Church Census. Bruce is unconvinced. No doubt the argument will continue, but to what avail? It is clear that the two scholars are talking past each other. Bruce is correct about overall decline; Goodhew is correct in saying that this is not the whole story. Both overstate their case. Indeed the real question lies elsewhere – in a gradual rebalancing of the whole picture. It is clear that fewer people are religious than used to be the case, but those who remain engaged are more likely to do so for reasons of conviction than for reasons of obligation. That makes a difference.

Notes

1 The French terms 'pratiquants' and 'non-pratiquants' are central to the work of early French sociologists of religion, many of whom specialized in the mapping of religious practice.

2 The title can be translated as *The Pilgrim and the Convert: Religion in Motion*. De facto, the book is one of a trilogy concerned with religion in late modern societies, especially France. See also Hervieu-Léger (2000, 2001).

3   In this usage 'ideal' means pure or distilled types not those found in real life, which is necessarily more ambiguous.

4   Two sources of information are helpful for this section. First the extensive information gathered on the Christianity and Culture website at the University of York – see www.christianityandculture.org.uk – and second the material on cathedrals and the greater churches in the Church Growth Research Programme – see http://www.churchgrowthresearch.org.uk/UserFiles/File/Reports/Publication_edition_Strand_3a.pdf. Both websites accessed 7 August 2014. The latter report was published after this chapter was drafted; it substantiates many of the points made here.

5   In this respect, Muskett's article builds very directly on to Rowe (2010).

6   This report is based on two bodies of data. The first was a local survey of 1933 adults, who were asked their opinions of one of six Church of England cathedrals (Canterbury, Durham, Lichfield, Leicester, Manchester and Wells) with which they were familiar. The second was a series of detailed case studies in the course of which 257 in-depth qualitative interviews were conducted among a wide range of people who work in and with the aforementioned cathedrals.

7   CASA was founded in 1967. More information about its interpretative work can be found on www.guidecasa.com (accessed 7 August 2014). I first came across this organization in Vézelay, France. Some 30 years later, the Christianity and Culture Centre in York (see note 4) came into being for a very similar reason. Specifically: '[M]any people are fascinated by the rich cultural heritage to be discovered in art, literature, music and historic buildings. However the fact that so much of this heritage has been substantially shaped by Christian belief and practice can pose a major problem of access and understanding for those who lack familiarity with Christian concepts or biblical themes.' See http://www.christianityandculture.org.uk/about (accessed 7 August 2014).

8   Author's translation from the original French.

9   See for example the Centre for Pilgrimage Studies website at the University of York and associated CD, which gathers together a huge amount of resources, www.pilgrimagestudies.ac.uk (accessed 7 August 2014).

10   The website of the Catholic shrine suggests that some 100 000 pilgrims arrive during the pilgrimage season, not least some 6000 Tamils, half of whom are Christian and half Hindu. See http://www.walsingham.org.uk/romancatholic/ (accessed 7 August 2014).

11   Anglican numbers are given as 10 000 residential pilgrims each year (almost 200 pilgrims can be accommodated at any one time). A further 300 000 visitors come on a daily basis. See http://www.walsinghamanglican.org.uk/welcome/index.htm (accessed 7 August 2014).

12   See greaterchurches.org for more information on at least some of these buildings (accessed 7 August 2014). The category 'greater churches' is included in the Church Growth Research Programme (see note 4).

13   An extended period of ethnographic fieldwork was carried out 1999–2000, with a follow-up visit in 2006. More detail about the methodology of this study can be found in Appendix 1 of Guest (2007).

14 In making these connections, it is important to bear in mind that Christian Smith's work focuses on the United States, where evangelicals are far more numerous than they are in the United Kingdom.

15 An additional example of distinctive Christianity can be found in Alpha, described by Matthew Bell as British Christianity's biggest success story. See http://www. independent.co.uk/news/uk/home-news/inside-the-alpha-course--british-christi anitys-biggest-success-story-8555160.html. The pivotal role of Holy Trinity Brompton, Alpha's birthplace, is worth noting in itself. See also www.alpha.org and Hunt (2004). Both websites accessed 7 August 2014.

16 For more details see www.greenbelt.org.uk, www.springharvest.org, www.new-wine.org and soulsurvivor.com (all accessed 7 August 2014).

17 Keswick Ministries is the current title of the Keswick Convention Trust. Its purpose is the 'advancement of the (Christian) religion by the emphasis of certain Christian doctrines, such objects being pursued by holding an annual Convention at Keswick, by promoting similar Conventions and meetings elsewhere, by distribution of suitable literature and by making grants of money for the said purpose'. See http://www.keswickministries.org/about-us/who-we-are (accessed 7 August 2014).

18 See http://www.greenbelt.org.uk/about/organisation/values/ (accessed 7 August 2014).

19 More information about this aspect of Greenbelt's work can be found on http:// www.greenbelt.org.uk/about/organisation/israel-palestine-programming/ (accessed 7 August 2014).

20 Interestingly this collection also contains a chapter on cathedrals. See Barley (2012).

21 For more information see http://www.freshexpressions.org.uk/about/whatis (accessed 7 August 2014). See also the very extensive material covered in the Church Growth Research Programme. Quite rightly Fresh Expressions and church plants constitute a major component within this work: http://www. churchgrowthresearch.org.uk/UserFiles/File/Reports/churchgrowthresearch_ freshexpressions.pdf for more details (accessed 7 August 2014).

22 See http://www.freshexpressions.org.uk/stories (accessed 7 August 2014).

23 See http://www.freshexpressions.org.uk/networks (accessed 7 August 2014).

24 See http://www.freshexpressions.org.uk/research. Note also the link to the Church Army's Research Unit in Sheffield – see http://www.churcharmy.org.uk/ ms/sc/reimaginechurch/sfc_database.aspx. Both websites accessed 7 August 2014.

25 For these details I am indebted to Paul Hammond (forthcoming). I was able to read an early draft of the relevant chapter of his doctoral thesis.

26 See for example the relevant section on the Church of England website – http:// www.churchofengland.org/our-faith/mission/missionevangelism/fresh-expres sions.aspx (accessed 7 August 2014).

27 See http://www.brierleyconsultancy.com/images/londonchurches.pdf, p. 11 (accessed 7 August 2014).

28 For example, the chapters by Hugh Osgood, Richard Burgess and Amy Duffour.

29 See http://www.brierleyconsultancy.com/images/londonchurches.pdf, pp. 5 and 11 (accessed 7 August 2014).

30   Any number of further examples could be found from a growing sociological literature on American congregationalism. An excellent source for this material can be found at http://hirr.hartsem.edu/cong/research1.html (accessed 7 August 2014).

31   For more details see http://www.sjp.org.uk/our-approach.html (accessed 7 August 2014).

32   See http://www.sjp.org.uk/groups.html (accessed 7 August 2014).

33   The initial exchange on the BRIN website can be found on http://www.brin. ac.uk/news/2012/church-growth-in-britain-since-1980 (accessed 7 August 2014). For the articles as such, see Bruce (2013a and 2013b) and Goodhew (2013).

8

Proliferations of the Spiritual

Two rather different understandings of religious pluralism have already been introduced (p. 136). They both extend beyond Christianity but in different ways. On the one hand are the proliferations of the spiritual that abound in modern Britain; on the other is the increasing presence of other-faith communities. For the sake of clarity, they will be taken in turn: this chapter deals with different manifestations of the spiritual, the next with religious minorities. In terms of timing, however, the two coincide. At precisely the moment that the Christian traditions began to lose the authority that they once had to discipline the beliefs and behaviour of the faithful, new groups of people were arriving in this country bringing with them the religious beliefs and practices present in their countries of origin. Both tendencies, moreover, took place against a background of increasing secularity.

A second ambiguity is equally pertinent and draws very directly on the work of James Beckford (2003). Not only is the term 'pluralism' used to *describe* very different situations, it is also used to evoke the moral and political values associated with these shifting profiles. In short, is the increasing variety in the religious life of this country a good or a bad thing? The inference is clear: there is a persistent confusion between what is and what ought to be, and until this is sorted out, there are bound to be misunderstandings in public as well as social scientific debate – a point that can be illustrated many times over. One way of proceeding is to use the term religious 'diversity' to capture the great variety of individuals, groups, organizations and communities that now cohabit in modern Britain, and to reserve the term 'pluralism' for the ideological or normative

Religion in Britain: A Persistent Paradox, Second Edition. Grace Davie.
© 2015 Grace Davie. Published 2015 by John Wiley & Sons, Ltd.

commitments associated with the acceptance or otherwise of this situation. In theory I concur with Beckford on this point (2003: 73ff), but the abundant literature now available in this field does not always sustain this distinction.

Keeping these difficulties in mind, this chapter will proceed as follows. It will start by looking briefly at the question of new religious movements – not to give a comprehensive account of these many and varied organizations, but to indicate what the debates that surround them tell us about the nature of British society.[1] Up to a point the same will be true of the 'new age' (the preferred term for the spiritual in the 1990s), but the latter raises very specifically the tensions that arise between older forms of religion and the more fluid nature of the spiritual. To what extent can these be combined and who is to decide where the limits lie? A related set of tensions can be found in the complex relationships between the material (i.e. the realities of everyday life) and the spiritual – strains that play on the notion of a market. Is a market in spiritual goods simply an extension of the market per se? Or is the emphasis on the spiritual by definition a rejection of the market in so far as it is indicative of a different set of values? Or is the converse closer to the truth: markets, it can be argued, are so pervasive that they corrupt the spiritual? Different commentators come to different conclusions.

The later sections of the chapter focus on the notion of spirituality itself: how should this be understood, where might it be found, how does it differ from religion and how has the idea been developed in academic study? The argument works in stages, looking first at the size of the constituency, then at the key characteristics of its practitioners and what they think, and finally at the resonance of the spiritual in public as well as private life. The chapter concludes with three case studies. It draws first on a much-quoted 'portrait' of religious life in Kendal, entitled *The Spiritual Revolution* (Heelas and Woodhead 2005), which takes as its theme the gradual shift from the religious to the spiritual in a small town in the Lake District. The second study looks at the situation in Glastonbury, another relatively small town, this time in the West Country, which contains an extraordinary range of religious and spiritual options – a market if ever there was one. The third illustration is a little different; it focuses on the everyday lives of disadvantaged young people, showing how these hover between the religious, the spiritual and the secular (Vincett and Olson 2012). Paradoxically the material that emerges from this case is in some ways very similar to the observations made some 25 years ago in connection with *Faith in the City* (see Ahern and Davie 1987). The methodology of Vincett's and Olson's enquiry is markedly more sophisticated than the work accompanying *Faith in the City*, but the continuities are clear.

New Religious Movements

The introduction to the first edition of this book pointed to a persistent paradox in the sociological approaches to religion in Britain. There was a marked imbalance in the material available in this field, in the sense that we were much better informed about the exotic fringes of religious life than we were about the beliefs and practices of ordinary British people. Or to put the same point in a more positive way, there existed at the time an important and growing body of sociological material on both sects and new religious movements carried out by some of the most distinguished scholars working in this field. These included Bryan Wilson (1961, 1967, 1982), James Beckford (1975, 1985) and Eileen Barker (1984). Particularly useful in this respect was Eileen Barker's *New Religious Movements: A Practical Introduction*, published in 1989 (Barker 1989a). As the title suggests, this provided in a readily accessible form a large amount of practical as well as sociological knowledge on this topic.

In this, Barker addressed questions about the numbers of people involved in new religious movements and about definitions – which groups or organizations should or should not be included in this inevitably amorphous category. The answer to the first question is very few; the answer to the second question is more difficult. At one end of the spectrum lie some relatively well established communities (Jehovah's Witnesses or Mormons for example), which are difficult to distinguish, sociologically if not theologically, from the smaller Protestant denominations. At the other extreme can be found what Paul Heelas has termed 'self-religions', which exist in abundance and are difficult to distinguish from the new age, at least in its 'psycho-spiritual' forms. In between are a huge variety of groups, distinct in many ways from the surrounding society but also from each other. The need to avoid generalizations is crucial, but is frequently overlooked in public discussion.

Barker's work has also found organizational expression in the Information Network on Religious Movements (INFORM).[2] This is an independent charity, founded in 1988 with the support of the Home Office and the mainstream churches. Once again its primary aim is practical: it exists to help individuals and families by providing them with information that is as accurate, balanced and up to date as possible about alternative religious, spiritual and esoteric movements. In order to do this, it eschews close definition: the phrase 'alternative religious, spiritual and esoteric movements' is simply a common-sense starting point to allow maximum accessibility. INFORM has proved its worth; it has become an important reference point for the media and government bodies as well as the general public and celebrated its silver jubilee in 2014. Its annual reports provide chapter and verse for this statement – they make fascinating reading and reveal the continuing resonance of at least some new religious movements in British life.[3]

What can a sociologist learn from this multifaceted phenomenon? Once again it is helpful to return to James Beckford's work and in particular to his comparative analyses. Beckford (1985) develops two themes in this respect, both which are relevant to the argument here and both of which have stood the test of time. The first compares the situation of new religious movements in Britain, France and what was West Germany. The key point is that 'the cult problem', if such it is, varies with the social, political and cultural characteristics that prevail in each of these countries. It follows that in order to understand 'the distinctive animus against certain NRMs' in different part of Europe, it is essential to examine not only their individual structures and teachings but also the religious – and indeed the political – situation in which they exist (Beckford 1985: 271). In other words, new religious movements like all religious phenomena have to be seen in context. Debates concerning such movements will have different outcomes depending upon the specificities of the setting in which the discussion occurs.

The second point is a corollary of the first. Beckford argues that new religious movements, though numerically of limited significance, can provide us with a powerful lens through which to view the wider society (see also Barker 1982). By looking at the way that societies react to new religious movements and the controversies that they generate, we can discover more about that society itself. What, for example, is regarded as normal or abnormal, as acceptable or unacceptable in the name of religion, or, to use another phrase, as tolerable or intolerable? Similarly a whole series of legal definitions relating to the rights or otherwise of individuals and/or religious groups follow from judgments in the courts concerning new religious movements. Controversies surrounding these movements become, therefore, 'the barometers of changes taking place in a number of different societies' (Beckford 1985: 11). And to pursue the analogy a little further, they may well offer signs of stormy weather ahead and nowhere more so than in questions of religious toleration.

What we discover from this approach is that the British are not altogether unfriendly towards religious diversity but some religions appear easier to accept than others. Barker (1989b) terms this 'tolerant discrimination'. Chapter 9 will develop this discussion in relation to other faith communities, a much larger constituency.

The New Age or Self-Spiritualities

The sociological debates surrounding the new age (and the many associated ideas) are different. The emphasis here is personal rather than organizational – individuals are free to explore a wide diversity of beliefs and practices guided by internal motivations rather than external constraint. It follows that questions concerning the acceptability or otherwise of a particular religious movement and the teaching associated with it are less relevant. The flash points, if any, occur in different ways: in the encounters with organized religion (notably in its more dogmatic versions), and in the relationships between the new age and mainstream society.

It is important, first, to grasp the nature of the topic. New age or self-spiritualities include a diverse, ill-defined and somewhat amorphous set of ideas held together by a relatively small number of consistent and cross-cutting themes – notably an emphasis on the self and self-discovery, and a desire to 'connect'. The former provides the essence of self-spirituality (the God in me, reaching fulfilment, realizing potential, 'I did it my way' and so on). The latter can be found in different settings: it reflects both the interconnected person (mind, body and spirit) and the interconnected universe (each individual is part of a cosmic whole). The fields in which such ideas both germinate and grow are diverse: they range along a continuum, which at the 'hard' end includes new forms of capitalism and management training (signifying the self as a business leader). The somewhat 'softer' end reveals a wide range of mostly holistic therapies (evoking the self in need of healing). In between can be found outlets in publishing (huge ones), in alternative forms of education (those that emphasize the self-discovery of the child), in green issues (the connected universe) and in alternative forms of medicine (the connected person).

The relationship with the mainstream is complex. It is clear that self-spiritualities are both friend and foe of more conventional forms of religion. They are 'friend' in the sense that they reject the emphasis on materialism as the primary goal of human existence. Happiness does not lie in the accumulation of possessions whether big (investments, houses and holidays) or small (shopping). Excessive consumption, in fact, is an indication of unmet need rather than fulfilment. They are a 'foe' in so far as traditional understandings of Christian teaching emphasize a defined body of teaching in which a transcendent rather than immanent God is central – in other words a God to whom the Christian submits, rather than the God within (a central tenet of new age teaching).

The distinction, however, is less than clear-cut. There are, and always have been, different – indeed contradictory – lines of thinking within the corpus of Christian doctrine, some of which make more room for the self than others. Reactions to the new age are correspondingly varied. At one end of the spectrum are the churches that affirm many, if not all, aspects of new age teaching as a source of inspiration or wisdom for the Christian. At the other are congregations that see new age ideas in a more negative light. More than mistaken, such ideas are perceived as dangerous – something to be avoided at all costs. Significant sections of the evangelical constituency take this view, but not all. The discussion in Chapter 7 reflected these distinctions, noting that it is the forms of Christianity that adopt some if not all aspects of self-spirituality – expressivism or self-reflection for instance – that are currently expanding. Those who take a harder line, rejecting *both* form and content of new age thinking, are less likely to prosper.

Such reactions should be seen against the mutations of modern society, at which point Paul Heelas' work becomes central to the argument. Heelas (1996, 2008) has been a close observer of alternative religions for at least two decades, during which time his thinking has evolved alongside the field itself. Heelas (2008), for example, establishes an interesting set of generational changes. First can be found a set of historical antecedents to the new age as such; these need not concern us here – except to remark that the ideas in question are by no means 'new'. They come and go periodically. But why, in the late twentieth century, did they move centre stage? According to Heelas, the first breakthrough came in the 1960s, a decade in which spiritual discovery coincided with the expansion of new religious movements already described. Both were indicative of counter-cultural trends as traditional institutions, including religious ones, came under attack.

But as the 1960s gave way to a rather less confident decade, new forms of self-spirituality appeared on the scene. Heelas uses the term 'seminar spirituality' to describe these shifts, initiatives which turned bit by bit into the 'soft production capitalism' of the 1980s. The crossings over into other disciplines are important at this point – into social psychology and management training, for instance, as the stress falls increasingly on releasing human potential for the benefit of business as well as leisure. Life and work were reconnected as each individual discovered the different ways in which he or she could contribute to the enterprise in question. Such organizations, however, were variously motivated: some were linked to capitalist endeavour and some were not. The 1990s introduced a further chapter in this story, expressed this time in a growing emphasis on well-being, a shift associated with the markedly subjective turn in modern culture. It is also the decade in which the ideas associated with self-spirituality became ever more visibly part of society's mainstream. No longer was it necessary to seek the products of the new age in alternative outlets or specialized shops; they were increasingly found in the high street.

What then is the position in the first decades of the twenty-first century? Is it the case that western populations are happy to embrace innovative forms of spirituality as more traditional practices fade? Or do these processes run in tandem? Who gains and who loses in these complex equations and who is to decide? It is at this point that we return to the concept of the market, noting that in many respects the debate surrounding this term echoes the ambiguities associated with the idea of pluralism. At one level a 'market' is simply a descriptive term that depicts a wide range of religious or spiritual options from which individuals can choose what suits them best. At another, it introduces a much sharper discussion about values and their applicability in different spheres.

The initial step is straightforward enough: not only do we purchase our material requirements from different outlets, we also shop around for our spiritual needs. Religious organizations respond variously to such requests by purveying particular products, some with greater success than others. There are, however, deeper questions to be asked and from different points of view. On the one hand are those who maintain that the sacred (in whatever form) challenges the notion of the market; by definition, it is concerned with non-materialist rather than materialist values. Such sentiments may be articulated verbally or expressed in practice. A good example of the latter can be found in the communities of new age individuals who adopt distinctive lifestyles – choosing to live simply or in accordance with ecological ideals.[4]

Jeremy Carrette and Richard King are not convinced. Indeed in *Selling Spirituality: The Silent Takeover of Religion* (2004), they reverse the entire argument – disclosing what they consider to be a silent take-over of 'the religious' by contemporary capitalist ideologies, notably neo-liberalism. Those who regard spirituality as the 'soft' face of capitalism, mitigating the worst effects of the market, and making the workplace more congenial in the name of authenticity are simply naïve. On the contrary, spirituality itself has become a product, constructed from elements of the major world-faiths which have been taken out of context. Thus packaged, it can be bought and sold as one commodity among others in the global marketplace. To substantiate their argument, Carrette and King expose the people and the brands which are profiting from this assault. The indictment is severe: if spirituality is to be reclaimed as a means of resistance to capitalism and its deceptions, it must become increasingly self-critical.

That however is not the only possibility. A rather more nuanced approach to the interconnections between religion, spirituality and the market can be found in the impressive collection of case studies brought together in Martikainen, Gautier and Woodhead (2011), Martikainen and Gautier (2013) and Gautier and Martikainen (2013). This body of writing stresses the multiplicity of ways in which the religious and the economic intersect in different parts of the world. That said, the dominant narrative concerns the effect on religion of wider economic changes, notably the spread of consumerism and neo-liberal ideology. For better or worse, we – like the rest of the world – live in a 'market society'.

What is Spirituality?

It is already clear that the line between the new age and spirituality is distinctly porous: each merges into the other and the terminology shifts over time. Some commentators – Wouter Hanegraaff (2009) for example – continue to use the term 'new age', but recognize that it can be understood in different ways; others – among them Steven Sutcliffe and Marion Bowman

(2000) – suggest that we have moved *Beyond the New Age* to what they call 'alternative spiritualities'. The underlying question persists, however. What is meant by alternative spirituality (whether singular or plural), and what is its significance in modern British society? And how is spirituality to be distinguished from religion? The following paragraphs engage these questions and work in stages. They look first at the constituency as a whole, in so far as it can be identified, and consider its size and significance. They then outline the key characteristics of this phenomenon, its internal divisions and emphases. Space will be given finally to the expression of spirituality in public life and to a growing corpus of academic material.

Spiritual people

'I am not religious, but spiritual', has become a cliché – and like most clichés, there is an element of truth in this. But how many people in British society hold this position? The question can be approached in two ways: either by looking at responses to large-scale enquiries such as those introduced in Chapter 4, or by extrapolating from a local study. Examples of the latter can be found at the end of this chapter.

In terms of the large-scale enquiries, it is commonplace to offer respondents a choice of answers regarding their belief, or otherwise, in God. The details vary, but by and large, the choice is between a 'personal God', 'some sort of spirit or life force' or neither – noting that the precise questions asked and the methodologies deployed vary considerably. As we saw earlier, the British population more or less divides itself into thirds – religious, spiritual and secular – proportions that are altering over time (see Tables 4.1 and 4.2 and Figure 4.1, pp. 74–6). Working in a similar vein and drawing on a wide range of sources (not all of them British) Vincett and Woodhead (2009: 323) offer the following estimates regarding the extent of spirituality, taking into account different levels of commitment:

1. the number of active, highly committed, regular participants stands at around 2–5 per cent of the population;
2. the level of adherence/affiliation (indicated by those claiming to be 'spiritual but not religious') stands at 10–20 per cent;
3. agreement with beliefs characteristic of spirituality – such as belief in 'some sort of spirit or life force' or 'God as something within each person rather than something out there' – lies somewhere between 20 per cent and 40 per cent.

A third source of data is rather different. Some idea of the categories that emerge in this amorphous field (together with their relative sizes) can be found by looking at the input into the 'Any other religion' line on the 2011

Census form. The numbers that emerge are noticeably small. There is abundant evidence here (i.e. in the list of entries) for the fragmentation of the religious sphere; there is very much less to substantiate claims about a shift from the religious to the spiritual.[5]

Additional information can be found in two Theos reports, both of which repay careful reading. The first, *The Faith of the Faithless* (Theos 2012b) builds on to the work on cathedrals, described in Chapter 7. As its title indicates it is primarily concerned with the faith or beliefs of those who place themselves outside 'any formal religious system'. A year later, *The Spirit of Things Unseen: Belief in Post-religious Britain* (Theos 2013c) offers a more comprehensive account in the sense that it examines the spiritual beliefs of the nation as a whole, noting the sections of the population who translate their ideas into action (gender is a significant variable in this respect). The focus lies on the middle ground – that is the space between what might be termed traditional religiousness and secular commitment. This is expressed as follows:

> For all that formalised religious belief and institutionalised religious belonging has declined over recent decades, the British have not become a nation of atheists or materialists. On the contrary, a spiritual current runs as, if not more, powerfully through the nation than it once did.
>
> For example, an overwhelming majority of people – 77% – believe that 'there are things in life that we simply cannot explain through science or any other means'. Only 18% disagree. Those who consider themselves to be a member of a religious group are more likely to agree with this (87%), but so do the majority (61%) of those who are not religious. (Theos 2013c: 12)

It is interesting to reflect on these statements. In many ways, these reports capture the beliefs and practices of the segment of society that interested me most some 20 years ago. The vocabulary has altered, as indeed has the way that we think about religion – a shift captured by the use of the term 'spiritual' rather than 'religious'. This in turn reflects a change in mood, characterized by Heelas and Woodhead (2005) as a 'subjective turn'. The underlying continuities are nonetheless important, one of which lies in the enduring significance of the 'centre' (however conceptualized) for a rounded understanding of religion in this country. This, moreover, is a contested space. As will become clear in due course, advocates of a more secular outlook will also be staking a claim.

Thinking spiritually

So far in this chapter, the spiritual has been contrasted with the material (in the discussion of the market) and with religion in its more traditional forms. This section considers the spiritual on its own terms. What are the characteristics of this way of thinking, and where can they be found in our society? Vincett and Woodhead (2009: 335) provide a starting point. They include the following attributes in their summary of this very varied field: an emphasis on inner, subjective and ineffable experience; the importance of the individual as the final arbiter of spiritual truth; an emphasis on holism and relationality; a stress on immanence rather than transcendence; and the importance of seeking and openness. They also describe a number of distinctive fields: two of these – 'mind, body and spirit' and Paganism – are worth exploring further.[6]

'Mind, body and spirit' practices cover a huge variety of activities and techniques, the majority of which have to do with healing or well-being.[7] Some of these will operate at the individual level; others involve groups and group work. All of them will engage the whole person. Take for example the Mind, Body and Spirit Festival, which began in 1977.[8] Since then the festival has stood as 'a catalyst for personal transformation, change, health and wellbeing, self-empowerment, community and the exchange of ideas and concepts'. The emphasis lies firmly on the spirit within and on an acceptance of new possibilities, in order to develop 'healthier, more creative and more fulfilling lifestyles'. This can be done in an infinite number of ways but the underlying themes are clear. They include: eco-living, natural health, complementary medicine, alternative technology, spirituality and personal growth.

Who is likely to be involved? On this point Vincett and Woodhead are clear. Women are disproportionately present in this world. Many of them, moreover, come from the caring professions. Indeed it is a moot point whether the relationality so evident in this sphere is in itself an attraction or whether it is derivative of those who engage in it. Either way a virtuous circle sets in. The age profiles should also be noted: most of these women are middle-aged. A string of questions follows from this. How should we interpret the choices of a small but significant minority of individuals who come from a particular demographic? Are their engagements with the spiritual a form of self-indulgence? Or are these women victims of low-level exploitation, as intimated by Carrette and King? A third option is more generous: the encounters engendered by the mind, body and spirit movement are one way among others of taking responsibility for yourself and for developing your potential to the full. And what is wrong with that?

Paganism has a different emphasis; it is often described as a nature religion or as a revitalization or reclamation of pre-Christian traditions (Harvey 2009). In its present forms it dates from the mid-twentieth century and brings together very ancient and more recent ideas. There is a natural affiliation with the ecological movement, indeed with anyone who cares about the natural environment. This is unsurprising given the significance for Pagans of this world rather than any other, and of immanence rather than transcendence. A stress on the interconnectedness of all things moves in a similar direction. These characteristics are common to all Pagans. Within the community as a whole, however, there are a number of 'traditions' or 'pathways'. Following Harvey, these include: Druidery, Goddess Spirituality, Heathenry, Wicca, a range of 'Ethnic' Paganisms and increasingly Eco-Paganism. His insightful chapter offers more information on each of these; it also includes a series of descriptive vignettes.

Overall Harvey describes Paganism as a new religion that fits well into modern or late modern society. He argues that its core characteristics – individualism, eclecticism, mass dissemination and egalitarian social structures – would be difficult to imagine in a previous age. The next question poses itself: should Pagans be seen as a part of late modern society or as a reaction to this? Harvey inclines to the latter view, noting the distinctive features of Paganism in ritual rather than preaching, in story-telling rather than formal teaching, and in a positive reading of enchantment. He also underlines a strong (almost Durkheimian) emphasis on participation, locality, belonging and relationships. All that said the degree to which these activities are seen as counter-cultural depends a good deal on how the mainstream (both societal and religious) constructs itself. This is as much a question of perception as of reality.

Either way, a notable episode occurred in 2010. The Charity Commission for England and Wales granted charitable status to the Druid Network after a four-year application process. The judgment is significant for the following reason: it indicated that the Network had met the four criteria established by the Commission in order to decide whether or not a system of belief constitutes a religion for the purposes of charity law.[9] The details of the reasoning are interesting in themselves, and can be found on the Charity Commission's website.[10] Even more significant is what this episode reveals about the place of alternative spiritualities in British society (Harvey and Vincett 2012). A degree of ambiguity remains. On one hand, the judgment implies not only greater acceptance but a more inclusive understanding of what constitutes a religion; on the other are the at times vehement reactions that followed. Leading the pack in this respect was Melanie Phillips in the *Daily Mail*.[11] Her language in an article that is well worth reading in full is not only strong, but political: 'The whole thing is beyond absurd. But it is also malevolent. For it is all of a piece with the agenda by the oh-so politically correct Charity Commission to promote the fanatical religious creed of the Left – the worship of equality.' And if the Druid Network has been accepted as a religion, who, Phillips asks, will be next? Quite clearly, the questions raised earlier in connection with new religious movements continue to resonate.

Public applications

A rather different facet of spirituality is revealed in the increasing use of the term in public discourse, sometimes alongside religion and sometimes instead of it, a shift in vocabulary worth noting. Three examples follow, all of which are extracts from public documents, drawn from different sectors of society and from secular rather than religious institutions. They could be repeated many times over. Such statements are clearly indicative of change; they need, however, careful interpretation. In many cases they are what they seem – in other words they represent a genuine commitment to inclusive and holistic principles of care in the institution in question. At times, however, the term 'spirituality' is used as an awkward proxy for 'religion', in an attempt to avoid the (supposedly) negative connotations of the latter. In reality, neither concept is properly understood, or is differently appropriated by different parties, leading to manifest confusions when the policy in question is put into practice. Gilliat-Ray's (2003) sensitive, but nonetheless critical, analysis of the application of spirituality in nursing care should be read with this in mind.

Whatever the case, the term 'spiritual' is widely used and in very different contexts. My first example is taken from the booklet given to prospective in-patients in a NHS hospital in the south west and reads as follows:

> Illness and injury can have an impact on your whole life, not just your body. And it can be hard to talk about your anxieties or fears with the people you are closest to. We are keen to help by supporting the full range and variety of spiritual and religious needs of our patients, their carers and staff.[12]

The subsequent paragraph provides further information about the chaplaincy team. The implication is clear: this aspect of hospital care lies within the purview of the chaplain, acknowledging – indeed underlining – the inclusive nature of chaplaincy work. A second illustration can be found on the website of the Department of Education and concerns the 'Aims, Values and Purposes' of the school curriculum. The Department stipulates that the teaching that we deliver to children should reflect the 'values in our society that promote personal development, equality of opportunity, economic wellbeing, a healthy and just democracy, and a sustainable future'. Specifically, these values should relate to 'ourselves, as individuals capable of spiritual, moral, social, intellectual and physical growth and development'. Exactly what is meant by 'spiritual' development is expanded on a subsequent page. It is markedly non-committal. Children must develop 'the knowledge, skills, understanding, qualities and attitudes they need to foster their own inner lives and non-material wellbeing'.[13] The third example has a sharper focus and comes from Scotland; it concerns the 'Policy on Spirituality in Social Care' endorsed by Aberdeen City Council. The introduction to this document stipulates the need to pay attention to spirituality. There is therefore 'an expectation that staff, who work within health and social care settings, will be able to, at the very least, acknowledge the spiritual lives of service users and understand something of the relationship between spiritual needs and wellbeing'.[14] The principles underlying this approach are clearly stated alongside its practical implications; the policy articulates very precisely what service users and staff should expect.

The academic study of spirituality runs parallel. It is given institutional form in the British Association for the Study of Spirituality (BASS), which was established in 2010 and exists to encourage and enhance the work undertaken in this field.[15] In order to do this effectively, there is a strong emphasis on crossing boundaries – between disciplines, between professions and between many different faiths and belief systems. The Association is closely linked with an academic journal (the *Journal for the Study of Spirituality*), which set out its stall in its first editorial.[16] This starts by outlining the different contexts in which the term 'spirituality' is currently deployed. These include 'established religions and wisdom traditions; professional settings such as education, medicine, health and social care; leadership, management and workplace studies; as well as healing therapies, life-coaching, and personal and professional development'. The editor also notes the point alluded to above – that is, the statutory duty to respond to the spiritual needs of patients, students or clients, noting at the same time the existence of countless more informal groups that focus on personal or spiritual development.

The corollary is clear. It is important to bring the very disparate work on spirituality together in terms of organization and publication. BASS and its associated journal exist for this purpose: specifically to create a forum for exchange and debate, and to encourage new syntheses in the understanding, research and practice of spirituality. The work finds its rationale in the notion that human beings are essentially spiritual creatures, driven by the need to ask 'fundamental' or 'ultimate' questions and to find meaning and value in human living. In this respect the inspiration is drawn from Zohar's and Marshall's writing on 'spiritual intelligence' (2000).

Religious and Spiritual Markets: Some Examples

The final section of this chapter draws some of these threads together and asks how a market in religion and/or spirituality works in practice. It does this by means of case studies. The first, the Kendal project, has become a landmark study for two reasons: partly because it told us new things about the nature of religious activity in Britain, but also because its authors offered an interesting interpretation of their data, drawing on innovative theoretical insights. Putting data and theory together, they explore the following claim: 'that traditional forms of religion, particularly Christianity, are giving way to holistic spirituality, sometimes still called "New Age"' (Heelas and Woodhead 2005: x).

The project has an empirical base. It begins by documenting in some detail the forms of religion practised in Kendal, a town of 28 000 people in the Lake District. A wide variety of approaches were employed to do this: an initial mapping, attendance counts, congregation counts, selected case studies for more detailed investigation and an in-depth study of a particular street.[17] From a snapshot of religious activity taken in one week (in November 2000) the authors established two religious heartlands: the congregational domain and the holistic milieu. Specifically, we discover that 2207 people (adult and younger) attended the 25 churches and chapels in Kendal on that particular Sunday – that is 7.9 per cent of the population (a percentage that appears to be shrinking year on year). The holistic milieu attracted 600 people in 126 separate activities during the same (typical) week – i.e. 1.6 per cent of the population (a percentage that continues to grow). Equally interesting were the results of the street survey. In one sense these are very clear: only two people (out of 56 interviewed) declared a definite lack of belief or anti-church sentiments. But how the rest of the figures are configured depends a good deal on how the 'grey' areas of belief are categorized – as support for relatively high levels of religiousness in its most general sense or as a marked drift from the Christian norm. Either could be argued from these data.

How should these findings be interpreted? Drawing on the work of Charles Taylor (1989, 1991, 2002, and in anticipation 2007), Heelas and Woodhead present what they call the 'subjectivization thesis' – that is, a radical shift in modern culture that represents a move away from life lived in terms of external or objective roles, duties or obligations, towards life lived in accordance with subjective rather than objective experience. Using their own terminology, 'life-as' becomes increasingly 'subjective-life'. In their view, moreover, it is the subjective turn that accounts for the decrease in the congregational domain and the increase in the holistic milieu, bearing in mind that the transformation is far from complete. Equally important, however, are the shifts *within* the congregational domain itself, once again from forms of religion which take relatively little account of the subjective lives of their members to those where the subjective or 'experiential' element is more developed – not least the evangelical charismatic churches, a relative success story in Kendal as they are elsewhere. In short, spiritualities which engage with the depths of personal experience are faring better than religions that demand conformity to higher truth.

It is clear that the findings of the Kendal Study endorse the gradual shift away from a culture of obligation to a culture of consumption and provide valuable data about the religious and spiritual choices of a relatively active minority. There are, however, further questions to address. In its published forms the material concentrates on the two heartlands and what can be learnt from these. It pays much less attention to the middle ground, those who self-identify as Christians, many of whom might turn to the Christian churches for the rites of passage. Precisely this point is well made by Alan Billings (2004) in a parallel account of religion in Kendal. The author, an experienced parish priest, pays careful attention to the occasional offices and the continuing role of the parish church in the lives of the local population – a feature missing from the more sociological Kendal Project. Indeed for a rounded view of religion in this unusually well-studied English town, both sources should be carefully noted. That done, the two religious economies outlined in previous chapters will be clearly visible.

Marion Bowman (1993, 2003–2004, 2005, 2008, 2013) has observed the religious scene in Glastonbury, a small town on the Somerset levels in the south west of England, over many years. She draws attention to its natural features, which include the Tor (distinctive in shape and visible for many miles), the chalybeate spring at the Chalice Well and the thorn trees that flower both in spring and in December. She also notes that attention to religion in this town is hardly new. Glastonbury Abbey dates back to Saxon times and lies at the centre of the town. Now ruined, it was among the richest in England and was closely associated with King Arthur. For this and other reasons, Glastonbury is a place where legends abound, both Christian and other, making it not only a hugely popular but a very varied pilgrimage site – reviving a much older tradition.[18] Pilgrims arrive from all over the world attracted by different things. Such visitors, moreover, are central to the local economy.

The Glastonbury Pilgrim Reception Centre opened in 2008.[19] Its website is a mine of information and lists the following as places to visit in the town: Bride's Mound, Chalice Well and Gardens, the Church of Saint John the Baptist, Glastonbury Abbey, the Glastonbury Goddess Temple, the Glastonbury Experience Courtyard, Glastonbury High Street, Gog and Magog, the Lake Village Museum, the Library of Avalon, the Somerset Rural Life Museum, Saint Margaret's Chapel and the Magdalene Alms Houses, the Glastonbury Tercentennial Labyrinth, Glastonbury Tor, Wearyall Hill and the White Spring. With the possible exception of the Lake Village Museum and the Somerset Rural Life Museum, every one of these has a religious or spiritual connotation which is carefully explained. The pages on Glastonbury 'faces', 'voices' and accommodation are similar. In addition the Centre proudly proclaims that over 70 different faiths, paths and beliefs co-exist in Glastonbury: 'a greater concentration per capita than anywhere else in the world'.[20] The goal of the Centre is to promote contact and understanding between people of different lifestyles, beliefs and faiths, and – it is clear – to encourage yet more pilgrims.

A walk down the high street, filled with retail outlets, alternative shops and specialist accommodation will substantiate these claims, leaving the visitor in no doubt that this is indeed a site of spiritual consumption. Bowman (2013) examines this concept in more detail in the light of the growing body of literature available in this field. Interestingly from the point of view of this chapter, she interrogates the connections between the spiritual and the market in some detail, noting that the purveyors of alternative spirituality in Glastonbury are becoming more rather than less business-minded – the counter-culture of the 1970s is not as visible as it used to be. That said the tensions between materialist and less materialist views remain as do the differences in perspective between Glastonbury's older residents ('Glastonians') and the more recently arrived 'Avalonians'. Most agree, however, that the town as a whole benefits from this activity. This is hardly surprising given that 40 per cent or so of its retail outlets can be categorized as 'alternative' shops, which sell goods 'intended to enhance and expand people's spiritual lifestyles and practices' (Bowman 2013: 210). Most striking in many ways is the combination of traditional forms of religion and new forms of spirituality, all of which co-exist in a limited space: lines are crossed and re-crossed all the time as pilgrims visit each other's holy places, pass each other in transit and eat in the same cafés and restaurants.

The final example appeals to me for a different reason. Having worked extensively on the nature of belief in the inner city in the mid-1980s (Ahern and Davie 1987), I was attracted to a project concerned with the religious or spiritual identities of young people who live in areas of considerable deprivation (Vincett and Olson 2012).[21] I warmed to the initial assumptions of the research team who wanted to know more about young people who felt themselves excluded from the traditional structures of religion. But did that make them irreligious? It seems not. What emerges in fact is a broad range of religious practices, some of which draw on 'traditional' religion, but in non-traditional ways. Both prayer and meditation, for example, are clearly evident as are practices that focused on recognized spaces, both old and new. Also present, however, were opportunities for spiritual exploration by individuals whose lives were necessarily insecure – many of them had confronted death or illness at an early age. Some reacted by rejecting religion; others were clearly more ambivalent, looking for resources to come to terms with their losses and to perpetuate links with family and friends who were no longer there. A belief in ghosts or spirits or angels followed from this.

But how were these young people to express such sentiments? And how were the research team to overcome the natural hesitation of groups of people who not only think of themselves as excluded but who are more likely to express their believing in practice than in words? The answer lay in a carefully planned project located in the more deprived areas of Glasgow and Manchester. An emphasis on 'space' is interesting and reflects the disciplinary location of the project in a department of geography. Equally attractive are the methodologies employed, which included not only considerable investments of time, but the development of an innovative strategy, designed to capture the non-verbal. Groups of young people were trained in video production and photography, which led to the production of two films and a travelling photography exhibition. The approach drew a positive reaction: 'The adults [involved in making the film] let us express what we felt about religion and spirituality. They kept the paperwork to a minimum and didn't take over. We learnt by talking to ourselves and others, brainstorming ideas and taking pictures.'[22]

The background to this project is worth noting. Effectively it constitutes the second part of a longer-term study on youth and religion. The initial piece of research concentrated on young people who were actively involved in a range of Christian churches or related organizations in Glasgow. In this course of this work, it became clear that the sample, though impressively articulate, was exclusively middle class. So what about the others, especially those pushed to the edges of society – those in other words who perceive local churches as places that exist for middle class people who live 'better' lives? Most important in my view is the recognition of agency in this project: that is the ability of the young people in question to reflect, to respond and to create. Such attributes are easily missed using conventional methodologies that rely too much on the spoken word. An inability to express oneself verbally does not constitute a dumbing down; it is simply a different way of doing things.

But is it new? Many of the findings in this study recall very directly the work that I did some 25 years ago, which drew in turn on wide reading. Current at the time was a memoir of life in Liverpool in the 1930s; the narrator is an articulate child who returns to the city with her family who had fallen on hard times during the recession. She replies to a question about church membership as follows: '"We are Church of England", I said. "That is, when we are clean and rich we are Church of England. I suppose at present we are nothing".' And a few pages further on, the narrator elaborates this contrast: 'The beauty of the language of King James's Version of the Bible and of the Church of England Prayer-Book and the rich poetry of the hymn-book were not lost upon me, and enriched my knowledge of the English tongue'. But in her changed circumstances, the mental stimulus and religious comfort offered by this heritage were no longer accessible. God, it seemed, was not only distant but angry. The sense of exclusion is palpable. That said the local church comes out of this account of pre-war Liverpool relatively well in terms of practical help to a family in need. The perceptions of a sensitive teenager who involuntarily crossed a social divide are nonetheless illuminating.[23]

Three points conclude my reflections on the more recent enquiry. I respond very positively to the researchers working in Glasgow and

Manchester when they indicate that, quite apart from religion, they learnt a great deal about deprivation in the course of their work. So did I. And like them, I also learnt first-hand of the resourcefulness (or agency) of individuals and communities who live at the margins of society. The third point is a little different. During the course of my work in the more deprived parts of Liverpool, I became increasingly aware that once belief or believing drifts from its institutional moorings, it becomes increasingly heterodox. Indeed it was my engagement with 'faith' in that city that set me on the trail of 'believing without belonging'. It is good to see an up-to-date study which develops this theme albeit deploying a different and perhaps more apposite terminology.

Notes

1   New religious movements hover on the cusp between this chapter and the next. They are indeed alternative forms of spiritual expression, but organizationally they pose similar questions to other faith communities.

2   For more information about the aims and objectives of INFORM, see www.inform.ac (accessed 7 August 2014).

3   These are available on http://www.inform.ac/about-inform (accessed 7 August 2013).

4   The Findhorn Foundation located in north east Scotland offers a possible example. This is 'a spiritual community, ecovillage and an international centre for holistic education, helping to unfold a new human consciousness and create a positive and sustainable future'. See www.findhorn.org for more information (accessed 7 August 2014). Castro (1996) provides a more critical account.

5   The data themselves, together with an interesting discussion of this point, can be found at http://www.brin.ac.uk/news/2012/census-2011-any-other-religion/ (accessed 7 August 2014).

6   Two other forms of spirituality are covered in Vincett's and Woodhead's account: the new age itself and what is termed theistic spirituality – a section which explores the links between spirituality and more traditional forms of religion.

7   Unsurprisingly there are close links between mind, body and spirit practices and complementary and alternative medicine (CAM).

8   For more detail about the festival, see http://www.mindbodyspirit.co.uk/about-us and http://www.mindbodyspirit.co.uk/about-us/our-history (accessed 7 August 2014).

9   More information about these criteria can be found on https://www.charitycommission.gov.uk/detailed-guidance/charitable-purposes-and-public-benefit/guidance-on-charitable-purposes/the-advancement-of-religion/ (accessed 7 August 2014).

10 See https://www.charitycommission.gov.uk/media/92221/druiddec.pdf (accessed 7 August 2014).

11   See 'Druids as an official religion? Stones of Praise here we come', *Daily Mail*, 4 October 2010. Available at http://www.dailymail.co.uk/debate/article-1317490/ Druids-official-religion-Stones-Praise-come.htm (accessed 7 August 2014).

12   The full text can be found on http://www.rdehospital.nhs.uk/patients/inpatient/ religion_12.html (accessed 7 August 2014).

13   See the section on Teaching and Learning on the Department of Education website. Specifically http://webarchive.nationalarchives.gov.uk/20130903160941/ http://www.education.gov.uk/schools/teachingandlearning/curriculum/ b00199676/aims-values-and-purposes/values and http://webarchive.national archives.gov.uk/20130903160941/http://www.education.gov.uk/schools/ teachingandlearning/curriculum/a00199700/spiritual-and-moral. Both websites accessed 7 August 2014.

14   The full document is available at http://committees.aberdeencity.gov.uk/ mgConvert2PDF.aspx?ID=11763 (accessed 7 August 2014). The quotation is taken from paragraph 1.3 of the Introduction.

15   The Society's website is located on http://www.basspirituality.org.uk/about-us. The rather older Network for the Study of Implicit Religion should also be noted; see http://www.implicitreligion.org/organise.htm. Both websites accessed 7 August 2014.

16   The full text of the editorial is available on http://www.basspirituality.org.uk/ wp-content/uploads/2013/08/JSS-1_1-Editorial.pdf (accessed 7 August 2014).

17   This information is taken from the Kendal Project website – see www.lancs. ac.uk/fss/projects/ieppp/kendal/methods.htm (accessed 7 August 2014). Not all these methodologies have been followed through in the publications that have emerged from the project.

18   It is worth noting that the modern version of the Christian pilgrimage dates back to the 1920s (rather like Walsingham, see pp. 139–40). See http://www. glastonburypilgrimage.com/history.html (accessed 7 August 2014). From the mid-1980s this has become steadily more ecumenical. Less inclusive, however, is the continuing reluctance to accept women as full members of the Anglican priesthood.

19   See www.unitythroughdiversity.org (accessed 7 August 2014).

20   More information can be found on http://www.unitythroughdiversity.org/ faiths-beliefs--spiritual-paths-in-glastonbury.html (accessed 7 August 2014).

21   See also http://www.religionandsociety.org.uk/research_findings/featured_findings/ loss_creativity_and_social_class (accessed 7 August 2014).

22   See note 21 together with Olson and Vincett (forthcoming).

23   See Forrester (1981: 127 ff.). Ahern and Davie (1987) provides the context for this extract.

Part IV

Public Religion and Secular Reactions

9

Managing Diversity

The following chapters should be seen as a pair; in many ways the narrative is continuous. Chapter 9 is concerned with the other-faith communities now present in British society and their impact on public debate. The discussion covers the changing situation in itself, the renewed attention to religion that this brings and the range of reactions that this prompts, secular as well as religious. Chapter 10 will develop these themes by examining the implications of religious and secular diversity for different sectors of British society, taking the law, politics, welfare and health care as examples.

One or two preliminaries are important. The argument builds on the facts and figures established in Chapter 3, which sets out the parameters of faith in British society: both its Christian past and growing plurality, noting the very marked regional differences that emerge in this respect and taking care not to exaggerate the size of the other-faith presence overall. Equally important is the material in Chapter 4, which depicts the drift within the Christian constituency towards the spiritual on one hand and towards the secular on the other – the latter will be further developed in this chapter. Third, the present discussion draws on the conceptual distinctions already introduced, notably the confusions surrounding the notion of pluralism (see Chapters 7 and 8). Is this a descriptive or normative concept? 'Tolerance', it is clear, opens another Pandora's box. Like pluralism, it means different things to different people – along a continuum which runs from the tacit acceptance of a restricted list of religious activities to a positive affirmation of forms of religion very different from the norm. Tolerance, moreover, operates at different levels: individuals who are tolerant of religious difference may exist in societies that have difficulty with the idea, and vice versa. Nor is there any

Religion in Britain: A Persistent Paradox, Second Edition. Grace Davie.
© 2015 Grace Davie. Published 2015 by John Wiley & Sons, Ltd.

direct correlation between pluralism (however understood) and toleration, though it is at least likely that those who affirm that religious diversity is beneficial rather than harmful are more likely to be tolerant of forms of religion that are able to co-exist. They will be less happy with forms of religion that aspire to monopoly status. The converse is equally true.

The discussion will proceed as follows. It will start by recalling the Rushdie controversy and its consequences – an episode which has already been mentioned a number of times and which opened a new chapter in the understanding of religious pluralism in British society. The Muslim community in all its diversity is central to this story, as is the notion of multiculturalism. An indirect consequence, however, has been a growing awareness among Christians that they too might consider themselves a minority – one moreover which is increasingly out of step with the mainstream of society. But are these observations accurate? In order to respond adequately, it is important to pick apart a number of different threads keeping the following questions in mind: which religious minorities do or do not feel themselves disadvantaged in modern Britain, and for what reasons? This is a rapidly growing research field that continues to evolve. External as well as internal events make a difference, not least in 2014 the escalating violence in the Middle East. Integral to the whole debate are a number of key concepts. Three of these will be examined in detail: discrimination, multiculturalism and secularism. The first needs careful consideration in that it is understood in different ways by different people. The second is a much-discussed term, which attracts strong views both for and against. The third is equally contested, stimulating a debate considered in the second half of the chapter. The starting point in this discussion is the secular rather than the religious, paying attention to the wide variety of views contained within this rubric. These range from the mildly agnostic to the vehemently anti-religious. What has become known as 'new atheism' is clearly significant in this narrative, but needs to be placed in context – it is not the whole story. A short conclusion gathers the threads together.

The Satanic Verses and its Aftermath

The bare bones of what has become known as 'the Rushdie affair' are simple enough.[1] In 1988 Salman Rushdie published *The Satanic Verses*, a novel deemed blasphemous by Muslims, whose initial and understandable outrage eventually included public book burnings. In February 1989, the Ayatollah Khomeini (of Iran) proclaimed a *fatwa* declaring the author guilty of blasphemy and Rushdie was forced into hiding. In December 1990, Rushdie publically embraced Islam – a key moment in the chain of events but one that was not reciprocated by the religious authorities in Iran who re-affirmed the *fatwa*.

Lives were lost in violent encounters outside Britain, including the stabbing to death of the translator of the Japanese edition. In short, this was an episode which appeared to violate almost every assumption of a modern, liberal and supposedly tolerant society. The fact that Rushdie was himself of Indian and Islamic origin simply made the sequence of events all the more complex.

It is the intractability of the underlying issues which requires attention. What in fact was at stake were the relative merits of two 'freedoms': freedom of religion on the one hand and freedom of speech on the other. The Muslim community invoked the former (faith should be inviolate), whilst Salman Rushdie and his supporters were claiming the latter (the right to publish freely). Pushed to extremes, the two collide – a situation which has recurred all over Europe (see below). Specific to the British controversy, however, was the moment in 1990 already alluded to. With every appearance of sincerity, Rushdie declared himself a Muslim, apologizing to his co-religionists for the problems caused by the book and acknowledging that some passages were offensive to believers. In effect this was an admission of blasphemy. Financial contributions from the book's royalties would be made to those who had suffered injury as a result of the protests; in other words reparations would be made. Though short-lived, Rushdie's attempt to build bridges seemed genuine enough and brought some comfort to the Muslim community in Britain. The point to note, however, is that the gesture provoked an equally potent reaction from the opposing camp, a counterpoint to the central debate. The rage of some secular liberals could hardly be contained at this stage, revealing an alarming illogicality at the heart of their campaign. Muslims should be tolerant of offensive books, but liberals cannot tolerate the writer who becomes a Muslim. Tolerance, it is clear, was a social construct, to be applied in some cases but not in others.

Just as troubling was the genuine incomprehension of the British public, who had great difficulty grasping the hurt of the Muslim community after the initial publication. Quite simply, the religious sensibilities of most British people were of a different order. Assuming a live-and-let-live approach to religious issues it was hard to understand why the publication of a book caused such anger when no one was obliged to read it against their will. So why not leave it at that? Part of being British, it seemed, was to accept a low-key approach to religion, with the strong implication that anyone who comes to live in these islands – for whatever reason – should conform, in public at least, to a similar view. But does this essentially conditional statement provide an adequate basis for a truly tolerant and pluralist society? The unexpected vehemence of the ensuing controversy suggests that it does not.

For all these reasons, the Rushdie affair has become a turning point in British society. It is the moment when ethnicity as a category cedes the place to religion – a shift of particular importance for Muslims, who were instinctively drawn together at this point. It is also the moment when the British public begins to realize that a significant minority in this country, and not only Muslims, wish to take faith seriously and to manifest their views in public as well as in private – a stance that challenges the status quo. Reactions to these adjustments vary: welcomed by some, they disturb others who resent the renewed attention to religion. Unsurprisingly, a cascade of publication has followed. Paul Weller's *A Mirror for our Times: 'The Rushdie Affair' and the Future of Multiculturalism* (2009) is a helpful guide in this respect. Published on the 20th anniversary of the initial controversy, the book has been widely acclaimed as a balanced account of the episode itself, its aftermath, its effects on policy and the secondary literature it has generated.

Weller begins by reconstructing the sequence of events following publication. Drawing on a huge range of resources,[2] he establishes a narrative which is noticeably more nuanced than that depicted by the media. The steps by which a primarily literary event became the trigger for a global crisis are not self-evident; each one of them needs careful explanation. The time-line however is simply the starting point. The chapters that follow reflect on broader issues: the nature of Islam, its place in British and European society and the implications for policy-making. The idea of 'a mirror for our times' frames this analysis (2009: 1–2); it is taken from the reflections of Bhikku Parekh – a prominent political scientist and a former chair of the Commission for Racial Equality. As early as 1989, Parekh saw in the Rushdie crisis a mirror which not only reflects but magnifies the underlying trends in British society. For this reason alone, it merits maximum scrutiny. In terms of policy, the key concept is 'multiculturalism', meaning by this an attempt not only to create but to sustain a society which is at ease with its own diversity. Already controversial, the idea has become more so in subsequent decades.

Before addressing this theme directly, it is important to fill in the background, noting first that equivalents to the Rushdie controversy happened in relatively quick succession right across Europe. A by no means exhaustive list would include the *affaire du foulard* in France, which also began in 1989; the murders of Pim Fortuyn (2002) and Theo van Gogh (2004) in the Netherlands, together with the subsequent defection of Hirsi Ali to the United States; the furore over the cartoons of Mohammed published by a Danish newspaper (in 2005), a debate which subsequently spread to Sweden (2007); the challenge to the legality of minarets in a Swiss referendum (2009); and finally the banning of the *burqa* or *niqab* in public in some parts of Europe. The details of these cases go well beyond the limits of this chapter, except to note that each of them raises issues which pertain to the country in question. That is equally the case in Britain. The underlying concerns are, however, common: they reflect the willingness (or not) of European societies to accommodate a minority whose religious assumptions challenge the status quo, and the capacities of that minority to live outside the *ummah*.[3] This is a two-way learning process which makes demands on both parties.

The second point concerns the global context: specifically a series of events which have made the building of a multicultural society and the values that go with this harder almost by the day. Most obvious in this connection were the traumatic events of 9/11 (2001) in New York and the 7/7 (2005) bombings in London.[4] The wider repercussions of the attack on the Twin Towers have already been noted (p. 37); Britain's interventions into Afghanistan and Iraq are, rightly or wrongly, seen in this light. The consequences of 7/7 are more local. Ironically, the bombings themselves occurred the day after London had won its bid to host the 2012 Olympic Games, in which the city's multicultural reputation had formed a central plank. Londoners, moreover, had to come to terms with the fact that the perpetrators were home-grown Islamic extremists – a realization that has led in turn to the sustained scrutiny of the Muslim community, which increasingly has been seen as a security threat.

The third point is a sidestep. It relates to an event which echoes the issues raised by the Rushdie controversy but within a different faith community. In December 2004, Birmingham's Repertory Theatre put on a play entitled 'Behzti', meaning 'Dishonour', written by a Sikh playwright (a woman) and concerned with the abuse of power in the name of religion. Some within the Sikh community were disturbed by scenes in the play which depicted both sex and violence in a Sikh temple. Peaceful protests and requests for minor changes in the text turned into more violent expressions of disapproval, leading eventually to the play being taken off, primarily for safety reasons, and renewed public discussion about freedom of speech in a democratic society. The point at issue, moreover, is exactly the same as it was a decade or so earlier: to what extent can a minority (or sections within a minority) prevent the publication or depiction of material that is deemed to be offensive to their religion? Conversely, can the majority afford simply to ignore the feelings of small, but nonetheless significant groups, whose religious views are different from the mainstream? Both views if pushed to the extreme are not only 'intolerant' but non-viable.

An odd coincidence – or perhaps not – occurred at this point. Also in December 2004, the Queen made religious tolerance in the United Kingdom the central theme of her Christmas broadcast.[5] The transmission was accompanied by images of the Queen visiting both a Sikh temple and a Muslim centre. Immediately acclaimed by the faith communities in Britain, the broadcast endorsed not only the presence of different religions in this country but the positive values associated with diversity. This was clearly a normative statement, presenting diversity as something that enriches a society, not as something to be seen as a threat. But a word of warning follows: 'We need also to realise that peaceful and steady progress in our society of differing cultures and heritage can be threatened at any moment by the actions of extremists at home or by events abroad.' The Queen was right: the 7/7 bombings took place a little over six months later.

An additional controversy was sparked in 2005. In the spotlight this time were a group of conservative Christians who were reacting to cultural events they considered blasphemous. One such was 'Jerry Springer the Opera', a British musical noted for its profanity and for its irreverent treatment of Judaeo-Christian themes. This highly successful show ran for two years in London before touring in the United Kingdom.[6] The west end however was one thing, BBC television quite another: multiple complaints were elicited when the show was broadcast on BBC2 in January 2005. The protests were led by evangelical pressure groups. Christian Voice, for example, led demonstrations against the screening and announced their intention to bring charges of blasphemy.[7] The Christian Institute attempted a private prosecution against the BBC which failed.[8] Protests continued nonetheless both on the web and at venues for the 2006 tour. Such actions raise once again complex questions concerning the place of religion in public life, the notion of blasphemy, freedom of speech, censorship, tolerance, mutual respect and equality. None of these are easy to resolve – a concern illustrated by the sharp growth in the literature relating to this field.

Researching Discrimination

It is already clear that some religious groups feel more vulnerable than others. In order to establish a framework within which to work in this respect, it is helpful to refer once again to Paul Weller – a close observer of this field. Two examples of his work will be highlighted here, which partially overlap. The first (Weller 2011) is a desk-based initiative, commissioned by the Equality and Human Rights Commission (EHRC), which reviews the research on religious discrimination in Britain from 2000 to 2010. It draws on a wide variety of sources, including a concurrent EHRC survey of research on religion, discrimination and good relations (Woodhead 2011). Weller begins by clearing the conceptual ground, adopting for the purposes of the report a working definition of religious discrimination – seeing this as 'unfair treatment' manifested in a variety of ways. Legal definitions, moreover, should be distinguished from socially articulated experiences of discrimination; they are not the same thing. Weller also notes that more research evidence exists for the Muslim community than for most other groups (Hindus, Sikhs or Buddhists).

Bearing these difficulties in mind, Weller records that there has been a gradual increase in tribunal cases since December 2003, when the Employment Equality (Religion or Belief) Regulations came into force (see below), recognizing that this may well be due to a greater awareness of legal remedy rather than a rise in the incidence of discrimination as such. More concrete is the evidence for Islamophobic 'spikes' (following 9/11 and 7/7) and for a gradual increase in recorded incidents of anti-Semitism, with an apparent peak in 2009. Unsurprisingly Muslims report both a greater frequency of discrimination and incidents of a more serious nature if compared to other religious groups. Since 2005 this has been compounded by the impact on public perceptions of terrorist incidents, and the increase in securitization which follows. Weller also notes a changing pattern amongst Christians – both in terms of perception and in terms of a readiness to advance claims in this field. Christians, however, wonder if their anxieties are taken as seriously as those which are raised by ethnic minorities.

Full details of the second piece of work, its approach and methods, and the extensive material emerging from it can be found on the project website.[9] Entitled 'Religion and Belief, Discrimination and Equality in England and Wales: Theory, Policy and Practice (2000–2010)', the project formed part of the Religion and Society initiative. Its scope was ambitious and drew in turn on an earlier empirical enquiry (1999–2001), thus enabling a valuable longitudinal perspective.[10] The summary findings of the later project provide a succinct and very useful overview of this substantial body of material. As before the starting point lies in the significant changes in the law which have taken place since 2003 and are designed to protect the holders of religious and non-religious beliefs from unfair treatment.[11] Encouragingly, it appears that the introduction of law in this field has been associated with positive changes in policy and practice, particularly in the public sector. That said, unfair treatment on the basis of religion or belief in important areas of individual lives remains an issue, noting however that – as generally reported – this has more to do with the attitudes and behaviour of individuals than with the policies or practices of organizations.

High profile controversies and legal cases reflect continuing sensitivities regarding particular issues, notably employer imposition of dress codes (Muslim head coverings for women and Christian crosses). The researchers also record an increased awareness among Sikhs regarding 'the 5Ks' of their religion (see pp. 60–1 of this book). Third, attention is drawn to the participants involved in 'non-religious' focus groups who felt that the new legislation does not always work well for this constituency, despite extensions in the meaning of 'belief'.[12] More generally, knowledge of the law and new legal rights remains imprecise, and once again there is an inevitable slippage between the spectrum of unfair treatment as identified by the researchers and its legal interpretation. The subsequent discussion both nuances and expands on these points, underlining the importance of sharing good practice, inclusive approaches to consultation and a paramount need for religious literacy. Worth noting in particular are the new challenges in the field of identity and law, not least the difficult balance between religion or belief on the one hand and gender and sexual orientation on the other – questions pursued in Chapter 10.

Weller's work is central to this field; it is however but one example among many in what Linda Woodhead calls 'an explosion of academic research on the topics of religion, equality and discrimination – and to a lesser extent, good relations' (2011: 3). In her view the 'immediate drivers' include the foundation of the EHRC in 2007 and the addition of 'religion' as one of the grounds of discrimination; efforts by this organization to promote research in the area including the establishment of a Religion or Belief Network; the operation of new legislation and the build-up of case law in both domestic and European courts; and considerable investment by research bodies in research on religious diversity and the 'problems' it raises, driven very largely by political concerns – prompted in turn by the visibility of Muslims in Europe, by acts of terrorism, and by growing anxieties about 'national identity' and 'social cohesion' (2011: 4). I very much agree with Woodhead's reflections on these matters, including her awareness that it can be hard at times to digest what is happening in a dramatically expanding field. Bearing this in mind, a selection of policy issues will be developed in Chapter 10 and theoretical questions will be addressed in Chapter 11. In the meantime, the notion of multiculturalism requires more detailed consideration.

Is Multiculturalism Possible?

A summary article by a leading scholar in this field and published in the *Guardian* provides a helpful starting point to a necessarily complex debate (Modood 2011b).[13] It was prompted by an intervention from the Prime Minister indicating that multiculturalism has failed. Modood disagrees, arguing as follows. Multiculturalism in Britain flourished in the mid post-war decades, but towards the end of the twentieth century it became increasingly suspect. As ever the publication of *The Satanic Verses* marks a turning point. Specifically, former advocates began to draw back as the multiculturalism that they had in mind no longer fitted with reality, which increasingly paid attention to religion. Modood puts it thus: 'steelbands, saris and samosas' no longer sufficed and 'for some liberals that meant an end to their support for the concept, as angry Muslims muscled in on something that was intended only for the likes of gay people or black youth. Their protests were supported as "right on", but a passionate religious identity was too multicultural for many.'

The idea persists nonetheless, argues Modood – a sentiment echoed by Dinham (2012). Notably New Labour clearly endorsed ethno-religious communitarianism – a stance which included the sanctioning of faith schools, the introduction of religious discrimination legislation and the inclusion of Muslims in networks of governance. It was, moreover, the Labour government that passed the first (2006) Equality Act, which (at last) put the claims of religion and belief on the same level as race. With respect to the Coalition,

David Cameron may not like the term multiculturalism or what it stands for, but his policies – the idea of the Big Society for instance – move in the same direction, in that they hand over resources and decision-making to 'neighbourhoods, communities, charities and organised religion'. This, Modood maintains, is a good thing and evidence of multiculturalism. Nothing, however, should be taken for granted: effective dialogue between groups must be balanced by careful attention to individual rights on the one hand and to the imaginative remaking of national identity on the other. Building a multicultural society is an on-going and very demanding process.

This short but timely intervention by Modood reflects two and half decades of research and writing pertaining to ethnic and religious minorities both in Britain and beyond.[14] Two (overlapping) themes are central to this work: multiculturalism on the one hand and moderate or accommodative secularism on the other. The continuing significance of both can be seen in the most recent edition of *Multiculturalism* (Modood 2013), in which Modood inserts two additional chapters.[15] The first, 'The strange non-death of multiculturalism', contrasts multiculturalism with three other modes of integration: assimilation, individualist-integration and cosmopolitanism. Each of these has a particular understanding of equal citizenship and should be deployed accordingly, taking care to respect the demands of the context and the preferences of the minorities in question, which may differ. This is not a case of one size fits all. In the second chapter, entitled 'Multiculturalism and the "crisis of secularism"' (see also 2011c), Modood argues that moderate (as opposed to radical) secularism can be fully justified in liberal, egalitarian, democratic terms, and in relation to citizenship. That said moderate secularism needs to be pluralized in order to accommodate growing religious diversity, not least a significant Muslim community.

Not everyone agrees with Modood. An interesting exchange in this respect can be found in a slim volume entitled *British Secularism and Religion* (Birt, Hussain and Siddiqui 2011). In this, Modood (2011d) sets out his ideas on 'Civic recognition and respect for religion in Britain's moderate secularism', echoing many of the points made above. Ted Cantle (2011) writes a rejoinder, arguing strongly for a much sharper distinction between the increasingly plural society now evident in Britain and the rational secular basis required for government and policy-making.[16] Predictably, there is no room for an establishment church in this arrangement in that no single faith should have a constitutional or practical advantage over any other. A similar distinction emerges in terms of concepts. Cantle favours the notion of interculturalism rather than multiculturalism, seeing the former as more in tune with current realities. Specifically interculturalism takes into account the dynamic nature of identity and works with all forms of difference, and on a global rather than national canvas – a shift which requires new ways of thinking about politics and power structures (Cantle 2012).

The academic debate continues in which a good deal depends on the precise definition of terms.[17] The statements of politicians are noticeably more direct. On the shortcomings of multiculturalism, for example, Angela Merkel has been as outspoken as David Cameron.[18] The stakes, moreover, are high. A string of issues are invoked, and at times confused, in these high profile pronouncements. These include immigration, integration (or the lack of it), national identity, Muslim extremism, radicalization and terrorist attacks. It is equally clear that the timing and circumstances of these interventions makes a difference – speaking opportunities are chosen with care in a milieu in which little is left to chance.[19] To be fair, David Cameron's speech in February 2011 makes a clear distinction between Islam as such and Islamist extremism, but this is not always what is 'heard', particularly by the right wing press. Indeed for many of the actors who compete in this very public arena, short-term advantage is noticeably more important than accurate representation. This is hardly a dispassionate debate.

Secular, Secularization, Secularity and Secularism

The notion of secularism has already been introduced; it will be developed further in the second part of this chapter. Before embarking, however, it is helpful to clarify the terminology. 'Secular' is normally used as an adjective to describe a condition or situation, noting that its meaning is not only imprecise (hovering between neutrality and hostility), but slips easily between the descriptive and the normative – the notion of a secular state, for example, can be used in either sense. 'Secularization' is quite different: it is a process, which takes place differently in different societies and encompasses a multiplicity of factors not all of which move in the same direction. Societies that demonstrate a marked decline in religious activity over a given period of time may or may not be associated with secular institutions and vice versa. 'Secularity' is less frequently used in popular parlance but denotes a state of affairs which is described as secular; by and large it is a neutral term. 'Secularism' in contrast is an ideology and implies a commitment – to the process of secularization, for instance, or to the affirmation of the secular in this or that sphere of society.

That at least is the theory. In practice it may be more complicated. For example in the articles brought together by Birt, Hussain and Siddiqui noted above, the terms 'secularity' and 'secularism' are differently deployed even within one volume. The collection is made up of two 'conversations' both of which pertain to British secularism and its relationship to Islam. The first is theological, the second political. The theological contributions contrast 'secularity' with 'secularism', using the former to invoke an accommodative arrangement that does not exclude religion from public life, whereas secularism has a tendency to be excluding and exclusive. In the political conversation that follows, Modood introduces two understandings of secularism, one radical or ideological and one moderate or accommodative. The first insists on an absolute separation between state and religion, the second is more flexible. Broadly speaking, France exemplifies the former and Britain the latter, a difference that can be explained historically.[20] The British case is then developed in detail paying particular attention to the Muslim minority and its struggle for ethno-religious equality.

A similar distinction can be found in a collection of essays by the former Archbishop of Canterbury (Williams 2012). Here the distinction is between 'procedural' and 'programmatic' secularism, seeing the former as a public policy 'which declines to give advantage or preference to any one religious body over others' (Williams 2012: 2). The example cited is India. As before, France is used to illustrate the more radical version – that is 'programmatic' secularism, which implies absolute loyalty to the state unimpeded by private convictions which have no place in the public square. Williams argues that the latter can be damaging to Christian living, indeed to faith more generally. The consequences are serious in the sense that a range of resources that enrich collective life are effectively side-lined, a process which 'thins-out' the fabric of public debate. In a functioning democracy, religion – theologically informed and properly argued – must be fully involved. For religious individuals or communities to stand on the edge demanding not to be offended is an insufficient response. Effective engagement means, however, learning the rules of the game, not least 'a strong common culture of ordinary courtesy and respect' (Williams 2012: 4). Particular attention must be paid to the sensitivities of minorities.

The initial chapter in this important collection is entitled 'Has secularism failed?' The question can be addressed in different ways. Among them is the indictment already noted: secularism fails in the sense that it excludes an important dimension of human living from the argument, thus impoverishing the debate as a whole. Even more significantly, Williams underscores the necessary collusion between 'victorious secularism' and violent forms of religiousness, in that the former provokes a counter claim: secularist certainties stand off against religiously controlled ones revealing layers of misunderstanding. Specifically, western liberals find it difficult to understand why Muslims cannot see their faith as one legitimate private opinion among others, a stance which not only fails to understand the essential 'grammar' of Islam but also to address the limits of the private and public as they pertain to these issues. It is hardly surprising that these misunderstandings provoke a reaction, as much political as religious. What ensues is accurately described as a (dangerous) dialogue of the deaf.

Being Secular in Modern Britain

In order to put these remarks in context, it is important to establish the size and nature of the secular constituency in this country. At one level the data in this respect are reasonably clear and reflect the profiles already established in Chapters 3 and 4. In terms of self-affiliation as measured by the Census, there has been a marked increase in the 'no religion' category. Between 2001 and 2011, this rose from 15 to 25 per cent, mostly at the expense of the 'Christian' section of the population (see Figure 3.1). There has been a similar drift in religious affiliation by year of birth (Figure 3.5), which indicates that the principal loser in this particular game is the Church of England. And if we take into account that the decline in churchgoing for the Church of England, though evident, is less steep (Figure 3.6), it seems reasonable to assume that the switch is largely from nominal Anglican to no religion. It is, moreover, age-related. There is a huge difference between those who are now approaching retirement, who remain relatively loyal to Christianity, and younger cohorts, who do not. It is also worth noting that the no religion constituency is disproportionately male. Belief, however, is more stable: between half and two thirds of the population continue to believe in a personal God or some sort of spirit or life force (Table 4.2), including a number who decline allegiance to a specified religion (see the data assembled in Chapter 8). The inference, however, is clear: growing numbers of British people, notably younger generations, are choosing to live their lives beyond the influence of organized religion.

That said, the range of views is a broad one. It is best seen in terms of a continuum which moves from a strong commitment to the religious at one end to an equally strong commitment to the secular, or to no religion at the other. Between the two extremes are various shades of grey, bearing in mind the added complication of the 'spiritual'. Is this or is this not religious? Indeed the more that you look at the possibilities, the more complicated things become. For a start, those who cluster towards the highly committed end of the spectrum may be strong adherents of very different faith communities. They may moreover be opposed to each other, although not necessarily so. And those in the middle are likely to be there for different reasons: nominal Christians are not a homogeneous category (Day 2011; Woodhead 2013a). Some moreover may declare themselves to be Christian as opposed to secular, while others think of themselves as Christian as opposed to Muslim. The implications vary accordingly. At the 'no religion' end of the spectrum, there are once again marked differences in motivation. These include unspecified indifference, a dislike of particular forms of religiousness and – at the extreme – an articulate disdain for religion as such. Much more positive is the reasoned commitment to secular or humanist values, recognizing that this in turn takes different forms (see below).

Unsurprisingly it is not at all easy to see where the religious shades into the secular (Woodhead 2014b). The key points have already been made: affiliation does not always match belief, commitments change over time and circumstances alter cases. The individuals (and indeed groups) 'introduced' in Chapter 4 illustrate the last of these. Young – or even less young – people who live their 'normal' or everyday lives beyond the limits of religion feel differently in times of crisis. Exactly the same finding emerged from the careful research conducted amongst the disadvantaged in Glasgow and Manchester, though their modes of access were not always conventional (pp. 170–2). A second set of variables are cultural rather than personal. The secular, just like the religious, is framed by history. British unbelievers, it follows, are different from their French or American counterparts. Indeed the whole spectrum from one end to the other is culturally patterned, which accounts for the fact that atheists are often very clear about the God in whom they do not believe. It also accounts for the preferred modes of expression in the middle ground. In Britain 'believers' outnumber 'belongers' though for how much longer is harder to say; the reverse is true in the Nordic countries.

Lois Lee's work has already been introduced (pp. 77–8), including her core insight: a shift from the 'hollowly secular' to the 'substantively nonreligious'. The change, moreover, has taken place at two levels – in the 'secular' constituency itself and in the social-scientific study of this. No longer are the 'nones' seen simply as a residual category (those who do not tick the 'religion' box); rather they are recognized as a varied group of people who are looking for new ways to express their 'non-religious' identities. Relatively few of them do this through formal organizations, though it is important to acknowledge the work of both the British Humanist Association (BHA) and the National Secular Society (NSS). The former, it is worth noting, campaigned actively as the 2011 Census approached. Individuals were encouraged not to tick the 'Christian' box out of habit but to check the 'no religion' category instead, the rationale being that over-representation of religion in the Census leads to distorted policy-making.[21]

Both organizations date from the mid to late nineteenth century: the NSS from 1866, and the BHA from 1896. In 1868 Charles Bradlaugh – a key figure in the NSS – also opened a 'Hall of Science' in Old Street (east London), which became a meeting place for secularists all over London, gathering significant numbers of people for a weekly lecture.[22] Organizationally, if not in other ways, the hall and its facilities were the equivalent of a nonconformist chapel. Interestingly, the idea of a meeting place for non-believers has enjoyed a 'revival' in recent years. A good example can be found in the 'Sunday Assembly', which describes itself as a godless congregation that celebrates life – the positive emphasis is important in a gathering that welcomes everyone, non-believer and believer alike. The tone is noticeably upbeat: affiliates are encouraged to live better, help often and wonder more.[23] The number of British assemblies (though tiny compared to churches) continues to increase.

This is one way to convey non-belief. Others are revealed in a growing number of research projects focusing on the daily lives of people who place themselves outside formal religion. Lois Lee's own work offers an excellent example. A primary aim of her approach is to uncover the banal; that is to 'make visible' the ways in which non-religion presents itself – to discover for example how it structures place, space and spatial practice, and how it makes use of bodily as well as intellectual practices. Indeed the stress lies firmly on the non-intellectual and non-verbal ways in which non-religion can emerge. Lee's work is conceptually as well as methodologically innovative. Specifically the distinction between matters of secularity and matters of non-religion permits a new understanding of religion itself. This is no longer seen as a unique or exclusive phenomenon, but becomes part of a larger whole, in which the religious, the spiritual and the non-religious not only co-exist, but are treated on equal terms.

Rebecca Catto and Janet Eccles (2011, 2013) offer further insight into this constituency. In the Young Atheists Research Project, funded by the Jacobs Foundation, they investigated the views of young people aged between 16 and 25 who hold atheist, humanist and secularist views or who engage with atheist, humanist or secularist organizations. The focus is firmly on the younger generation who are more inclined to be non-religious than their elders, but about whom we know relatively little. The following points emerge from their enquiry, noting that the sample was small. Young non-religionists appear to be more flexible and more open to different perspectives than their older equivalents; they prefer, moreover, to engage with online communities than to belong to official organizations. They are mainly British-born, white, middle class and well educated and are clearly influenced by this background (family as well as education). Some, it seems, have reacted against a Christian upbringing; others have been influenced by the new atheists. In short, their routes to non-belief vary. The socially acceptable nature of non-religion amongst younger generations in Britain is important; to the extent that non-religion can be an easier option for this age group than being Christian.

These examples are but two of many; the study of non-religion and the secular is a burgeoning field, rather similar to the burst of interest in the spiritual. Their organizations, moreover, are comparable. The focus this time is the Nonreligion and Secularity Research Network (NSRN) established in 2008, which exists to gather existing material in the field and to promote further discussion in conferences, lectures and workshops.[24] The agenda is a wide one and welcomes a broad range of perspectives: 'the atheistic, agnostic, religiously indifferent or areligious, as well as most forms of secularism, humanism and, indeed, aspects of religion itself'. International links have been established which have led in turn to an online journal in 2012.[25] This publication welcomes articles which focus on the secular at one of three levels: the micro or individual level, the meso or institutional level, or the macro or national and international levels. The inter-connectedness of the field is the crucial point.

New Atheism

No chapter on the secular or secularism would be complete without a section on the new atheists, notably the four horsemen of the apocalypse: Richard Dawkins, Christopher Hitchens, Daniel Dennett and Sam Harris. Here are some of the most widely read, provocative and contentious writers of the twenty-first century both in Britain and beyond. Their work and the varied reactions to this have generated a vigorous – not to say acrimonious – debate, both in print and online, which shows no signs of abating. The new atheists and their ideas are loved and loathed in equal measure. The following is a highly selective account. It looks very briefly at the arguments of the new atheists themselves, before turning to the most intriguing element of the debate: their extraordinarily rapid reception in the Anglophone world and the social movement this has engendered. It concludes with a sharply critical voice.

At the centre of new atheism lies the conviction that religion should not simply be tolerated but should be countered, criticized and exposed by rational argument. Religion in other words is toxic; this is not a question of live and let live but of active campaigning to expose both the falsity of religious argument and the damage that ensues. The logic proceeds as follows. Starting from the assumption that there is no supernatural or divine reality of any kind, religious belief is deemed irrational. At the same time the assertion of a universal, objective and above all secular moral standard renders religion at best irrelevant and at worst harmful. Underpinning this approach is an appeal to the natural sciences, both to justify the critique of religion and to promote the theory of evolution. Evidence-based knowledge is the only knowledge that counts, and empirical science is the basis of knowledge. Science, moreover, reveals no knowledge of God – hence the assumption of God's non-existence. Religious belief, however, is approached differently; it is seen as the product of biological evolution. There is in other words a purely natural explanation for this persistent and 'irrational' phenomenon.

The above account is skeletal, but as Stephen Bullivant points out, from 'a sociological point of view, the most interesting aspect of the new atheism is not its ideas … but the *reception* of those ideas' (Bullivant 2010: 110). There is persuasive support for this statement in the extraordinary popularity of new atheist publications. To take the most obvious example, Richard Dawkins'

The God Delusion (2006) not only marked a watershed in the advent of new atheist ideas, but became a publishing sensation in its own right; it remained on the *New York Times* bestseller list for 51 consecutive weeks. It has since been translated into more than 30 languages. It is very unlikely that all of Dawkins' readers are necessarily converts to his thinking, but sales figures such as these give pause for thought: is this an idea whose time has come? Many people would reply positively. Dawkins moreover is not an isolated example; such figures could be multiplied many times over.

In a later piece, Bullivant uses these extraordinary sales figures to question a pervasive view: that is to refute the idea of indifference to either religion or atheism (Bullivant 2012). In so doing, he echoes an important theme in this book. The argument works in stages, beginning with the obvious paradox. The statistics of religious activity continue to decline – there can be no doubt about that – but the interest in religion does not. Bullivant substantiates this claim by focusing on three bodies of data: the 'new visibility of religion' in general, including media attention to Islam; a selection of national events, drawing on the same type of material as I have done in relation to vicarious religion; and, crucially, recent fieldwork by Lois Lee. The latter is particularly interesting in that it reveals the meticulous attention paid by Lee's respondents to both religion and non-religion, even if they declare at the outset of an interview that they are uninterested. Probe a little and they clearly care deeply, one way or the other. The second aspect of Bullivant's argument is even more significant in that it demonstrates the real focus of new atheist thinking. These writers are not reacting to the highly religious nature of their fellow citizens since that no longer exists; they are reacting instead to 'specific, public, disproportionately visible, and often "problematic", manifestations of modern religion' (Bullivant 2012: 102). This in itself distorts the argument.

New atheism can be viewed from several perspectives. By and large, however, more attention has been paid to the ideas themselves than to the goals, organization and structure of the ensuing movement. Steven Kettell (2013a) aims to fill this lacuna, noting in particular the political dimensions of new atheism. Central in this respect is an evident concern about the influence of religion in public life – not least its continuing role in the state (specifically an established church and the presence of bishops in the House of Lords); in welfare (the growing significance of faith-based organizations in the delivery of care); in health care (notably issues relating to the beginning and end of life); in education (faith schools and compulsory worship); and in civil rights (for example, religious exemptions from equalities legislation, and discrimination on issues such as housing, employment and the marriage of same-sex couples). The list, it is clear, is a long one and it will be revisited (selectively) in Chapter 10. In the meantime, it is interesting to note the significance of the internet both as a forum for debate and as a principal means of communication in a markedly decentralized organizational structure.

Criticisms of new atheism abound. Only one will be referenced here, chosen on the grounds that the argument is explicitly sociological. David Martin (2014) is affronted by new atheism for the following reason: it is a 'critique of religion that privileges the negative narrative over the positive, and does so from a "scientific" viewpoint which contravenes every norm of social scientific investigation' (2014: 38). Specifically the difference between the scientific intentionality appropriate to socio-historical issues and the scientific intentionality appropriate to natural phenomena is systematically ignored. Arguments about causation relating to social science are necessarily specific given the nature of human living. What happens in one situation may be entirely different in another given the particular constellation of factors (historical, economic, political, social, cultural and so on) in that place. In short '[t]he human world can only be understood *scientifically* if you understand means and ends, meanings, motives and intentions as these are variably realised in widely different contexts' (2014: 38).

This is particular apparent in the new atheist assumptions about religion and violence. Connections are asserted regardless of circumstance and no account is taken of the nature of the conflict in question, its justification or otherwise, the relationship of religious constituencies to this, the nature of their involvement, and the manner in which this changes over time. It is the patient sifting of the detail that matters, not the ever-louder repetition of unproven assertions. The situation is made worse, however, by retaliation in kind – a point already made by Archbishop Williams (p. 187): extreme forms of secularism feed off extreme forms of religion and vice versa. Martin – his frustration clearly visible – puts it thus: '[w]e have the strange spectacle of struggles between standard science and "Creation science" equally based on false premises about the nature of Christianity: the blind "New Atheists" wrestle with the blind "Creationists" and they both stand and fall together as they stumble into the ditch' (2014: 44).

Gathering the Threads

Is it possible to bring the many different threads in this chapter together? It began with the Rushdie controversy, an unusually visible marker of a shift that was already underway. By the 1990s it was no longer possible to take for granted the status quo, meaning by this a degree of consensus regarding the 'handling' of religion in British society. New questions had to be asked and new formulae found in order to deal not only with growing secularization but also with increasing religious diversity. No new consensus has emerged. Indeed the discussion at times has been heated: discrimination persists, multiculturalism is declared dead and secularism can be as intolerant as certain forms of religion. There are however more hopeful signs: in new legislation regarding equalities, in genuinely constructive thinking about diversity and in more accommodative forms of secularism. The following chapter will look at the implications of these shifts for different sectors of British society.

To end this chapter on a positive note, it is worth referencing a recent and very refreshing study of young people. *Youth on Religion* (Madge, Hemming and Stenson 2014) outlines the findings of a major research project which investigated the ways in which young people in three multi-faith locations in England negotiate their religious identities in the course of their daily lives – in the family, in school, in the community and as individuals. These articulate and thoughtful respondents are realists. They recognize that religion remains an important factor in the global order taken as a whole, and in the country and communities of which they are part. At the same time they are clearly aware of their differences, both cultural and religious. They are trying nonetheless to build an effective and harmonious society in the places where they live, and by and large they do this very well. Good for them.

Notes

1　Nye's and Weller's chapter on controversy (2012) offers useful background reading both for this and other episodes covered in this chapter. More specifically, Weller (2009: 2) notes that many Muslims prefer not to use the term 'Rushdie affair' given that it points to the author rather than the book. For this constituency 'the *Satanic Verses* controversy' is a more accurate description.

2　See, for example, the extensive reference list in the opening pages of Weller (2009) and its meticulously ordered bibliography.

3　In the sense of living outside a society in which a Muslim way of life is taken for granted.

4　The bombings in Madrid (in 2004) and in Bali (2002 and 2005) should also be taken into account.

5　The full text can be found at https://www.royal.gov.uk/ImagesandBroadcasts/ TheQueensChristmasBroadcasts/ChristmasBroadcasts/ChristmasBroadcast2004. aspx (accessed 7 August 2014).

6　A useful chronological account can be found on Wikipedia. See http://en.wikipedia. org/wiki/Jerry_Springer:_The_Opera (accessed 7 August 2014).

7　See http://www.christianvoice.org.uk/?s=jerry+springer+the+opera (accessed 7 August 2014).

8　See the continuing series of posts on The Christian Institute website: http://www. christian.org.uk/search.htm?cx=003034083221446362013%3Asqtyasn8ir4& cof=FORID%3A11&q=jerry+springer+the+opera&sa.x=13&sa.y=7 (accessed 7 August 2014).

9　See http://www.derby.ac.uk/religion-and-society. The Project Summary Findings and the Research Informed Policy Brief are particularly helpful (accessed 7

August 2014). See also the substantial monograph arising from the project: Weller *et al.* (2013).

10   Details of the earlier project can be found in Weller, Feldman and Purdam (2001).

11   See for example the 2003 Employment Equality (Religion or Belief) Regulations, the Incitement to Racial and Religious Hatred Act, 2006, and the 2006 and 2010 Equality Acts. More information about this legislation is given in Chapter 10, pp. 198–9.

12   The argument turns on which philosophies or world views are considered the equivalents of religion, and are therefore accorded similar privileges.

13   This article, entitled 'Multiculturalism: not a minority problem' is available at http://www.theguardian.com/commentisfree/2011/feb/07/multiculturalism-not-minority-problem (accessed 7 August 2014).

14   Full details of Professor Modood's research and publications are available on his personal website, www.tariqmodood.com (accessed 7 August 2014).

15   The first edition appeared in 2007.

16   Professor Ted Cantle is an acknowledged expert on intercultural relations. He is best known as the author of what became known as the Cantle Report on community cohesion, which was produced for the Home Office following the 2001 race riots in Bradford, Burnley and Oldham.

17   For example, is interculturalism an extension of multiculturalism or something new altogether? See the interesting exchange in the *Journal of Intercultural Studies*, 33(2), beginning with Meer and Modood (2012).

18   See for example Angela Merkel's forthright comments at http://www.theguard ian.com/world/2010/oct/17/angela-merkel-german-multiculturalism-failed, as well as David Cameron's own remarks on http://www.bbc.co.uk/news/uk-poli tics-12371994. The full text of David Cameron's speech can be found at http://webarchive.nationalarchives.gov.uk/20130109092234/http://number10.gov.uk/news/pms-speech-at-munich-security-conference/. All websites were accessed on 7 August 2014.

19   It is important to note where the speech was made and to whom. Concurrent events and the possibly policy implications should also be taken into account. In February 2011 the Labour MP for Luton South, Gavin Shuker, asked if it was wise for Mr Cameron to speak about multiculturalism on the same day that the English Defence League staged a major protest in his (Gavin Shuker's) constituency. The policies alluded to in the text (the Prevent Strategy) were equally controversial.

20   There is truth in this contrast but it should not be taken too literally. Specifically, there are those who argue that the French case is less clear-cut than is sometimes imagined. This is unsurprising in that there is more than one way of interpreting the notion of *laïcité*, the French version of secularism.

21   See http://census-campaign.org.uk (accessed 7 August 2014). The slogan 'If you're not religious for God's sake say so!' was considered mildly controversial.

22   At its peak the hall held well over 1000 people. See Royle (1980: 46).

23   The Sunday Assembly was started in London by two British comedians, Sanderson Jones and Pippa Evans, in January 2013; it has now become an

international network of atheist churches. See http://sundayassembly.com/ about/ (accessed 7 August 2014). See also De Botton (2013).

24 For more information, see http://nsrn.net/about, which includes a regularly updated bibliography (accessed 7 August 2013).

25 For more information see http://nsrn.net/journal and http://www.secularism-andnonreligion.org (both websites accessed 7 August 2014).

10

Religion in Public Life

The previous chapter examined a variety of strategies for the management of religious diversity in British society; these ranged from a genuine respect for markedly different viewpoints to the outright condemnation of religion as such. This chapter takes a different approach, concentrating on sectors rather than strategies. The coverage is necessarily selective but is arranged under the following headings: religion and the law, religion and politics, religion and welfare, and religion and health care. The section on the law comes first in that it develops most directly ideas and themes that have already been introduced.

Religion and the Law

The renewed attention to religion by a wide variety of lawyers, both practising and academic, is striking; there have been fundamental changes in this field (Theos 2012c, 2014c). Three examples illustrate the point. First, constitutional lawyers have been heavily engaged in those parts of the world where a change in regime has permitted the free, or freer, exercise of religion. The post-1989 democracies are a case in point, but the discussions have wider resonance. Central to the debate are questions of inclusion and exclusion: which forms of religion 'count' and which do not and who has the authority to decide? Second, family lawyers are tracking the evolution of this key component of society as profound shifts are taking place. A number of these are due to advances in medical technology which have introduced not only new structures of family life but entirely new sets of relationships. Careful attention to beginning- and end-of-life issues is part and parcel of

Religion in Britain: A Persistent Paradox, Second Edition. Grace Davie.
© 2015 Grace Davie. Published 2015 by John Wiley & Sons, Ltd.

the same story. It is hardly surprising that sharp exchanges ensue given the traditional teachings of the churches – and of the Catholic Church in particular – regarding the nature of the family and the sanctity of human life. These boundaries are carefully guarded. Third, human rights lawyers have seen their work develop exponentially, both in general and in the field of religion. Key in this respect is a series of competing rights – between for example the freedoms associated with belief and the freedoms of artistic or literary expression, or between the rights of those who resist same-sex relationships for religious reasons and gay and lesbian people. An important subtext in this respect concerns the degree to which religion is considered 'special', a question that raises crucial issues regarding the status of religion (ethics, epistemology and practices) in western legal and political theory.[1]

The Human Rights dimension will be taken as the principal example in this chapter, paying attention to the development of the Equality and Human Rights Commission (EHRC) in the United Kingdom,[2] to the European Convention on Human Rights (ECHR), and to the role of the European Court of Human Rights (ECtHR) in enforcing this agenda. The tricky relationship between the United Kingdom and Europe is central to this discussion. Equally relevant is the growing jurisprudence emerging from the ECtHR, which has far-reaching implications for the member states as a whole. Indeed a whole set of issues come together at this point: the law itself, the work on discrimination outlined in Chapter 9, ambivalence towards Europe, the increasing significance of religion in public life, and the marked shifts in academic attention that have emerged as a result.

Substantive changes in the law pertaining to human rights, including its application to religion, have taken place in Britain in the first decade of this century. In 2003, the Employment Equality (Religion or Belief) Regulations addressed religious discrimination and harassment on grounds of religion or belief for the first time, but only in terms of employment and vocational training. The 2006 Equality Act extended this to cover the provision of goods and services, and four years later the 2010 Equality Act not only consolidated existing legislation, but established the Public Sector Equality Duty (PSED), which came into force in April 2011.[3] Alongside these changes, the Human Rights Act of 1998 introduced the right of freedom of thought, conscience and religion (Article 9 of the European Convention of Human Rights) into the United Kingdom in 2000. Article 9 has two clauses. Article 9(1) ensures an absolute right to hold a religion or belief and a qualified right to manifest this in worship, teaching, practice and observance; Article 9(2) states that the freedom to manifest a religion or belief is subject to 'necessary' limitations. The distinction is important.

In parenthesis it is worth noting that additional shifts in the law took place in the same time period. In 2008 Parliament voted to abolish the common law offences of blasphemy and blasphemous libel in an amendment to the Criminal Justice and Immigration Bill. The Blasphemy Laws constituted an important element in the Rushdie controversy, revealing a manifest injustice. The legislation only protected Christians (and historically only the Church of England), not religion as such. Effectively this left two possibilities: the legislation had either to be abolished or extended. Given that the body of law in question was considered by many (including those in the churches) to be prejudiced, outdated and a threat to free speech, the former was the only option. New legislation concerning religious hatred and religiously aggravated offences has, however, been put in place. The Racial and Religious Hatred Act was passed in 2006, at the third attempt – a struggle that reflects the controversial nature of the underlying issues. As Nick Spencer puts it: 'the debate is caught painfully between those who will countenance not only no offence but no criticism of their religious beliefs, and those who, in response, take effort and pleasure at provoking them. This is not a recipe for social harmony' (Theos 2014c: 54).

The Equality and Human Rights Commission, established in 2007, is responsible by law for seven equality strands (age, disability, gender, race, religion or belief, sexual orientation and transgender); it became a National Human Rights Institution in 2009. De facto it is the successor organization to the following bodies: the Commission for Racial Equality, the Disability Rights Commission and the Equal Opportunities Commission. Since its inception the EHRC has operated in a variety of ways in relation to religion and belief. These include legal interventions – both direct and indirect. Regarding the former, Perfect (2013) offers two examples, both of which relate to the unlawful discrimination against same-sex couples by Christians offering services in the public domain. The most important of these involved Martyn Hall and Steve Preddy, civil partners who were denied the use of a double room they had previously booked online by the owners of a small hotel in Cornwall.[4] Among the latter, which are much more common, are expert submissions to the courts. One of these was a formal submission in the key case of *Eweida et al. v United Kingdom*, a case decided at the ECtHR in Strasbourg in January 2013. It will be discussed in more detail below.

Additional aspects of the EHRC's activity include the gathering and sifting of evidence, including a number of the reports referenced in Chapter 9,[5] and the commissioning of new work. Particularly significant in this respect is an enquiry into the law in relation to equality, human rights and religion or belief, and how this is understood and applied in the workplace and in public services (Donald, with Bennett and Leach 2012). Running alongside these research-based activities is the policy and guidance dimension. A good example can be found in the commissioning of the Religious Literacy Leadership Programme at Goldsmiths, University of London (see Chapter 6) to work in partnership with the Coexist Foundation. Four dialogue events and a final conference were arranged in 2013 to examine the following themes: religion and belief in the public sphere; religion and the media; religious diversity in the workplace and in service delivery; and balancing competing interests. Those invited included participants from religion or belief organizations, employer organizations and trade unions, advice and equality bodies and government officials.[6] The findings emerging from these and other consultations – though not always clear-cut – enable the EHRC to decide its priorities and to identify the guidance documents that are most effective. Good examples of the latter can be found in the guidance published following the *Eweida et al. v United Kingdom* judgment and in the material produced in connection with the 2013 legislation on marriage of same-sex couples.[7]

The European Court of Human Rights was established in 1959 on the basis of Article 19 of the European Convention on Human Rights.[8] It became a full-time institution in 1998 and its jurisdiction is recognized by all 47 member states of the Council of Europe. It exists to apply the ECHR. Specifically:

> Its task is to ensure that States respect the rights and guarantees set out in the Convention. It does this by examining complaints (known as 'applications') lodged by individuals or, sometimes, by States. Where it concludes that a member State has breached one or more of these rights and guarantees, the Court delivers a judgment finding a violation. Judgments are binding: the countries concerned are under an obligation to comply with them.[9]

Most of the work of this important institution has little to do with religion so need not concern us here. That said the following points are worth noting. It is clear, first of all, that the tensions between the different 'freedoms' noted in the discussion above can be found within the ECHR itself. Freedom of thought, conscience and religion (Article 9), for example, can at times sit awkwardly alongside both Freedom of expression (Article 10) and the Prohibition of discrimination (Article 14).

Some, if not all, of these issues are raised in a fascinating series of cases brought against the United Kingdom in 2010. The four cases have already been mentioned – they are known as *Eweida et al. v United Kingdom*. The final judgment was delivered in 2013. In terms of the argument presented here, it is important to note that all of the applicants were Christians, and all of them were concerned with violations of Article 9, in some cases in conjunction with Article 14. Each case was distinct but together they raise profound questions about the rights, and the limits to these rights, of employees to oblige their employers to alter conditions of employment, in order to accommodate their religious convictions or practices. Two cases (Eweida and Chaplin) relate to the right or otherwise to wear a cross or crucifix in the work place, and two (Ladele and McFarlane) reflect the changing situation with regard to same-sex relations in British society. Could Ladele (a registrar) refuse in the course of her duties to conduct same-sex civil partnership ceremonies? And should McFarlane's employer (a national counselling service) accommodate his conscientious objection to giving sex therapy advice to gay couples? In both the latter, the rights of Christians are set against the rights of same-sex individuals. Eweida's case was upheld by the court; the other three were not. The judgments can be read in full including the partly dissenting opinions;[10] they were carefully followed in the British press. The cases, moreover, have been subject to different interpretations by different legal commentators (see Catto and Perfect forthcoming). The case of Ladele is particularly controversial in that it raises very directly the clash between religious freedom and anti-discrimination norms.[11]

An increasingly important dimension of cases such as these concerns the gradual interaction between the jurisprudence that is emerging from the ECtHR in terms of religion and national bodies of law. An innovative research project has been established with precisely this in mind.[12] It will examine the domestic impact of the ECtHR case law on religion. Specifically 'it explores the mobilization of local and national level actors in the wake of a number of high-profile ECtHR religious freedom cases in order to determine the nature and extent of European juridical influence on religious pluralism' (Fokas 2013). The cases selected for detailed study in this project do not include the United Kingdom, but the underlying question is crucial in so far as the judgments at Strasbourg will be formative in the shaping of domestic law, and that in turn will have a profound influence on the management of diversity. This influence is both direct and indirect. As Fokas notes, not only do the Court's judgments affect policy-making as such, they also determine the discursive frameworks within which citizens are able to act. For example, a 'traditional' – essentially pragmatic – solution to the situations in which Ladele and McFarlane found themselves might have taken the form of a re-arranged schedule, in order to accommodate their scruples. In Ladele's case at least, this could easily have been done without prejudice to the service provided. It was not, however, considered a satisfactory solution, a decision upheld in Strasbourg. It is quite clear that there is less room for manoeuvre now than there was previously.

Unsurprisingly, there is a growing body of research in this field, which has produced in turn a formidable literature. Important foci for this work can be found in newly created centres for the study of law and religion, both in Britain and elsewhere. The first in the United Kingdom was established in Cardiff in 1998. Its activities relate to the theory and practice of substantive law, 'the focus being principally upon religious law and national and international law affecting religion, with regard to their historical, theological, social, ecumenical and comparative contexts'.[13] The range of activities is extensive and includes the hosting of a growing Law and Religion Scholars Network (LARSN).[14] Rather more recently (in 2006) a similar Centre emerged in Bristol, bringing together the expertise of various scholars. Here there is a strong emphasis on human rights and the place of religion in the European Union.[15] An additional forum for debate came into being in *The Oxford Journal on Law and Religion*, launched in 2012 in response to the recent 'proliferation of research and writing on the interaction of law and religion cutting across many disciplines'.[16] Textbooks are beginning to emerge, for example Edge (2006) and Sandberg (2011, 2014).

Religion and Politics

The relationship between religion and politics is distinct from that between church and state. The latter was discussed at some length in Chapter 5, and constitutes, if you will, the 'stage' on which political events take place. The stage moreover is relatively durable, which is not to say that it cannot change. The debate about establishment should be seen in this light. That said, the line between structures or institutions and the policy-making that goes on within them is a fine one – a statement that has relevance for both religion and politics. Take, for example, the striking similarity between traditional forms of religion and the major political parties. Both are under pressure and for much the same reasons. The following paragraphs from Matthew Parris's lament for the Conservative Party illustrate the point perfectly. They are supported by the data available on membership of the political parties in general (i.e. not just the Conservatives):[17]

> How many metaphors, how many sagging graphs and tumbling bar-charts will it take until the Tories stop whistling and looking away, and get to grips with the reality of the approaching death of the 20th-century model of a national party?
>
> A once-great national club, various in the ages, types and opinions of its members, mildly political but united by little more than a broadly conservative outlook, a fitful interest in current affairs and the pleasures of fellowship, was already in its twilight when, in 1978, as their new parliamentary candidate, I encountered the West Derbyshire Conservative Association: all 40 branches and 2000 members – can you believe?
>
> We had fun together but even then I could see the writing on the wall. Today the association – splendid people, the same people, just thirty years older – remains stronger than many.
>
> The national party is evaporating away, and what's left is a miscellany of types: the very old, the very loyal, the absolute bricks, the rather lonely, the slightly embarrassed guest and … yes, it has to be said, a goodly clutch of ideological obsessives. (Parris 2013)

No one reading these words can avoid a comparison with the church, and most obviously the Church of England, which is in markedly better shape that the Conservative Party but is suffering from the same complaint: manifestly so, right down to the detail (age, gender, trends and types). It is equally clear that the metamorphoses that are taking place in both spheres have as much to do with the changing nature of society as they do with the changing nature of religion or politics. Regarding the latter, these shifts are partly ideological in that the capital-labour axis which underpinned the major political parties no longer resonates, and partly organizational as traditional organizations of all kinds give way to new modes of action. Political parties cede the place to single issue groups, which come and go, and which thrive on virtual rather than traditional means of communication. Shifts in religion run parallel.

All that said old affinities die hard. In *Voting and Values in Britain: Does Religion Count?* (Theos 2014a), Ben Clements and Nick Spencer use the British Election Study and data from the British Social Attitudes surveys to examine the relationships between religious (and indeed non-religious) commitment and political activity. The first section of their work looks at voting behaviour in which persistent correlations emerge. Specifically, self-identifying Anglicans have been more likely to vote Conservative than Labour for most of the post-war period, the exceptions being in 1966 and 1997; self-identifying Catholics have generally preferred to vote Labour since 1959, and often by large margins (the exception in this case is 1979); and self-identifying nonconformists have shown greater voting fluidity than either Anglicans or Catholics, with a marginally stronger association with the third party. The report contains considerable detail on this situation, refining the variables in a variety of ways (notably the degree of religious commitment) and including data on the minority faiths.[18] It seems moreover that these patterns are driven by economic issues; there is little sign of the 'values voting' so prevalent in the United States. Immigration, however, is rising rapidly as a salient issue – a topic with important repercussions for both religion and politics.

The second part of Clement's and Spencer's (Theos 2014a) analysis deals with values rather than voting, examining the religious constituency in terms of three axes: left–right, libertarianism–authoritarianism and welfarist–individualist. The findings are complex and to be fully appreciated they need to be read in detail. They reveal nonetheless significant denominational differences in the appropriation of values, bearing in mind the disparity between nominal and practising respondents – attendance just as much as affiliation makes a difference in these intricate equations. Somewhat similar questions are asked by Linda Woodhead in an article concerned specifically with Anglicans, drawing this time on two YouGov polls that took place in 2013. The first focused on ethics and personal life; the second on ethics and public life.[19] Deploying sophisticated statistical analyses, Woodhead (2013f) uses these data innovatively: the emphasis here is not so much on values as a values gap. She discovers a marked disjunction between church leaders on the one hand and the 'faithful' on the other – and in two respects. Official church policy, as upheld by church leaders is markedly more conservative in terms of personal morality that the opinions of the Anglican faithful captured in the survey. In terms of social ethics, however, the reverse is the case. The values gap remains but Anglicans in general turn out to be more conservative (in the sense of less welfarist) than their leaders. The former reflects the very rapid changes in attitudes to gender and sexuality which have left the church at odds with the mainstream; the latter is reminiscent of the old adage: *Guardian* in the sacristy and *Telegraph* in the pew.

Towards the end of her article, Woodhead considers the consequences of this situation. Does it matter that the church leaders in question are noticeably out of step not only with public opinion, but with a significant section of its own members, affiliates and sympathizers (not all 'Anglicans' are the same)? Woodhead implies that this is the case, a tension made sharper by the claims of the Church of England to be a national church. I understand her approach, but wonder if there are other ways to consider these disparities, recalling in particular the discussion in Chapter 4 on vicarious religion. Church leaders are indeed 'different' from the rest of society, but are expected to be so – that is the whole point. There are, however, limits to this position, raising once again the question introduced at the end of Chapter 6. At what point and in what circumstances should the churches adjust their views to the wider social changes? And who is to decide? Answers vary, but one fact is abundantly clear: that is, the markedly different timescales of the political world if this is compared with the religious.

What might be termed the different 'rhythms' of political, religious and indeed journalistic life are nicely illustrated in the following. Martin (2004) draws on the thinking of Max Weber (1948) to understand more fully the tensions between the Christian, the politician and the academic or journalist, taking each of these as a representative of a professional group. What Martin describes are, of course, 'ideal-types' in the Weberian sense of the term.[20] That said a perceptive reader, acquainted with the British political scene post 9/11, could very easily give names to these protagonists, but the real point lies elsewhere: that is, in appreciating the different parameters within which the politician, the Christian and the journalist work and the near impossibility of crossing the boundaries between them. Politicians, for example, must be pragmatic; they must know when and how to compromise and how to effect the 'best possible' within the present situation. The Christian, on the other hand, deals in absolutes (the Sermon on the Mount, the Prince of Peace) – ideas which do not, indeed cannot, translate into political realities, either in secular life or in ecclesiastical policy-making.

(The latter in many ways can be even more deadly than the former.) The journalist or commentator, finally, is free in three respects: he or she is *free to* subject both the politician and the Christian to merciless scrutiny, whilst remaining *free from* the obligations of office. Third, the journalist is free to move on to the next debate at will, leaving others to sweep up the china. A failure to grasp these essential differences of role leads not only to serious misunderstandings but to policy disasters, a point fully grasped by Max Weber but equally relevant today.

An additional body of material that explores the role of faith and faith communities in British society has been brought together by Jonathan Birdwell with Stephen Timms (2013) in *The Faith Collection*, a report published by Demos – a left-leaning think tank. The document in question is substantial and contains within it two earlier reports: 'Faithful Citizens' and 'Faithful Providers'. The first of these explores the connections between faith and civic and political engagement in this country. The second examines the role of faith groups in delivering public services. Central to both is the observation that religiously active individuals are more likely than the population as a whole to express their convictions in voluntary action – a theme to be developed in the following section. Here, attention is focused on the extended introductory essay by Stephen Timms MP and Paul Bickley entitled 'Faithful Politics'.

Their opening statement is a bold one. 'The research in this collection supports the argument that members of faith groups, and faith-based organisations, have a strong contribution to make to progressive politics' (2013: 11). In so saying the authors recognize the paradox evident throughout this book: that is, the decline in active membership in most, if not all, churches in this country, alongside the growing significance of religion in public – and therefore political – life. The consequences of this combination for those committed to progressive politics need spelling out, as does the potential of the religious institutions themselves. It ill behoves politicians to thumb their noses at the latter given the parlous state of their own organizations (see note 17). Indeed the reverse should be the case: people of faith should – like everyone else – be encouraged to join political parties, including those on the left. 'Faith' in other words is a resource rather than a problem and should be as central to the Labour Party as to any other. It follows that the seductions of programmatic secularism should be avoided at all costs; it is a creed likely to alienate valuable sources of support. In short: 'a progressive party in Britain, like Labour, looking for new supporters, new ideas and new energy needs to include faith groups in its work. It needs to be respectful, and careful to avoid needlessly alienating them, as has sometimes happened in the past' (2013: 31).

Keeping this in mind, it is interesting to note the thrust of an important project based in the Centre for Ethnicity and Citizenship in Bristol. Entitled

'Muslim Participation in Contemporary Governance',[21] it looks at involvement from the other side. Specifically the project explored modes and practices of state–Muslim engagement in the fields of equalities, faith-sector governance and counter-terrorism, considering the national level on one hand and three local areas (Birmingham, Leicester and Tower Hamlets) on the other. The project ran from 2010 to 2013; the data collected covered the period from 1997 onwards. The final report merits very careful attention – it raises a host of significant questions. Among these are difficult issues concerning representation in Islam; the importance of religious as opposed to ethnic identities; shifting understandings of equalities, diversity and cohesion; relationships with other faith actors, notably the Church of England; and the implications of the 'Prevent' strategy. The continuities with Chapter 9 are immediately apparent.

An important follow-up to the Bristol project can be found in 'Public Spirit', an online forum for debate that invites 'researchers, policymakers, politicians and practitioners from the voluntary and community sectors to debate recent developments in faith and public policy'.[22] The intention is to cross-cut both political affiliations and religious traditions. A glance at the aims of this initiative reveals by now familiar themes: increasing interest in religion, its growing visibility in public life, alongside a public conversation about faith, which all too often is 'fractious and ill-informed'. That in turn has negative consequences for policy-making. The inference is clear: in order to be effective, high-quality research in this field must be presented in an accessible format. Academics have new things to learn in this respect.

Religion and Welfare

The welfare state has, or more accurately has had, iconic status in this country. Its establishment was a major achievement of post-war Britain. There is however a growing awareness that comprehensive care from the cradle to the grave for all citizens is not only unrealistic, but in some ways undesirable in that it creates dependencies from which it is difficult to escape. A second narrative runs parallel: it is found in the idea that the welfare state in a certain sense replaced religion. There is truth in this, but it is not the whole truth. It is true that the welfare state became a recognized public utility that eclipsed much of the care delivered through the parish system – a move for the better for many reasons. It is not true that the churches took no further part in welfare. Faith groups have maintained 'a constant and consistent presence often working in the most disadvantaged areas where all other agencies have withdrawn' (Dinham 2013, forthcoming; see also Dinham and Jackson 2012). Disentangling these threads and the ideologies attached to them is a complex process.

The detail of these relationships is more easily appreciated in a comparative perspective. The work brought together in two pan-European projects is useful in this respect. Two points are particularly important: first is the distinctive position of Britain as a European society, but pulled nonetheless towards the United States; second is the evident relationship between the dominant theology – or more precisely ecclesiology – historically present in the society and the welfare state which subsequently evolves. The projects in question were Welfare and Religion in a European Perspective (WREP) and Welfare and Values in Europe (WaVE). The first concentrated on the historic churches; the second included valuable material on a wide variety of minorities, not least their entitlement (or not) to welfare as judged by different groups of people. Both projects were based in Uppsala University in Sweden and both included an English case study.[23] Right from the start, moreover, this became a distinctive case in that it represented the 'liberal model' in Esping-Andersen's typology of welfare regimes (Esping-Andersen 1989).

This statement requires expansion. The 'liberal model' in this much-discussed analysis is typical of Anglo-Saxon countries in which responsibility is taken by the state for basic social issues, but independent agencies are given considerable scope. It is noticeably different from the 'conservative or corporatist model' found in continental Europe – for example, in Germany, France, Austria and Belgium. In this formulation, a rather more authoritarian state has primary responsibility for the social welfare framework, while voluntary bodies (including large numbers of paid professionals) also play a significant role. The liberal case should also be distanced from the 'social-democratic model' typical of the Nordic countries – Sweden, Norway, Finland, Denmark, Iceland and, to some extent, the Netherlands. Here the state has overall responsibility for social welfare, while voluntary organizations provide complementary services only.

These clarifications are important. The crucial point, however, lies deeper and derives from the innovative work of Manow (2004), Kahl (2005) and van Kersbergen and Manow (2009), all of whom highlight the significance of religious ideas in the formative period of the welfare state from the nineteenth century onwards. For example, van Kersbergen and Manow demonstrate convincingly that the Lutheran countries of northern Europe, including Germany, were the first to develop systems of welfare and social insurance. Catholic and 'reformed' countries adopted these ideas somewhat later. The explanation for the differences in timing can, moreover, be found in the religious factor. Steered by the notion of 'two kingdoms', the Lutheran churches welcomed the welfare state, or – at the very least – offered little resistance to its creation and development. The Catholic Church, conversely, actively hindered the intrusion of the state into the aspects of society that had long been regarded as central to its own identity (notably the family).

Much less predictably, rather similar hesitations can be found in countries influenced by 'reformed' as opposed to Lutheran theology (the Netherlands, Switzerland and, to some extent, England), but for rather different reasons. Once again, there was resistance to state welfare, but this time in the name of theological as well as political individualism. Self-reliance, rather than social care, becomes the supreme virtue.[24]

The literature on religion and welfare in Britain is growing fast. Among the major contributions are Harris (1998), Prochaska (2006), Dinham (2009), Dinham, Furbey and Lowndes (2009), Beaumont and Cloke (2012), Jawad (2012), a themed section in *Social Policy and Society* (2012),[25] a collection of opinion pieces brought together in Theos (2014b) and the continuing work of the William Temple Foundation.[26] Added to these are a string of government and voluntary sector reports, some national and some regional.[27] Formats vary: some texts are single-authored and develop distinctive themes; others are compilations of case studies with reflective pieces fore and aft. Either way, the disciplinary range is wide. It includes different branches of theology and ethics, economic and social history, economics, organizational dynamics, social policy, political and sociological analysis, and political and social theory. Equally varied are the viewpoints of the authors. Some come from inside the faith communities and care deeply about their futures; others have encountered the abundance of faith-based organizations in the course of their fieldwork and wondered how to incorporate such groups in their analyses. This, moreover, is a rapidly developing field in which new ideas are emerging all the time.

That said, a number of themes recur. On the first point everyone agrees: there is a huge amount of activity in this field which, in itself, requires an explanation. Why in other words has there been growth rather than decline in the presence of faith communities in the welfare provision of a modern western democracy, which is becoming more rather than less secular? Two interrelated responses emerge: a shortage of money and an increase in demand both of which strain the system. The first is driven by the swings and fortunes of the global economy, which have become more rather than less acute. They began in the 1970s, following the oil crisis, and have ebbed and flowed ever since. The 2008 recession simply made a tricky situation more difficult. Policy issues, including austerity measures, need to be seen against this background – they are not the whole story. The increase in demand is paradoxical: in itself it is the result of successful welfare in the sense that we live longer than we used to. Long-living, however, has become a 'problem'. Without doubt, it is the far-reaching changes in demography noted in Chapter 2 that are driving the debate about pensions and social care. The always delicate balance between the working and the non-working sectors of society is central to this discussion, which will be even more relevant with respect to health care.

A second set of issues concerns the appropriateness, or not, of faith-based provision in welfare – a topic which provokes heated debate. Societal responses range from warm approbation to serious critique. 'Faithful Providers' (see above) is an example of the former; Kettell (2013b) offers a more critical view, interrogating the assumptions on which much of this work is based. Searching questions arise in these discussions. These include sensitive issues surrounding inclusion, exclusion and conditionality (see below), and issues relating to professional codes, training, evaluation and quality control. Dinham (forthcoming) digs deeper still, raising questions that recall an underlying theme of this book. In the mid twentieth century the welfare state displaced religion and religious sensibility as the primary language of care. Some 50 years later an increasingly mixed economy of welfare re-admitted religiously based actors, almost by accident. An entirely new situation began to emerge: much greater diversity than previously, alongside a diminishing capacity to address the implications that follow. There is therefore an urgent need to re-skill both public professionals and citizens to deal with the issues – essentially those of religious literacy – as they present in the world of welfare.

Equally ambivalent are the reactions of the faith-based organizations themselves. Some are prepared to take public money, despite the restrictions that this entails; others feel that public funding would necessarily compromise their primary mission, which is to save souls rather than bodies. Government criteria do not always sit easily alongside faith commitments. An additional point runs parallel. Faith-based organizations can be anxious lest their role as providers compromises their critical or prophetic obligations. It is not always possible to reconcile the two. Indeed the tension between them reflects a persistent dilemma. If faith-based organizations step in to resolve a crisis (in, for example, provision for the homeless or the organization of food banks), are they effectively letting the government off the hook? Would it not be better to use their energies in political critique rather than daily provision? As is so often the case, answers differ.

Two examples conclude this section. Myriad others could have been chosen, so why these? The first, Street Pastors, brings to our attention the striking capacities of the churches to mobilize volunteers; the second, a study of care for the homeless, raises the vexed question of conditionality – is it, or is it not the case that there are strings attached to faith-based welfare?[28]

Street Pastors defines itself as 'an interdenominational network of Christian charities operating across the UK and worldwide. It is a Church response to urban problems, engaging with people on the streets to care, listen and dialogue'.[29] The idea as such came from the West Indies and was pioneered in London in 2003 by Les Isaac, the director of the Ascension Trust.[30] Initially devised to ameliorate gang violence, it now directs itself to anyone in need on a Friday or Saturday night – be they homeless people settling down for the night or clubbers trying to get home after an evening of heavy drinking. The Pastors work in teams and patrol their patch (usually the city centre) from late evening to the early hours. Help is very practical: water, blankets, flip flops and bus timetables are distributed to those who require them by individuals who are more ready to listen than to judge.

Currently (i.e. in 2014) there are some 250 Street Pastor teams in different parts of the United Kingdom, staffed by 9000 trained volunteers. An interesting study of one of these took place in Kingston-on-Thames in 2012 (Collins-Mayo, King and Jones 2012).[31] The researchers found that the safety and well-being of individuals out at night is improved: in the sense that the streets are 'domesticated'; that the presence of older people makes a difference; that opportunities for antisocial behaviour are reduced by low-level interventions; that Street Pastor volunteers are recognized, respected, valued and trusted by both the public and other interested parties including the police; and that volunteers are careful to maintain a boundary between normative Christian mission and proselytizing, but are willing nonetheless to engage with the existential or spiritual questions of the people that they meet. It is interesting to note that the time on the street is systematically supported by prayer (Collins-Mayo 2013).

An inevitable question arises. Why do people do this? Why are significant numbers of individuals willing to give up time and energy to offer practical help to mostly young people, who – more often than not – have got themselves into difficulties? The answer lies in the classic combination that faith communities (Christian and other) offer: at one and the same time, they preach an ethic of care and offer a network of opportunities through which to express these sentiments (Gill 1992, 1999). The Kingston research demonstrates this perfectly. Recruitment happens through the local churches; specifically 34 per cent of the volunteers said that they heard about Street Pastors through a presentation given at church and a further 20 per cent through church notices. One volunteer encourages another and they subsequently tell their friends. This moreover is not an isolated example; the same story could be told over and over again regarding the recruitment of volunteers in faith-based welfare of all kinds and at many different levels.

The second illustration looks at the role of faith-based care for the homeless, asking specifically whether or not faith makes a difference? The study in question was part of the Religion and Society Programme and looked at a range of providers – both secular and religious – who were offering services to homeless people in London and Manchester.[32] The picture that emerged was interesting. Faith-based organizations continue to play an important role in the care for the homeless, but the differences between these organizations and secular agencies were not at all clear-cut – boundaries were blurred both within and across sectors. That said, faith-based initiatives tended to be smaller and rather more informal than secular ones, which offered more specialized services. The researchers also found different degrees of 'interventionism' across agencies, in the sense that some organizations demanded more in the way of lifestyle changes than others. Interestingly the rather more interventionist end of the continuum was dominated by secular agencies, whilst the faith-based providers were bunched at the other.

The team concluded that the widespread distrust of faith-based providers found in the sector is out of touch with reality. In this case at least, there was no suggestion of 'conditionality', in the sense of providers using public money to propagate religion; nor was there evidence of exclusion on religious or other grounds. That however is not the whole story. Johnsen (2012) raises further and penetrating questions about interventionism, noting the tendency of government to promote 'rehabilitative' measures', an approach resisted by at least some faith-based organizations. What emerges is in many ways paradoxical. Faith-based providers are indeed out of step with the mainstream, but for an unexpected reason: they intervene too little rather than too much.

Religion and Health Care

Debates about welfare merge into concerns about health and health care. That is so in practice as well as in academic discussion. There is, for example, real concern about older people who are occupying hospital beds when their requirements are social rather than medical, but moving from one agency to another is easier said than done. Faith-based organizations are able to bridge this gap in the sense that they fill the same sorts of needs in both cases: most obviously companionship and support for the vulnerable however defined. Such needs moreover are growing as the years pass – unsurprisingly given the combination of financial and demographic pressures already outlined. A further resemblance concerns institutional arrangements. Both welfare and health care are distinct from the world of education, in the sense that there was a rather more comprehensive transfer of responsibility to the state in the immediate post-war period. There is nothing comparable in either case to the church schools which remain a significant element within public education (see Chapter 6).

All that said, there are distinctive issues to consider regarding the connections between religion, spirituality and health, including the meaning of health itself. The most widely-used definition is that established by the World Health Organization: 'Health is a state of complete physical, mental and social well-being and not merely the absence of disease or infirmity'. It was agreed in 1948 and has remained unchanged ever since.[33] It is noticeably broad and leads naturally into holistic understandings of health which bring together the physical, mental and social. The links with well-being and the connectedness of mind, body and spirit, beloved of the new age and its off-shoots, are immediately apparent and relate in turn to the growing material on complementary and alternative medicine. Recent shifts in mainstream medicine away from the biomedical model towards Paul Tournier's 'medicine of the person' run parallel (Cox, Campbell and Fulford 2006).

This however is jumping ahead in a story which reflects very clearly the transitions in modern western society from pre-modern, to modern, and to what is often termed post-modern – a narrative that was central to the theoretical chapter that concluded the first edition of this book. It recalls an important dimension of the process of secularization, in which sectors of society that historically were dominated by the church, became bit by bit autonomous spheres each with its own professional codes. Understandings of the healing process evolved accordingly, a shift in which the religious and spiritual dimensions diminish and the scientific advances – systematically and with evident success. We live much longer than we used to and, at least in the western world, we expect to be in good health. There is however a downside, which is increasingly remarked on. High-tech medicine may have made huge advances; it has however depersonalized the patient, who resents the notion that he or she is simply through-put in a system, which records success in terms of targets and tick boxes rather than comfort or care.

Unsurprisingly, the situation has provoked increasingly visible reactions, accurately perceived as post-modern, in the sense that they come after. They do not constitute a return to the past – few right-thinking people want that; they do, however, prioritize models or ways of doing things that foreground the patient's needs. Many of these incorporate elements of the spiritual or sacred in the healing process, notably the holistic tendencies mentioned above. Just as significant are new ways of dealing with birth and death. For example, new approaches to childbirth allow far greater autonomy for the mother as opposed to the medical professional, and careful attention to the dying has led to innovative institutions which react against the (sometimes extreme) medicalization of the hospital environment. The hospice movement is the most obvious illustration of the turn towards holistic care, in which death becomes once again the natural end of life; it is not simply a failure of modern medicine.[34] Three further examples will flesh out these ideas: first, a growing body of material on the care of older people; second, some interesting developments in mental health; and third, a case study which crosses conventional boundaries. Each will be taken in turn.

Research carried out in the Department of Psychology in Southampton, notably the interdisciplinary work of Peter Coleman, affords an excellent example from gerontology. Coleman's interests include developmental, spiritual and mental health issues associated with ageing. Two of his many publications illustrate the point. *Belief and Ageing: Spiritual Pathways in Later Life* (Coleman 2011) is based on 40 years of empirical work and the reflection that goes with this. Drawing on this work, Coleman argues that both gerontologists and welfare professionals should pay far more attention to belief (and indeed non-belief) as a constituent of well-being in later life. The lack of interest in this field reflects the seductions of secular frames of reference, ways of thinking which diminish the importance of meaning and belonging – unhelpfully given that these increase rather than decrease with age. More recently Coleman led a fascinating study on ageing, ritual and social change in different parts of Europe (Coleman, Koleva and Bornat 2013).[35] The content of this book is a little less relevant to the health of older people except in a general sense, but the narrative is utterly compelling as elderly people in very different parts of Europe, including Britain, describe their engagements (or otherwise) with religion at key moments in their lives. This project represents comparative work at its very best.

One way of capturing the shifts in mental health is to note the presence of the Spirituality and Psychiatry Special Interest Group (SPSIG) within the Royal College of Psychiatry. The SPSIG was founded in 1999 as a forum for psychiatrists eager to explore the influence of religion in the field of psychiatry. The field encompasses religion (the major world faiths), no religion and spirituality. The group offers an integrative approach to mental health care, which allows patients to articulate their spiritual concerns, thus permitting the discussion of fundamental questions such as the purpose and meaning of life. Both pathological and normal human experiences are carefully considered – the goal being to understand better the ways in which the two do or do not overlap. Crucial in this respect is a shift in perspective: religion and spirituality are no longer seen as harmful or delusional (or at least not necessarily so); they become instead part of an individual's core values and beliefs, offering the potential for healing rather than harm.[36] There is a rapidly growing literature in the field, evidenced by the very extensive publications archive maintained by the SPSIG. The collection edited by Cook, Powell and Sims (2009) offers a more detailed account of the Special Interest Group and the reasons for its existence; the subsequent chapters cover the key specialties of psychiatry.

The final example is rather different – it is in effect the exception that proves the rule. Burrswood hospital in Kent is run as a charitable trust that exists to deliver high quality care to patients through the marriage of medicine and Christian ministry. At the same time it promotes the knowledge and provision of such care, acting as a resource to others who wish to develop such ministries.[37] Here in short is a modern hospital in which the boundary between medicine and religion has effectively collapsed. It was founded in 1948 by Dorothy Kerin – a Christian visionary with a personal experience of healing. Right from the start, Kerin advocated 'whole person care', relating physical illness to an individual's spiritual, mental or emotional state. The scope of the work is varied, but the treatment of chronic fatigue syndrome or myalgic encephalomyelitis (ME) has emerged – unsurprisingly – as a much-needed specialism. Burrswood hospital lies squarely between two structures: it is firmly endorsed by the Church of England; it is also recommended on NHS websites, bearing in mind that most patients are privately funded.

As ever the academic debate both reflects and contributes to these changes. Take, for example, the impressive range of handbooks that have been published in recent years. The *Handbook of Religion and Health*, edited by Koenig, King, and Carson (2012) and the *Oxford Textbook of Spirituality in Healthcare* edited by Cobb, Puchalski and Rumbold (2012) exemplify the genre.[38] The first is a primarily American text, a fact that makes a difference in terms of practice, but less so with respect to the range of topics deemed important. These include the historical connections between religion and health; the difference between 'religion' and 'spirituality' as they are applied in this field; mental health; the mind–body relationship; and the impact of religion on physical as well as mental wellbeing. Attention is also paid to research methods and clinical practice. The second text is more focused and concerns the relationship between spirituality and health care as such, given its growing importance in research, policy, clinical practice and training. It is crucial that we understand how spirituality is not only experienced but expressed in illness, suffering, healing and loss. What resources should be made available in this field and how should these be organized? These questions increase in significance almost by the day.

In Conclusion

The questions raised in this chapter are central to the understanding of religion in this country. Taken together, moreover, they indicate very clearly the positioning of Britain between Europe and the United States. The section on religion and the law, for example, highlighted the role of the ECHR and the European Court that enforces this agenda. The British are markedly ambivalent towards both.[39] But like it or not, Britain lies for the time being within the purview of the Court. Indeed in terms of structures or institutions, Britain is similar to its European neighbours on a number of counts: it has a historically dominant church or churches, a welfare state and a comprehensive health system. The paragraphs above have shown moreover that these features are related to each other. The welfare state for example is conditioned by the particular nature of the church(es) that preceded it, and both are distinctive in European terms.

That there are elements in Britain that pull in a different direction is widely acknowledged. As Woodhead and others have shown (pp. 203–04), the population is less welfarist in its inclinations than it used to be and self-reliance continues to resonate as a virtue – both in and beyond the Conservative Party. Britain is also a nation of volunteers, many of whom are highly trained and in positions of considerable responsibility.[40] In these and other respects, the affinities with the United States are clearly visible. That said there are limits to this relationship as well. British people are as bewildered as anyone else at the reluctance of a sizeable section of the American population to accept Obamacare and the principles that lie behind this, and there is no equivalent in this country to the values voting that undoubtedly influences the outcomes of American elections. Nor is there any sign of a new Christian right despite unfounded claims to the contrary (Theos 2013a). In short, there is no getting round it: Britain is a very particular case.

Notes

1   A fascinating and long-term enquiry into precisely this subject is currently in progress. Cécile Laborde is directing a project funded by the European Research Council entitled 'Is Religion Special? Secularism and Religion in Contemporary Legal and Political Theory'. For more details, see http://www.ucl.ac.uk/spp/people/cecile-laborde (accessed 8 August 2014).

2   More information about the religion and belief strand of the Equality and Human Rights Commission can be found at http://www.equalityhumanrights.com/your-rights/equal-rights/religion-and-belief (accessed 8 August 2014). For the material in this section, I am indebted to David Perfect, who works on the religion or belief strand. A useful summary of the Commission's work in this respect can be found in Perfect (2013).

3   The PSED requires public authorities to pay due regard to the need to eliminate discrimination, advance equality of opportunity and foster good relations.

4   The EHRC funded and led the successful discrimination claim that Hall and Preddy took to the County Court in 2011; they also funded their defence when the owners unsuccessfully appealed to the Court of Appeal in 2012 and to the Supreme Court in 2013.

5   These include Woodhead with Catto (2009), Woodhead (2011) and Weller (2011).

6   The dialogues were facilitated by Adam Dinham, the Director of the Religious Leadership Literacy Programme. Further information including reports from each event can be found on the following website: http://www.religiousliteracy.org/ehrc-dialogues (accessed 4 August 2014).

7   For the Guidance published following the *Eweida et al.* judgment, see http://www.equalityhumanrights.com/publication/religion-or-belief-workplace-guide-employers-following-recent-european-court-human-rights-judgments. The Marriage (Same Sex Couples) Act 2013 Guidance is available at http://www.equalityhumanrights.com/your-rights/equal-rights/sexual-orientation/marriage-same-sex-couples-act-2013-guidance. Both websites accessed 8 August 2014.

8   See the website of The European Convention on Human Rights, available at http://www.echr.coe.int/Documents/Convention_ENG.pdf (accessed 8 August 2014).

9   See The European Court of Human Rights: Questions and Answers, available at http://www.echr.coe.int/Documents/Questions_Answers_ENG.pdf (accessed 8 August 2014).

10   The details of these cases can be read on http://hudoc.echr.coe.int/sites/eng/pages/search.aspx?i=001-115881#{"itemid":["001-115881"]}   (accessed February 18 2014).

11   See for instance McCrea (2014) and Leigh and Hambler (2014), who take different views.

12   More information about the project can be found at http://erc.europa.eu/erc-stories/european-perspectives-religion-public   and   http://www.eliamep.gr/en/descriptions/project-descriptions/grassrootsmobilise/ (accessed 8 August 2104).

13   See http://www.law.cf.ac.uk/clr/aboutus/ for more information (accessed 8 August 2014).

14   See http://www.law.cf.ac.uk/clr/networks/lrsn2.html. The LARSN maintains an invaluable database of religion or belief judgments – see http://www.law.cf.ac.uk/clr/networks/lrsncd.html. Both websites accessed 8 August 2014.

15   Further details can be found at http://www.bristol.ac.uk/law/research/centres-themes/law-religion.html#01 (accessed 8 August 2014).

16   See http://www.oxfordjournals.org/our_journals/ojlr/about.html (accessed 23 August 2014). This journal was not however the first in the field. *The Ecclesiastical Law Journal* and *Law and Justice* already existed.

17   Up to date information on membership of political parties can be found at http://www.parliament.uk/business/publications/research/briefing-papers/SN05125/membership-of-uk-political-parties (accessed 8 August 2014).

18   The minority faiths vary in their voting preferences. Conclusions, however, must remain tentative given the size of the sample. Clements (forthcoming) provides more detailed information on religion, voting behaviour and party choice.

19   The data from the YouGov polls can be found at http://d25d2506sfb94s.cloudfront.net/cumulus_uploads/document/mm7go89rhi/YouGov-University%20of%20Lancaster-Survey-Results-Faith-Matters-130130.pdf (fieldwork: 25–30 January 2013) and http://d25d2506sfb94s.cloudfront.net/cumulus_uploads/document/4vs1srt1h1/YG-Archive-University-of-Lancaster-Faith-Matters-Debate-full-results-180613-website.pdf (fieldwork: 5–13 June 2013). Each survey contained an extensive battery of questions. Both websites accessed on 8 August 2014.

20   See Chapter 7, note 3 on ideal types. The academic or journalist in this example denotes the outside commentator rather than the participant.

21   This project was part of the Religion and Society Programme. Full details, including the final report can be found at http://www.bristol.ac.uk/ethnicity/projects/muslimparticipation. See also http://www.publicspirit.org.uk/presence-voice-and-impact. Both websites accessed 8 August 2014.

22   See the information given on http://www.publicspirit.org.uk/about-public-spirit (accessed 8 August 2014).

23 Full details of both projects and subsequent publications can be found on http://www.crs.uu.se/Research/former-research-projects/ (accessed 8 August 2014). The case study in question was English rather than British.

24 It is hard to avoid the conclusion that this was one reason why the political views of Mrs Thatcher resonated with a sizeable section of the British population. There was no equivalent to Mrs Thatcher in continental Europe.

25 The themed section was entitled 'Social Policy and Religion in Contemporary Britain' and appeared in *Social Policy and Society*, 11(4), 2012.

26 For an up-to-date list of publications, see http://williamtemplefoundation.org. uk/our-work/research/ (accessed 8 August 2014).

27 A number of these are listed in Dinham (2013) and Dinham and Jackson (2012). Evans (2008) and Russell-Jones (2013) contain data on faith-based activities in Wales. See also the work of 'Faith in Community Scotland' – www. faithincommunityscotland.org (accessed 8 August 2014).

28 Interestingly exactly the same questions are asked in the two reports brought together in Birdwell, with Timms (2013). 'Faithful Citizens' talks in detail about volunteering and 'Faithful Providers' rejects the claim that faith-based organizations are prone to proselytizing and/or discrimination.

29 For more information about Street Pastors and the Ascension Trust, see http:// streetpastors.co.uk/Home/tabid/255/Default.aspx and www.ascensiontrust. org.uk (both websites accessed 23 August 2014).

30 See note 29.

31 A summary report is available at http://kingston.streetpastors.org.uk/wp-content/uploads/2012/04/Kingston-University-Briefing-on-Street-Pastors.pdf (accessed 8 August 2014).

32 More details can be found at http://www.religionandsociety.org.uk/research_findings/featured_findings/faith_based_services_for_homeless_people_do_not_bible_bash (accessed 8 August 2014). See also Cloke, Johnsen and May (2012).

33 See the preamble to the Constitution of the World Health Organization as adopted by the International Health Conference, New York, 19–22 June 1946.

34 Dame Cicely Saunders is generally considered the founder of the Hospice movement. She was trained as a nurse, as a medical social worker and finally as a physician. She founded St Christopher's Hospice in 1967, bringing together expert symptom control, compassionate care, teaching and clinical research.

35 More details about the project can be found at http://www.religionandsociety.org. uk/research_findings/featured_findings/religious_rituals_continue_to_mark_the_life_course_especially_in_ex_communist_countries and http://www.southampton. ac.uk/mrasc/introduction (both websites accessed on 8 August 2014).

36 Interesting research on the mental health care of asylum seekers, refugees and immigrants has been done in Sweden. Religio-cultural issues are central to this work. See http://www.crs.uu.se/Research/impactofreligion/Theme_4/immigration_healthcare_and_existential_questions/?languageId=1 for more detail (accessed 8 August 2014).

37 This information is taken from the Burrswood website. See http://www. burrswood.org.uk/about_burrswood/our_organisation (accessed 8 August 2014).

38 The *Handbook of Religion and Health* was first published in 2001.

39   The issue of voting rights for prisoners is particularly controversial. See Donald, Gordon and Leach (2012: 126–127) and http://www.bbc.co.uk/news/uk-politics-25421082 (accessed 8 August 2014) for more details.

40   Take for example the responsibilities of the Chair of the Governing Body of a state school in the United Kingdom. This work is demanding, time-consuming and highly skilled, but unpaid.

Part V

Thinking Theoretically

11

Religion and Modernity Continued

The Preface to this edition of *Religion in Britain* indicated that three things have changed since its predecessor went to press; all three, moreover, concern the shifting relationships between religion and modernity and how these should be understood. The first has to do with the religious situation as such. The second reflects the growing interest of a wide variety of academic disciplines, including those oriented to policy, in what is happening. The third is a little different; it is also more personal in that it relates to the perspectives that I am able to bring to the questions that emerge – at one and the same time these are both broader than they used to be and more focused.

The goal of the preceding chapters has been to describe and to explain the religious situation in Britain in the early years of the twenty-first century, paying attention to the range of factors set out in Chapter 1. The discussion has made reference to the burgeoning literature in the field, which draws in turn on a rapidly expanding corpus of research, itself part of the changes that are taking place. Rather less has been said about the responses of social science to the subsequent challenges – the principal topic for this chapter, which among other things will indicate the ways in which I, trained in the discipline of sociology, respond to what I see happening both in Britain and elsewhere. Before embarking on this agenda, however, a couple of preliminaries are important. The first is to indicate where more might have been said; the second is to summarize the overall picture that has emerged from the evidence presented above.

Any book of this nature which attempts an overview of the religious life of a nation in a single volume is necessarily selective. Additional themes could always be added – lists that will vary from reader to reader depending on what interests them most. As the author, however, I am particularly

Religion in Britain: A Persistent Paradox, Second Edition. Grace Davie.
© 2015 Grace Davie. Published 2015 by John Wiley & Sons, Ltd.

aware of three topics that have not been discussed in the detail that they deserve: the significance of gender and social class in the profiling of religion, and the shifting relationships between religion and the media in its broadest sense.

I have written about gender elsewhere (Davie 2013; Walter and Davie 1998), but in the preceding chapters I have discussed this more as a bone of contention (Chapter 6) than as a powerful factor in the patterning of religion as such. Regarding the latter, more emphasis had been placed on generations and generational change than on the differences between men and women, recognizing that the two overlap (see Brown 2001; Aune, Sharma and Vincett 2008; Trzebiatowska and Bruce 2012; Voas, McAndrew and Storm 2013). My justification is the following: the evolution of gender roles is of crucial importance in the understanding of religious development, but it is not specific to Britain. Indeed the consistency of gender differences across frontiers, in the sense that women are more religious than men over a wide variety of indicators throughout the Christian west, is striking – it is, for example, one of the factors that bridges the gap between Europe (including Britain) and the United States. More apposite in this book would have been a fuller appreciation of the subtle and developing interactions between gender and generation and between gender and ethnicity in relation to the wide variety of faith communities in this country, both Christian and other. This, however, is very specialized work.

More could also have been said about social class, which (unlike gender) is quintessentially British. The issue was developed as a significant sub-theme in the first edition of the book, which noted the different patterns that emerged regarding belief and belonging in different sections of society. 'Believing without belonging' was characteristic of what might be termed the traditional working class – in, for example, Richard Hoggart's descriptions of working people in Leeds in the immediate post-war period, recalled in Chapter 2. Both class and class structures, however, have metamorphosed in recent decades, making the analysis considerably more complicated than it used to be. Class, moreover, is criss-crossed by other variables, notably ethnicity – which is itself giving way to religion in the understanding of social and cultural difference. The latter point is crucial and has been alluded to in several places.

The third lacuna relates to the media both in their traditional and more innovative forms. The important study led by Kim Knott has been referenced in Chapter 3, primarily to indicate the distorted profiles of religion that emerge in both the newspapers and television (Knott, Poole and Taira 2013).[1] A careful perusal of the data emerging in this field reveals, however, additional details that should be taken into account, not least the marked contrast between local and national outlets. Local newspapers, for instance, are noticeably more balanced in their accounts of religion than their national equivalents, offering on a moderately regular basis sympathetic accounts of what is happening in a particular city or neighbourhood. Quite different are the questions raised by the increasing presence of new media, outlets which have developed exponentially since 1994, and which interact in innovative ways with new forms of religious life – so much so that religion online morphs bit by bit into online religion, generating an entirely fresh set of commentaries. Also significant is the mediatization of religion as such. For all these reasons, serious efforts have been made since the 1990s to place religion on the agenda of media studies, and media on the agenda of religious studies – exchanges that are bearing rich fruit (Lövheim 2013).[2]

Any number of side-steps could have been made at this point: on the one hand to a fuller discussion of the internet and its implication for religion as for so much else, and on the other to the world of popular culture (film, music, video and so on). The compressions of time and space are but the starting point in either case, linking the local with the global in a couple of clicks.

Thinking in the Round

Turning now to the positive – what has been covered – the first challenge is to capture the overall picture, bearing in mind that this is easier said than done. As has been made clear from the outset, the various factors identified in this book push and pull in different directions. There are however pertinent questions to ask. One of these relates to defaults: if twenty-first century Britain is no longer Christian in any meaningful sense, what is it? Is it secular? Is it diverse? Or is it simply indifferent? And in what direction is it heading? The evidence is mixed in the sense that every statement requires qualification. Britain is markedly more secular than it used to be, but by no means totally so; it is also more diverse, but unevenly – the regional variations are considerable. Indifference, moreover, interweaves with unattached belief on the one hand, and more articulate versions of the secular on the other. Each of these elements depends, moreover, on the others. Secularization is most certainly advancing, but is itself coloured by the specificities of British Christianity, as indeed are the forms of secularism that are emerging in this part of the world. Increasing religious diversity is a fact, but it too is distinctive in terms of the religious minorities now present in Britain and their relationship to the host society. There are parallels in Europe, but both form and content vary.

Bearing such complexity in mind, the constellation that is developing might be summarized as follows. The centre of British society is gradually shifting away from Christianity, but remains deeply coloured by it. New forms of accommodation are beginning to evolve, which are more likely to be secular than religious in nature – take, for example, the discourses associated with equality or human rights – but unless they can find space for the seriously religious of different faiths, they will be unlikely to endure for long. Within these new formulations, engaged Christians are likely to become one minority amongst others, but will have the weight of history on their side – an advantage that brings with it considerable responsibility. In short the cultural deposits can still be felt but in new ways: in what might be termed a hierarchy of minorities, one of which finds expression in an established church. The latter, quite rightly, has lost any sense of dominance, but retains its constitutional privilege. The advantages of this position (a 'weak' established church) have already been mentioned (pp. 97–8).

A cluster of interrelated questions follows from this summary. How much has changed? At which point or points did this happen? And how can we disentangle perception from reality? The different approaches to the 1960s outlined in Chapter 2 offer a good example. Quite clearly a profound metamorphosis was taking place in British society at that time, but its significance for the process of secularization is disputed. Callum Brown sees the 1960s as pivotal; others take a longer view. And what was the position of the churches? Did they lead the way or were they simply responding to what was happening round them? Probing further, did the change in ideas espoused by a selection of senior churchmen bring about the slide in churchgoing or were these individuals reacting to a decline in religious activity that was already evident? Whatever the case, there is abundant evidence that church leaders in the 1960s were persuaded that Britain – along with other western societies – had entered a new and profoundly secular age. Their perceptions of what was going on around them sound extraordinarily similar to what we currently hear.[3]

Other commentators find significant turning points in later decades. Linda Woodhead is one such, seeing the 1980s as the 'hinge'. Crucially important in this connection is the gradual assertion of the market, rather than the state, as the dominant mode of organization in both religion and welfare – a shift that begins in the 1970s (Woodhead 2012). Up to a point I agree: this after all is the shift evoked in the movement from obligation to consumption. I would also argue (with Woodhead) that religion based on choice rather than habit or obligation does not mean that religion is necessarily trivialized. Seriously made choices have implications for public as well as private life. Nor is the market *necessarily* pernicious. I would, however, put more weight than Woodhead does on the continuing notion of religion as a public utility and the mentalities that go with this. Old habits die hard in the sense that there are still large sections of the population who expect their parish church, just like the NHS, to be there at the point of need for those who want it. Among the latter are many who do not have the luxury of choice.

A related set of issues is noted by Woodhead in her commentaries on the work emerging from the Religion and Society Programme. Her plenary address to the closing conference on 'New Forms of Public Religion' offers a good example.[4] This evokes two 'styles' (or ideal types) of religion. 'Old style' religion denotes the organizational modes extant since the Reformation (essentially medium-sized local membership organizations that aggregate into national structures); these are underpinned by uniform creeds, the essence of which is set out in printed form. The membership of these churches is relatively passive and salvation is seen in transcendent rather than immanent forms. 'New style' religion moves away from the medium-sized membership structure towards more episodic modes of existence. Some are very large (festivals or gatherings), and some are very small (cell groups); the latter can exist within the former. In 'new style' religion, moreover, authority is dispersed and communication takes place through a wide variety of media; the agency of the individual believer is considerably enhanced. The stress lies in finding yourself rather than in a definitive form of salvation. The echoes with Woodhead's earlier work on spirituality (Heelas and Woodhead 2005) are clearly evident.

It is important to note that the two types or styles of religion run alongside each other. This has been the case for centuries rather than decades and will continue to be so for the foreseeable future. The combination underpins the structure of this book. That said Woodhead sees the 1980s as the tipping point, when 'new style' religion not only accelerates markedly, but becomes normative. Once again my view is similar. This is unsurprising given that the shift from one type of religiousness to another constituted a central theme in the concluding chapter of the first edition of this book, which traced the shifts from modernity to post-modernity and its implications for religiousness in modern Britain. Broadly speaking, Woodhead's first type fits well with my descriptions of 'modern' society, the second with 'post-modern', noting that the latter provoked a variety of reactions. On the one hand were those who chose to go with the flow and to create forms of religion that were consonant with the fluidities of modern living. On the other were those who found this difficult, seeking instead forms of religion that protected the individual and his or her co-religionists from the uncertainties of late or post-modern living.[5] In the latter lies the essence of fundamentalism, which can take both religious and secular forms.

A rather different approach can be found in the work of Marion Bowman, a specialist in alternative forms of religion. Like Woodhead and myself she recognizes the complexity of religious life in this country, but emphasizes a different, very revealing point. Indeed, Bowman is hesitant about using the term 'alternative' altogether in the sense that this implies that something else is mainstream. But what? For this reason, she prefers to speak of 'integrative spirituality', chosen to capture a sense of 'bricolage' and creative blending – recognizing, however, that none of this is new. Current formulations may be innovative, but the combinations of formal and less formal, of official and less official have always been present in vernacular religion, which from time immemorial has run alongside what might be termed conventional forms of religiousness. From this perspective, Glastonbury (an important focus of Bowman's fieldwork) is seen in a new light; by looking carefully at what happens here we are able to make sense of more general trends particularly in relation to plurality, both past and present (Bowman 2015).

The discussion, moreover, will continue as each generation, be they practitioners or commentators, tries to get a grip on what is happening around them. Lying behind my own thinking is, however, a deeper question: a sociological awareness that whoever holds the middle ground possesses a particular kind of legitimacy – with respect to religion as in so much else. It is for this reason that my work over 20 years has concentrated on this section of society and on finding concepts that help to grasp this better. I continue to reflect on these issues. In Chapter 4, for example, I explained my reasons for moving away from 'believing without belonging', introducing instead the idea of 'vicarious religion'. I do not want to go back on this judgement, but I am beginning to wonder whether 'believing without belonging' might have a new lease of life as we concentrate more on the secular: those in other words who have placed themselves outside any form of religious community, but who continue to prevaricate on a wide range of issues. Woodhead (2014b) terms these people the 'fuzzy nones', noting that most 'nones' do not decisively reject God. What they do resist is any kind of identification with 'religion' (whether general or specific) or with the label 'religious'.[6]

Whatever the case, the evolving situation in Britain has to be seen against the considerably more dramatic events taking place elsewhere in the late twentieth and early twenty-first centuries. Three of these were world-changing: the Iranian Revolution of 1979, the collapse of communism in 1989 and the attack on the Twin Towers in 2001. Given their gravity, each of these episodes merits careful analysis in its own right, but they have in common a crucial feature: their unexpectedness. Manifestly, both policy-makers and pundits were caught unawares. Why was it, for example, that the Shah of Iran, a western figurehead, was obliged to flee before an Ayatollah motivated by conservative readings of Islam? And why did observers of all kinds fail to anticipate the concatenation of events that led to the fall of the Berlin Wall and the collapse of communism as a credible narrative, within which the election of John Paul II was a significant element? And why finally did the events of 9/11 come like a bolt from the blue? By this stage there was a growing awareness of events in the Muslim world and their significance for western policy,[7] but nobody – nobody at all – expected hijacked planes to fly into iconic buildings in New York. Hence the abruptness of the wake-up call: religion was undeniably important in that it was clearly able to motivate widely different groups of people to act in dramatic and unforeseen ways – a realization that prompted renewed attention to an aspect of society that had been ignored for too long.

The wrong inference was drawn, however. All too quickly commentators began to assume that religion was resurgent or back, reasoning that we are now in a post-secular, rather than a post-religious, situation. To argue thus, however, is to conflate two rather different things. Was it really the case that religion (or God) was back?[8] Or was it simply that the disciplines of social science in the west, along with a wide variety of policy-makers, had now become aware (or re-aware) of something that had been there all the time? Was it, in other words, perceptions that had altered rather than reality? It is, I think, a complex mixture of both. New forms of religion have asserted themselves in different parts of the world; that is beyond doubt. It is incorrect to assume, however, that the new manifestations emerged from a vacuum. In almost all global regions, the presence of religion has not only been continuous but taken for granted; only in Europe might this statement be questioned, and then only partially. These are the issues to consider in the second half of this chapter.

Reacting to Unexpected Events

As already indicated, the equivalent chapter to this one in the first edition of this book was concerned with the changing nature of society in the late twentieth century, and the effect that this was having on the religious dimensions of human living. It also paid attention to the sociological insights that were emerging to make sense of the new reality. The watchwords in this respect were post-modernity and post-modernism, using the former to grasp the changing nature of society's structures and the latter to capture the epistemological shifts that went with these – taking care not to equate one with the other. That particular debate has largely run its course, but others have emerged to take its place. Notable here is a presumed shift from the secular to the post-secular as western commentators were brought up short by the persistence of religion in the twenty-first century. The assumption that to be modern meant to be secular was no longer sufficient to deal adequately with events that were taking place across the globe, not to mention their repercussions nearer home.

Understanding the various stages of this story, including their implications for sociological analysis, is the goal of the paragraphs that follow. The argument works in stages. The situation as such will be summarized very briefly – simply to set the scene. Attention will then be paid to the flood of research that this new awareness of religion has prompted, both in Britain and beyond. Most important of all, however, is a growing realization that the step-change in research activity is itself generating new and urgent questions for the social scientific community, many of which remain unanswered.

The current state of affairs, set out at length in the previous chapters, can be précised thus. Religion (in all its diversity) is no longer invisible either to society as a whole or to the academic community. It is increasingly present in public debate, despite the fact that indices of religious activity are falling rather than rising. Immigration – the process by which the 'world' arrives on our doorstep – is a crucial element in this narrative, noting that the initial debate in this respect took place in terms of ethnicity rather than religion. This was so for an obvious reason: racial or ethnic differences were easier for social scientists to deal with within their existing paradigms than their religious equivalents. Bit by bit, however, the mismatch between the perceptions of western scholars, and the preferred identities of the incoming communities that were establishing themselves had to be acknowledged, a shift in which the presence of Islam was central. As a result religion and religious differences became increasingly relevant to the agendas of many European societies, including Britain. Such issues, however, were more often than not constructed as a 'problem', an image exacerbated by the violence of events elsewhere.

What followed was essentially a delayed reaction. Denial that religion was a salient public matter gradually gave way to alarm, producing in a remarkably short space of time the phenomenon referenced in Chapter 9: namely an impressive array of generously funded research programmes, a wide variety of government initiatives and an avalanche of publications. The details of this 'research mountain' can only be summarized here. The crucial point to appreciate, however, is that the Religion and Society Programme in Britain, on which I have drawn repeatedly, is simply one of many (Davie 2011). Very similar undertakings can be found in the Netherlands, Switzerland, Denmark, Sweden and Canada.[9] Simultaneously the Sixth and Seventh Framework Programmes of the European Commission supported an extended series of projects relating to the growing diversity of Europe and its consequences for economic, political and social life.[10] The policy implications of the European programmes were firmly underlined in the relevant research calls.

Indeed the subtext of all this activity – national as well as international – is unmistakable and revolves around the following question: is the growing religious diversity present in this part of the world damaging to social cohesion, and if so, what is to be done? The multiple projects assembled in the initiatives listed above interrogate these questions in a wide variety of fields (politics, democracy, law, education, welfare), in which key values (tolerance, acceptance, respect, rights, responsibilities, inclusion, exclusion) are thoroughly explored. Unsurprisingly much of this work foregrounds the presence and aspirations of minorities and the reactions of host societies to these groups. Identities can no longer be taken for granted in a continent where movement and migration are commonplace, including – it should be noted – the movement of significant numbers of people from one part of Europe to another. Fluctuations in the economy are central to what is happening in that they exacerbate the associated tensions.

A number of significant points emerge from this all too rapid overview. First it is important to differentiate between projects and programmes. There have always been research *projects* relating to religion, many of which have yielded significant data, not to mention new ways of thinking. These have been valuable initiatives. In the last decade, however, something rather different has appeared: that is, a series of research *programmes*, which are designed to gather together a wide variety of projects and to ensure that the latter add up to more than the sum of their parts. It is the systematic approach to the study of religion which is new. This development, together with the strikingly generous funding that supports it, is growing in momentum. Second, the fact that so much research activity occurred at more or less the same time is not, I contend, a coincidence; it has been brought about by similar anxieties about the place of religion in modern European societies and is motivated by alarm rather than curiosity.

Whatever the motivations, the implications are far-reaching. The numbers of scholars involved in these programmes, their individual and joint publications, the conferences that they both host and attend and the impact that their work will have outside as well as inside the academy have undoubtedly made a difference. New knowledge has been generated in abundance, a new generation of researchers has been trained, and new possibilities for collaboration are emerging all the time. As a result new fields of study are becoming apparent almost by the day. Four of these formed the substance of Chapter 10: the growing significance of religion for law and law-making, the need for politicians (and thus political scientists) to adjust their perspectives, the renewed attention to religion in connection with welfare, and fresh initiatives in health care and healing. All four, moreover, require the input of very different groups of scholars and in themselves have generated new forms of inter-disciplinarity. The interactions of law and social science are particularly striking in this respect.

Responding to New Questions

It is hardly surprising that new sets of questions are emerging from these partnerships, two of which will be prioritized in this section. The first is the notion of the post-secular itself, asking whether or not this is a helpful approach to the understanding of religion in the twenty-first century; the second considers the capacities of the social sciences to respond creatively to what is happening. The discussion as a whole recalls my earlier writing in this field but moves beyond this. At the same time it poses fresh challenges for the new – and very impressive – generation of scholars who are currently entering the field.

The term 'post-secular' moved centre-stage following a series of interventions by the distinguished philosopher, Jürgen Habermas. One of these was the address that he gave following the award of the Holberg prize in 2005.[11] Habermas' lecture, entitled 'Religion in the Public Sphere' began thus: 'We can hardly fail to notice the fact that religious traditions and communities of faith have gained a new, hitherto unexpected political importance'. It continues: 'The fact is at least unexpected for those of us who followed the conventional wisdom of mainstream social science and assumed that modernization inevitably goes hand in hand with secularization in the sense of a diminishing influence of religious beliefs and practices on politics and society at large' (Habermas 2005: 10). In short, religion has reappeared as a political force; this was not expected to happen; and the reason for the unexpectedness was the confident assertions of mainstream social science, which assumed that the processes of modernization and secularization were concomitant.

A second intervention can be found in a cogently argued article published in the *European Journal of Philosophy*, which addresses the idea of the post-secular in terms of John Rawls' celebrated concept, the 'public use of reason' (Habermas 2006: 3). The challenge that emerges is provocative: Habermas invites of secular citizens, including Europeans, 'a self-reflective transcending of the secularist self-understanding of Modernity' (2006: 15) – an attitude that quite clearly goes beyond 'mere tolerance' in that it necessarily engenders feelings of respect for the world view of the religious person. There is in fact a growing reciprocity in the argument. Historically, religious citizens had to adapt to an increasingly secular environment in order to survive at all. Secular citizens were better placed in that they avoided, almost by definition, 'cognitive dissonances' in the modern secular state. This however is no longer the case as religion and religious issues increasingly pervade the agenda. An additional question follows from this. Are these issues simply to be regarded as relics of a pre-modern era, or is it the duty of the more secular citizen to overcome his or her narrowly secularist consciousness in order to engage with religion in terms of *'reasonably expected disagreement'* (Habermas 2006: 15), assuming, in other words, a degree of rationality on both sides? It seems that the latter expectation has prevailed.

Habermas' claims are challenging in every sense of the term and merit very careful reflection. They constitute an innovative response to the changes in the global environment – one moreover in which the relative secularity of Europe is increasingly seen as an exceptional, rather than prototypical, case. Unsurprisingly his interventions have provoked a lively debate, which for the most part lies beyond the scope of this chapter.[12] The contributions of three scholars are, however, central to the argument presented here. The first two – Hans Joas and David Martin – address a similar question, asking whether either the secular or the post-secular is a unitary concept. The third – James Beckford – has comparable concerns but pushes the argument further. Helpfully in terms of the present discussion, he grounds his criticism in a detailed analysis of the British case.

Hans Joas has written extensively in this field, in a body of work which interrogates the connections between modernization and secularization. In the course of this enquiry he pays close attention to the imprecise use of both these concepts, noting in particular up to seven different meanings of the term 'secular' (Joas 2002; Joas and Wiegandt 2009). Such complexities, he argues, must be squarely faced. It is in working through them that a better understanding of late modern society will emerge, not in an exaggerated contrast between an oversimplified, and thus distorting, understanding of either the secular or post-secular. David Martin argues similarly in a discussion which draws on five decades of scholarship. As early as the 1960s, Martin urged caution regarding the idea of secularization, underlining the manifest confusions surrounding this term, not to mention its ideological overtones. Some 50 years later, he advises similar prudence with respect to the post-secular, fearing that the same confusions might happen again. Specifically, he affirms the persistence rather than the resurgence of religion, including its presence in public debate – for which reason he questions the notion (the idea itself) of privatization. Is this the correct word to describe what has happened even in Europe (Martin 2011: 6–7)? Much of the evidence suggests otherwise. The interactions of the religious and the secular should rather be seen in the long term. 'Religious thrusts' and 'secular recoils' have happened for centuries rather than decades and – crucially for Martin – they work themselves out differently in different places. It follows that the indicators regarding religion in the modern world need careful and contextual scrutiny; the shorthand of 'God is back' cannot do justice to this urgent and complex agenda.

The development of religion in Britain in the late twentieth and twenty-first centuries – including its 'thrusts and recoils' – has been set out in the preceding chapters, in which the distinctiveness of the British situation (and within this England, Scotland Wales and Northern Ireland) has been repeatedly emphasized. Martin's work has been central to this analysis. In his presidential address to the 2011 meeting of the Society for the Scientific Study of Religion, James Beckford (2012b) adds a further layer to this critique. He begins by comparing the present situation to earlier debates, specifically by comparing the post-secular to the ambiguities surrounding the post-modern a decade or so earlier. His reactions, moreover, are not only similar but characteristically thorough in both cases. Each concept is subject to rigorous interrogation in order to expose their frailties.[13] For example, with regard to the post-secular, Beckford starts by identifying the multiple strands embedded within this much-used term, not all of which are compatible with each other. The discussion, it follows, is necessarily confused in that different scholars are talking about different things. Two points are worth noting in particular: first, that different disciplines adopt this term in different ways; and second, that a frequently normative discourse does not always pay attention to empirical detail.

In the second part of his address – and to bring home the point about empirical detail – Beckford explores recent changes in the management of religion in Britain. He notes three aspects in particular: an increase in religious diversity, the application of equalities legislation to 'religion or belief' and the promotion of social enterprise policies across government departments, all of which have been covered in previous chapters and all of which have increased the visibility of religion in public debate. But is the term post-secular helpful in this context? Beckford is not convinced, for reasons which are markedly similar to those evoked by Joas and Martin: namely that the concept of the post-secular mirrors simplistic accounts of the secular. To be properly understood, both ideas must be earthed in a detailed, historically informed account, which will reveal – amongst other things – what counts as 'religion' in public life in any particular case. All too often this is simply taken for granted.

I take their point, but as a postscript to this discussion I will add a personal note. I welcome the current debate concerning the post-secular and the growing body of literature that surrounds it (see, for example, Molendijk, Beaumont and Jedan 2010; Baker and Beaumont 2011). Both are signs that religion is taken seriously – that is a good thing. I accept, moreover, that the notion of the post-secular needs considerable refinement in order to be used effectively. That said, I need a term to capture the two things that are happening simultaneously in British society: the decrease in religious activity measured over a wide range of variables, alongside the growing significance of religion in public debate. If I cannot use the term post-secular to describe this, how am I to evoke the paradox that underpins the argument of this book?

Turning now to the more general capacities of social science to respond creatively to what is happening, it is important to bring together the two themes that have been central to my thinking in the last 20 years. The first finds its focus in describing and explaining the religious situation in different parts of the modern world. The widening canvas on which I have worked in this respect was outlined in the Preface. The second theme concerns the development of the sociology of religion as a sub-discipline, asking in particular whether the ways of thinking embodied in this field are up to the task required of them. Are they, in other words, fit for purpose? In 2007, I published the first edition of *The Sociology of Religion*, in which I considered the agenda of the sociology of religion to be critical – in two senses (Davie 2007c). It was vital that we understood the place of religion in the twenty-first century and its continuing role in the lives of countless individuals and the societies of which they are part. I was, however, critical of a sub-discipline that did not always rise to this challenge – all too often sociological analyses were locked into old paradigms that had difficulty dealing with the rising significance of religion both in Britain and elsewhere. A second edition of *The Sociology of Religion* was published in 2013. The marked acceleration in research and research funding described in this chapter took place between the two editions.

An obvious question follows from this. Has the step-change in research activity stimulated a similar step-change in sociological thinking about religion? On the positive side, it is my firm belief that the sociology of religion – indeed the study of religion in general – is now in better shape that it was a decade ago. I embrace this shift unreservedly, but remain sceptical about the motivations for much of the work being done. By and large, religion is still perceived as a 'problem' – and in order to be better managed, it must be thoroughly researched. Such a statement requires, however, immediate qualification. It is more applicable in some places than in others, to some disciplines than to others, and to some researchers than to others. Broadly speaking the potential of religion to become a positive resource is most easily appreciated by those who know it best. Thinking globally, American scholars find it easier than their European counterparts, while those who work in the developing world find it easier still – notably anthropologists, missiologists and (some) development workers.[14] The reason is clear enough: researchers who 'live' in the field (in whatever capacity and in whatever kind of society) are more likely to display a respect for their subjects and the lifestyles they embrace, including their religious dimensions. Respect includes of course a critical perspective – at times a sharp one.

Such principles can be applied nearer home. It is this reasoning that leads me to commend a younger generation of scholars who are better trained than I was in the imaginative methodologies that are required to assess the significance of religion in the everyday lives of individuals and communities in different parts of Britain. A number of these approaches emerged from the Religion and Society Programme and have been referenced in this book; they are brought together in Woodhead (forthcoming). A second example of innovative thinking in this respect can be found in the online training in 'Research Methods for the Study of Religion' offered to postgraduates through the Department of Theology and Religious Studies at the University of Kent.[15] As the introduction to this project makes clear: 'The role of empirical research in the study of religion has become increasingly important in recent years.

In the discipline of Religious Studies, more postgraduate students are undertaking field-work based projects, and in other social science disciplines there has been a renewed interest in religion as an area of study.' The range of methods explored in this training initiative is noticeably varied, but together they add up to an impressive set of resources for the postgraduate (or researcher) embarking in this field. Once again it is the systematic approach to the topic that is striking.

Two points, it follows, are beyond doubt. Increasing numbers of researchers from many different disciplines are currently engaged in the study of religion and much of their work is innovative in terms of method as well as substance. But for social scientists in particular this suggests a further challenge: the need to penetrate the philosophical core of the associated disciplines and to enquire what difference the serious study of religion might make to their ways of working. Before confronting this question directly, however, a revealing parenthesis should be noted. A great deal of the activity outlined in this book is taking place in departments of theology and religious studies rather than in departments of sociology, a statement supported by tracking the recent appointments in the empirical study of religion (sociological, psychological or political). Exceptions can be found – for the most part in newer universities – but more often not these openings have emerged in centres for the study of religion rather than in clusters of social science.[16]

The reason all too often lies in a persistent – and at times damaging – reluctance on the part of sociology and other social sciences to admit that to be seriously religious is indeed compatible with being fully modern. Despite everything, the combination remains a sticking point. In many ways this is hardly surprising: the disciplines in question have emerged more or less directly from the European Enlightenment, implying that they are underpinned by a markedly secular philosophy of social science. As Jürgen Habermas and Hans Joas have implied, from the nineteenth century onwards it was simply assumed that modernization would bring about secularization. The fact, moreover, that this branch of learning expanded exponentially in the 1960s is no coincidence (see p. 32): the social sciences, both pure and applied, thrived on the secular assumptions of this decade and are reluctant to give them up. Unpicking connections as deep-seated as these will not be easy. It will require the disciplines in question to rethink the foundations of their respective fields of study, in order to accommodate fully the implications of religion and religious issues in their analyses of modern societies. This, moreover, means accepting religion as it is, not as we would like it to be. Above all, it must be driven by data, and the critical thinking that surround this, not by the overly secular assumptions of 'traditional' paradigms. Meeting this challenge is, in my view, the primary task for the new generation of scholars embarking in this field.

I will make a more limited claim for this book. If nothing else I hope that it will improve the religious literacy of those that read it. That in itself will make a difference.

Notes

1   For a broader overview of the religion and media field, see Knott and Mitchell (2012).
2   The full title of Lövheim's edited text, *Media, Religion and Gender: Key Issues and New Challenges*, reveals her concomitant interest in gender.
3   See, for example, the evidence gathered together in Brewitt-Taylor (2013). Senior churchmen of differing denominations (John Robinson, Michael Ramsey and Donald Soper, for example) were convinced that they were living in a 'secular age', to the extent that they found the persistence, rather than the loss, of interest in Christianity the thing to be explained.
4   See http://www.religionandsociety.org.uk/events/programme_events/show/new_forms_of_public_religion (accessed 8 August 2014) for the details of the conference and for the podcast of Professor Woodhead's address.
5   The similarities with Danièle Hervieu-Léger's 'pilgrim' and 'convert' are evident at this point. See Chapter 7.
6   The situation in the United States is similar (Pew Forum on Religion and Public Life 2012).
7   Samuel Huntington's (1993, 1996) work can be taken as an example. His thinking on the clash of civilizations dominated debate in the 1990s, both in the United States and beyond.
8   The shorthand of 'God is Back' is taken from the title of a widely read book; see Micklethwait and Wooldridge (2009).
9   For the work in the Netherlands, see http://www.nwo.nl/en/research-and-results/programmes/the+future+of+the+religious+past; in Switzerland, see http://www.nfp58.ch/e_index.cfm; in Denmark, see Christoffersen *et al.* (2010) and Christoffersen, Modéer and Andersen (2010); in Sweden, see http://www.crs.uu.se/Research/impactofreligion; ; and in Canada, see http://www.religionanddiversity.ca. In Denmark and Sweden the approach was a little different; it was clustered in a particular university rather than spread over several institutions. All websites were accessed on 8 August 2014.
10 See http://cordis.europa.eu/home_en.html (accessed 8 August 2014) for more information about the European Commission's Framework Programmes.
11 See http://www.holbergprisen.no/en/juergen-habermas/holberg-prize-symposium-2005.html (accessed 8 August 2014) for the details of the symposium that took place on this occasion. Professor Habermas's lecture can be downloaded in full.
12 The very disparate elements brought together in these exchanges are well summarized in Beckford (2012b).
13 Beckford's attention to conceptual clarity is central to his work as a whole. It was equally clear, for example, in his approach to pluralism (see pp. 155–56).

Quite apart from this, the parallels between the post-modern and the post-secular can be extended to a whole series of similar terms which denote the changing nature of late modern societies and the cultural expressions associated with these developments. This is a controversial field.

14   The benefits or otherwise of engaging religion for development were discussed at a Westminster Faith Debate. See http://faithdebates.org.uk/debates/do-benefits-of-engaging-religion-for-development-outweigh-dangers/# (accessed 7 August 2014).

15   The details of this impressive training programme can be found at http://www.kent.ac.uk/religionmethods/index.html (accessed 8 August 2014).

16   Generalizations of this nature need to be treated with caution. I find it interesting, however, that a wide-ranging 'Programme in the Study of Religion and Non-Religion' has been launched in the Department of Anthropology at the London School of Economics, rather than in Sociology, which was a centre for the sociology of religion in the mid post-war decades. It was here that David Martin and Eileen Barker (among others) did some of their most influential work. For more details of the programme as such, see http://www.lse.ac.uk/anthropology/research/PRNR/Home.aspx (accessed 8 August 2014).

References

Abercrombie, Nicholas, John Baker, Sebastian Brett and Jane Foster. 1970. 'Superstition and Religion: The God of the Gaps.' In *A Sociological Yearbook of Religion in Britain 3*, edited by David Martin and Michael Hill, pp.91–129. London: SCM Press.

Ahern, Geoffrey and Grace Davie. 1987. *Inner City God: The Nature of Belief in the Inner City*. London: Hodder and Stoughton.

Ammerman, Nancy. 1997. *Congregation and Community*. New Brunswick, NJ: Rutgers University Press.

Ammerman, Nancy. 2005. *Pillars of Faith: American Congregations and their Partners*. Berkeley, CA: University of California Press.

ap Siôn Tania. 2009. 'Ordinary Prayer and the Rural Church: An Empirical Study of Prayer Cards.' *Rural Theology*, 7, 1: 17–31. DOI: 10.1558/ruth2009v7i1.17.

ap Siôn, Tania. 2010. 'Implicit Religion and Ordinary Prayer.' *Implicit Religion*, 13, 3: 275–294. DOI: 10.1558/imre.v13i3.275.

Arweck, Elisabeth, ed. Forthcoming. *Young People's Attitudes to Religious Diversity: Findings from a Mixed-Methods Research Project*. Farnham: Ashgate.

Arweck, Elisabeth and Robert Jackson, eds. 2013. *Religion, Education and Society*. London: Routledge.

Aune, Kristin, Sonya Sharma and Giselle Vincett, eds. 2008. *Women and Religion in the West: Challenging Secularization*. Farnham: Ashgate.

Baker, Christopher and Justin Beaumont, eds. 2011. *Postsecular Cities: Religious Space, Theory and Practice*. London: Continuum.

Ball, Jonathan. 2013. '"O Hear Us When We Cry to Thee": Liturgy in the Current Operational Context.' In *Military Chaplaincy in Contention: Chaplains, Churches and the Morality of Conflict*, edited by Andrew Todd, pp.113–132. Farnham: Ashgate.

Religion in Britain: A Persistent Paradox, Second Edition. Grace Davie.
© 2015 Grace Davie. Published 2015 by John Wiley & Sons, Ltd.

Barker, Eileen. 1982. 'A Sociologist Looks at the Statistics.' In *The UK Christian Handbook, 1983 Edition*, edited by Peter Brierley, pp.5–9. London: Marc Europe.

Barker, Eileen. 1984. *The Making of a Moonie: Choice or Brainwashing*. Oxford: Blackwell.

Barker, Eileen. 1989a. *New Religious Movements: A Practical Introduction*. London: HMSO.

Barker, Eileen. 1989b. 'Tolerant Discrimination: Church, State and the New Religions.' In *Religion, State and Society in Modern Britain*, edited by Paul Badham, pp.185–208. Lewiston: Edwin Mellen Press.

Barley, Linda. 2012. 'Stirrings in Barchester: Cathedrals and Church Growth.' In *Church Growth in Britain*, edited by David Goodhew, pp.77–90. Farnham: Ashgate.

Beaumont, Justin and Paul Cloke, eds. 2012. *Faith-based Organizations and Exclusion in European Cities*. Bristol: Policy Press.

Beckford, James. 1975. *The Trumpet of Prophecy: A Sociological Study of Jehovah's Witnesses*. London: Blackwell.

Beckford, James. 1985. *Cult Controversies*. London: Tavistock.

Beckford James. 1991. 'Politics and Religion in England and Wales.' *Daedalus*, 120, 3: 179–201.

Beckford, James. 2003. *Social Theory and Religion*. Cambridge: Cambridge University Press.

Beckford, James. 2005. 'Muslims in the Prisons of Britain and France.' *Journal of Contemporary European Studies*, 13, 3: 287–297.

Beckford, James, 2007. 'Prison Chaplaincy in England and Wales: From Anglican "Brokerage" to a Multi-faith Approach.' In *Democracy and Human Rights in Multicultural Societies*, edited by Matthias Koenig and Paul de Guchteneire, pp.267–282. Paris and Aldershot: UNESCO and Ashgate Press.

Beckford, James. 2012a. 'Reified Knowledge about "Religion" in Prisons.' In *Religion and Knowledge. Sociological Perspectives*, edited by Mathew Guest and Elisabeth Arweck, pp.25–38. Farnham: Ashgate.

Beckford, James. 2012b. 'Public Religions and the Postsecular: Critical Reflections.' The SSSR Presidential Address. *Journal for the Scientific Study of Religion*, 51, 1: 1–19. DOI: 10.1111/j.1468-5906.2011.01625.x.

Beckford, James. 2013. 'Religious Diversity in Prisons: Chaplaincy and Contention.' *Studies in Religion/Sciences Religieuses*, 42, 2: 190–205. DOI: 10.1177/0008429813479293.

Beckford, James and Sophie Gilliat. 1998. *Religion in Prison: 'Equal Rites' in a Multi-Faith Society*. Cambridge: Cambridge University Press.

Beckford, James, Danièle Joly and Farhad Khosrokhavar. 2005. *Muslims in Prison: Challenge and Change in Britain and France*. Basingstoke: Palgrave Macmillan.

Béraud, Céline, Claire de Galembert and Corinne Rostaing. 2013. *Des hommes et des dieux en prison*. Convention de recherche entre le Ministère de la Justice-DAP et le CNRS-ISP (UMR 7220), no. 210.09.15.34.

Berger, Peter, Grace Davie and Effie Fokas. 2008. *Religious America, Secular Europe: A Theme and Variations*. Farnham: Ashgate.

Berman, Gavin and Aliyah Dar. 2013. 'Prison Population Statistics.' Commons Library Standard Note. Available at http://www.parliament.uk/business/publi cations/research/briefing-papers/SN04334/prison-population-statistics. Accessed 12 August 2014.

Billings, Alan. 2004. *Secular Lives, Sacred Hearts*. London: SPCK.

Birdwell, Jonathan, with Stephen Timms, eds. 2013. *The Faith Collection*. London: Demos.

Birt, Yahya, Dilwar Hussain and Ataullah Siddiqui, eds. 2011. *British Secularism and Religion: Islam, Society and the State*. Markfield: Kube Publishing Ltd.

Bluck, Robert. 2012. 'Buddhism.' In *Religion and Change in Modern Britain*, edited by Linda Woodhead and Rebecca Catto, pp.131–143. London: Routledge.

Bocock, Robert and Kenneth Thompson, eds. 1985. *Religion and Ideology*. Manchester: Manchester University Press.

Bowman, Marion. 1993. 'Drawn to Glastonbury.' In *Pilgrimage in Popular Culture*, edited by Ian Reader and Tony Walter, pp.29–62. Basingstoke and London: Palgrave Macmillan.

Bowman, Marion. 2003–2004. 'Taking Stories Seriously: Vernacular Religion, Contemporary Spirituality and the Myth of Jesus in Glastonbury.' *Temenos*, 39–40: 125–142.

Bowman, Marion. 2005. 'Ancient Avalon, New Jerusalem, Heart Chakra of Planet Earth: Localisation and Globalisation in Glastonbury.' *Numen*, 52, 2: 157–190. DOI: 10.1163/1568527054024722.

Bowman, Marion. 2008. 'Going with the Flow: Contemporary Pilgrimage in Glastonbury.' In *Shrines and Pilgrimage in the Modern World: New Itineraries into the Sacred*, edited by Peter Jan Margry, pp.241–280. Amsterdam: Amsterdam University Press.

Bowman, Marion. 2013. 'Valuing Spirituality: Commodification, Consumption and Community in Glastonbury.' In *Religion in a Consumer Society: Brands, Consumers and Markets*, edited by François Gautier and Tuomas Martikainen, pp.207–224. Farnham: Ashgate.

Bowman, Marion. 2015. 'Christianity, Plurality and Vernacular Religion in Early Twentieth Century Glastonbury: A Sign of Things to Come?' In *Christianity and Religious Plurality*, Studies in Church History 51, edited by Charlotte Methuen, Andrew Spicer and John Wolffe. Woodbridge: Boydell and Brewer.

Breaking New Ground: Church Planting in the Church of England. 1994. London: Church House Publishing.

Brewitt-Taylor, Sam. 2012. '*Christian Radicalism' in the Church of England, 1957–70*. Unpublished DPhil thesis, University of Oxford.

Brewitt-Taylor, Sam. 2013. 'The Invention of a "Secular Society"? Christianity and the Sudden Appearance of Secularization Discourses in the British National Media, 1961–4.' Duncan Tanner Essay Prize Winner 2012. *Twentieth Century British History* 24, 3: 327–350. DOI: 10.1093/tcbh/hwt012.

Brierley, Peter. 2006. *Pulling Out of the Nosedive: A Contemporary Picture of Churchgoing – What the 2005 English Church Census Reveals*. London: Christian Research Association. Available at http://www.brierleyconsultancy. com/nosedive.html. Accessed 12 August 2014.

Brierley, Peter. 2011. *UK Church Statistics, 2005–2015*. Tonbridge: ADBC Publishers.

Brierley, Peter. 2013. *Capital Growth: The London Church Census*. Tonbridge: ADBC Publishers. Available at http://www.brierleyconsultancy.com/capital growth.html. Accessed 12 August 2014.

Brierley, Peter. 2014. *UK Church Statistics No 2, 2010–2020*. Tonbridge: ADBC Publishers. Available at http://brierleyconsultancy.com/statistics.html. Accessed 16 October 2014.

Brierley, Peter and Val Hiscock, eds. 1993. *UK Christian Handbook 1994–5 Edition*. London: Christian Research Association.

Brown, Callum. 1987. *The Social History of Religion in Scotland*. London: Methuen. [A revised edition was published in 1997 under the title *Religion and Society in Scotland since 1707*. Edinburgh: Edinburgh University Press.]

Brown, Callum, 2001. *The Death of Christian Britain*. London: Routledge. [A revised edition was published in 2009.]

Bruce, Steve. 1986. *God Save Ulster. The Religion and Politics of Paisleyism*. Oxford: Clarendon Press.

Bruce, Steve. 2002. 'Praying Alone? Church-Going in Britain and the Putnam Thesis.' *Journal of Contemporary Religion*, 17, 3: 317–328. DOI: 10.1080/1353790022000008244.

Bruce, Steve. 2013a. 'Secularization and Church Growth in the United Kingdom.' *Journal of Religion in Europe*, 6, 3: 273–294. DOI: 10.1163/18748929-00602005.

Bruce, Steve. 2013b. 'Further Thoughts on Church Growth and Secularization.' *Journal of Religion in Europe*, 6, 3: 316–312. DOI: 10.1163/18748929-00602007.

Bruce, Steve and David Voas, 2010. 'Vicarious Religion: An Examination and Critique.' *Journal of Contemporary Religion*, 25, 2: 243–259. DOI: 10.1080/13537901003750936.

Bullivant, Stephen. 2010. 'The New Atheism and Sociology: Why Here? Why Now? What Next?' In *Religion and the New Atheism: A Critical Appraisal*, edited by Amarnath Amarasingam, pp.109–124. Leiden: Brill.

Bullivant, Stephen. 2012. 'Not so Indifferent After All? The New Visibility of Atheism and the Secularization Thesis.' *Approaching Religion*, 2, 1: 100–106.

Cameron, Helen. 2001. 'Social Capital in Britain: Are Hall's Membership Figures a Reliable Guide?' Paper presented to the 2001 ARNOVA Conference, Miami, FL.

Cantle, Ted. 2011. 'Secular Governance in a Multi-Faith Society.' In *British Secularism and Religion: Islam, Society and the State*, edited by Yahya Birt, Dilwar Hussain and Ataullah Siddiqui, pp.55–76. Markfield: Kube Publishing Ltd.

Cantle, Ted. 2012. *Interculturalism: The New Era of Cohesion and Diversity*. Basingstoke: Palgrave Macmillan.

Carrette, Jeremy and Richard King. 2004. *Selling Spirituality: The Silent Takeover of Religion*. London: Routledge.

Castro, Stephen. 1996. *Hypocrisy and Dissent within the Findhorn Foundation: Towards a Sociology of a New Age Community*. Forres: New Media Books.

Catto, Rebecca. 2008. *From the Rest to the West: Exploring Reversal in Christian Mission in Twenty-first Century Britain*. Unpublished PhD thesis, University of Exeter.

Catto, Rebecca, 2012. 'Reverse Mission: From the Global South to the Mainline Churches.' In *Church Growth in Britain*, edited by David Goodhew, pp.91–103. Farnham: Ashgate.

Catto, Rebecca and Janet Eccles. 2011. 'Beyond Grayling, Dawkins and Hitchens, a New Kind of British Atheism.' Comment is Free at *The Guardian*. Available athttp://www.theguardian.com/commentisfree/belief/2011/apr/14/atheism-socialnetworking. Accessed 12 August 2014.

Catto, Rebecca and Janet Eccles. 2013. '(Dis)Believing and Belonging: Investigating the Narrative of Young British Atheists.' *Temenos*, 49, 2: 37–63.

Catto, Rebecca and David Perfect. Forthcoming. 'Religious Literacy, Equalities and Human Rights.' In *Religious Literacy in Secular Society: Theories, Policies and Practices of Faith in the Public Realm*, edited by Adam Dinham and Mat Francis. Bristol: Policy Press.

Chambers, Paul. 2012. 'Economic Factors in Church Growth and Decline in South and South West Wales.' In *Church Growth in Britain*, edited by David Goodhew, pp.221–236. Farnham: Ashgate.

Chambers, Paul and Andrew Thompson. 2005. 'Public Religion and Political Change in Wales.' *Sociology*, 39, 1: 29–46. DOI: 10.1177/0038038505048999.

Chapman, Mark, ed. 2011. *The Established Church: Past, Present and Future*. Edinburgh: T&T Clark International.

Christoffersen, Lisbet, Hans Raun Iversen, Hanne Petersen and Margit Warburg, eds. 2010. *Religion in the 21st Century: Challenge and Transformations*. Farnham: Ashgate.

Christoffersen, Lisbet, Kjell A. Modéer and Svend Andersen, eds. 2010. *Law and Religion in the 21st Century: Nordic Perspectives*. Copenhagen: DJOF Publishing.

Clements, Ben. Forthcoming. *Religion and Public Opinion in Britain: Change and Continuity*. Basingstoke: Palgrave Macmillan.

Cloke, Paul, Sarah Johnsen and Jon May. 2012. 'Ethical Citizenship? Faith-based Volunteers and the Ethics of Providing Services for Homeless People.' In *Faith-based Organisations and Exclusion in European Cities*, edited by Justin Beaumont and Paul Cloke, pp.127–154. Bristol: Policy Press.

Cobb, Mark, Christina M. Puchalski and Bruce Rumbold, eds. 2012. *Oxford Textbook of Spirituality in Healthcare*. Oxford: Oxford University Press.

Coleman, Peter. 2011. *Belief and Ageing: Spiritual Pathways in Later Life*. Bristol: Policy Press.

Coleman, Peter, Daniela Koleva and Joanna Bornat. 2013. *Ageing, Ritual and Social Change: Comparing the Secular and Religious in Eastern and Western Europe*. Farnham: Ashgate.

Coleman, Simon. Forthcoming. 'Locating the Church: From Parish to Pilgrimage?' In *Contemporary Issues in the Worldwide Anglican Communion: Powers and Pieties*, edited by Abby Day. Farnham: Ashgate.

Collins-Mayo, Sylvia. 2013. 'Street Prayer: A Case Study of the Use of Prayer by Street Pastors.' In *Annual Review of the Sociology of Religion, 2013, Volume 4:*

Prayer in Religion and Spirituality, edited by Giuseppe Giordan and Linda Woodhead, pp.173–188. Leiden: Brill.

Collins-Mayo, Sylvia and Pink Dandelion, eds. 2010. *Religion and Youth*. Farnham: Ashgate.

Collins-Mayo, Sylvia, Andrew King and Lee Jones. 2012. *Faith in Action: Street Pastors Kingston Social and Spiritual Impact Project*. Final Report available from Sylvia Collins-Mayo, Kingston University. A Research Briefing is available at http://kingston.streetpastors.org.uk/wp-content/uploads/2012/04/Kingston-University-Briefing-on-Street-Pastors.pdf. Accessed 12 August 2014.

Collins-Mayo, Sylvia, Bob Mayo and Sally Nash. 2010. *The Faith of Generation Y*. London: Church House Publishing.

Connor, Phillip. 2014. *Immigrant Faith: Patterns of Immigrant Religion in the United States, Canada, and Western Europe*. New York: New York University Press.

Conroy, James. 2012. 'What's Happening to Religious Education in Schools is a Disaster for Britain.' Contribution to the Westminster Faith Debate on 'What's the Place for Faith in Schools.' Available at http://faithdebates.org.uk/wp-content/uploads/2013/09/1329132950_Conroy-final.pdf. Accessed 12 August 2014.

Conroy, James, David Lundie, Robert Davis, Vivienne Baumfield, L. Philip Barnes, Tony Gallagher, Kevin Lowden, Nicole Bourque and Karen Wenell. 2013. *Does Religious Education Work? A Multi-Dimensional Investigation*. London: Bloomsbury.

Cook, Chris, Andrew Powell and Andrew Sims, eds. 2009. *Spirituality and Psychiatry*. London: RCPsych Publications.

Cox, James, Alastair Campbell and Bill Fulford, eds. 2006. *Medicine of the Person: Faith, Science and Values in Health Care Provision*. London: Jessica Kingsley.

Currie, Robert, Alan Gilbert and Lee Horsley. 1977. *Churches and Churchgoers*. Oxford: Clarendon Press.

Davie, Grace. 1994. *Religion in Britain since 1945: Believing Without Belonging*. Oxford: Blackwell.

Davie, Grace. 2000. *Religion in Modern Europe*. Oxford: Oxford University Press.

Davie, Grace. 2002. *Europe: The Exceptional Case. Parameters of Faith in the Modern World*. London: Darton, Longman and Todd.

Davie, Grace. 2006. 'Religion in Europe in the 21st Century: The Factors to Take into Account.' *European Journal of Sociology*, 47, 2: 271–296. DOI: 10.1017/S0003975606000099.

Davie, Grace. 2007a. 'Pluralism, Tolerance and Democracy: Theory and Practice in Europe.' In *Democracy and the New Religious Pluralism*, edited by Thomas Banchoff, pp.233–241. New York: Oxford University Press.

Davie, Grace. 2007b. 'Vicarious Religion: A Methodological Challenge.' In *Everyday Religion: Observing Modern Religious Lives*, edited by Nancy Ammerman, pp.21–36. New York: Oxford University Press.

Davie, Grace. 2007c. *The Sociology of Religion*. London: Sage Publications. [A revised edition was published in 2013.]

Davie, Grace. 2008. 'Debate.' In *Praying for England: Priestly Presence in Contemporary Culture*, edited by Samuel Wells and Sarah Coakley, pp.147–170. London: Continuum.

Davie, Grace. 2010a. 'Vicarious Religion: A Response.' *Journal of Contemporary Religion*, 25, 2: 261–266. DOI: 10.1080/13537901003750944.

Davie, Grace. 2010b. 'An English Example: Exploring the Via Media in the Twenty-First Century.' In *Between Relativism and Fundamentalism*, edited by Peter Berger, pp.35–55. Grand Rapids, MI: Eerdmans.

Davie, Grace. 2011. 'Thinking Sociologically about Religion: A Step Change in the Debate?' (ARDA Guiding Paper Series). State College, PA: The Association of Religion Data Archives at the Pennsylvania State University. Available at http://www.thearda.com/rrh/papers/guidingpapers.asp. Accessed 12 August 2014.

Davie, Grace. 2012. 'A European Perspective on Religion and Welfare: Contrasts and Commonalities.' *Social Policy and Society*, 11, 4: 989–999. DOI: 10.1017/S1474746412000267.

Davie, Grace. 2013. *The Sociology of Religion. A Critical Agenda*, 2nd ed. London: Sage Publications.

Davie, Grace. 2014. 'Managing Pluralism: The European Case.' *Society*, 51, 6: 613–622. DOI: 10.1007/s12115-014-9834-6.

Davie, Grace and Derek Hearl. 1991. 'Politics and Religion in the South West.' In *Centre and Periphery: Brittany and Devon and Cornwall Compared*, edited by Michael Havinden, Jean Quéniart and Jeffrey Stanyer, pp.214–212. Exeter: University of Exeter Press.

Davie, Martin. 2008. *A Guide to the Church of England*. London: Mowbray.

Davison, Andrew and Alison Milbank. 2010. *For the Parish: A Critique of Fresh Expressions*. London: SCM Press.

Dawkins, Richard. 2006. *The God Delusion*. Boston, MA: Houghton Mifflin Harcourt.

Day, Abby. 2011. *Believing in Belonging: Belief and Social Identity in the Modern World*. Oxford: Oxford University Press.

Day, Abby. 2013. 'The Problem of Generalizing Generation.' *Religion and Society: Advances in Research*, 4, 1: 109–124. DOI: 10.3167/arrs.2013.040107.

Day, Abby. Forthcoming. *The Religious Lives of Generation A: Laywomen in the Church*. Oxford: Oxford University Press.

De Botton, Alan. 2013. *Religion for Atheists: A Non-Believer's Guide to the Uses of Religion*. Harmondsworth: Penguin.

Dinham, Adam. 2009. *Faiths, Public Policy and Civil Society: Problems, Policies, Controversies*. Basingstoke: Palgrave MacMillan.

Dinham, Adam. 2012. 'The Multi-faith Paradigm in Policy and Practice: Problems, Challenges, Directions.' *Social Policy and Society*, 11, 4: 577–586. DOI: 10.1017/S1474746412000255.

Dinham, Adam. 2013. 'Welfare is Sacred.' *Public Spirit*. Available at http://www.publicspirit.org.uk/welfare-is-sacred. Accessed 12 August 2014.

Dinham, Adam. Forthcoming. 'Religious Literacy and Welfare'. In *Religious Literacy in Secular Society: Theories, Policies and Practices of Faith in the Public Realm*, edited by Adam Dinham and Mat Francis. Bristol: Policy Press.

Dinham, Adam and Mat Francis, eds. Forthcoming. *Religious Literacy in Secular Society: Theories, Policies and Practices of Faith in the Public Realm*. Bristol: Policy Press.

Dinham, Adam and Robert Jackson. 2012. 'Religion, Welfare and Education.' In *Religion and Change in Modern Britain*, edited by Linda Woodhead and Rebecca Catto, pp.272–294. London: Routledge.

Dinham, Adam, Robert Furbey and Vivien Lowndes, eds. 2009. *Faith in the Public Realm: Controversies, Policies and Practices*. Bristol: Policy Press.

Donald, Alice, Jane Gordon and Philip Leach. 2012. *The UK and the European Court of Human Rights*. Manchester: Equality and Human Rights Commission, Research Report 83.Available at http://www.equalityhumanrights.com/publica tions/our-research/research-reports. Accessed 12 August 2014.

Donald, Alice, with Karen Bennett and Philip Leach. 2012. *Religion or Belief, Equality and Human Rights in England and Wales*. Manchester: Equality and Human Rights Commission, Research Report 84. Available at http://www. equalityhumanrights.com/publications/our-research/research-reports. Accessed 12 August 2014.

Edge, Peter. 2006. *Religion and Law: An Introduction*. Farnham: Ashgate.

Esping-Andersen, Gøsta. 1989. *The Three Worlds of Welfare Capitalism*. Cambridge: Polity Press.

European Commission. 2012. Eurobarometer 73.1 (Jan–Feb 2010). TNS OPINION & SOCIAL, Brussels [Producer]. GESIS Data Archive, Cologne. ZA5000 Data file Version 4.0.0. DOI:10.4232/1.11428.

Evans, John. 2008. *Faith in Wales: Counting for Communities*. Cardiff: Gweini (The Council of the Christian Voluntary Sector in Wales).

Faith in the City. 1985. The Report of the Archbishop of Canterbury's Commission on Urban Priority Areas. London: Church House Publishing.

Faith in the Countryside. 1990. The Report of the Archbishops' Commission on Rural Areas. London: Church House Publishing.

Filby, Eliza. 2015. *God and Mrs Thatcher: Conviction Politics in Britain's Secular Age*. London: Biteback Publishing.

Fokas, Effie. 2013. Intervention in a debate on 'Rethinking Religious-secular Intersec-tions.' Unpublished paper given at the Impact of Religion: Challenges for Society, Law and Democracy Conference, Uppsala, Sweden.

Forrester, Helen. 1981. *Twopence to Cross the Mersey*. London: Fontana/Collins.

Francis, Leslie. 2003. 'Religion and Social Capital: The Flaw in the 2001 Census in England and Wales.' In *Public Faith? The State of Religious Belief and Practice in Britain*, edited by Paul Avis, pp.45–64. London: SPCK.

Gautier, François and Tuomas Martikainen, eds. 2013. *Religion in a Consumer Society: Brands, Consumers and Markets*. Farnham: Ashgate.

Gill, Robin. 1992. *Moral Communities*. Exeter: Exeter University Press.

Gill, Robin. 1993. *The Myth of the Empty Church*. London: SPCK. [A revised edition was published in 2003.]

Gill, Robin. 1999. *Churchgoing and Christian Ethics*. Cambridge: Cambridge University Press.

Gill, Robin. 2002. 'A Response to Steve Bruce's "Praying Alone?"' *Journal of Contemporary Religion*,17,3:335–338.DOI:10.1080/1353790022000008262.

Gill, Robin. 2012. 'Mission-Shaped by Society: York Revisited.' In *Theology Shaped by Society: Sociological Theology*, Volume 2, pp.113–156. Farnham: Ashgate.

Gill, Robin, Kirk Hadaway and Penny Marler. 1998. 'Is Religious Belief Declining in Britain?' *Journal for the Scientific Study of Religion*, 37, 3: 507–516. DOI: 10.2307/1388057.

Gilliat-Ray, Sophie. 2000. *Religion in Higher Education: The Politics of the Multifaith Campus*. Aldershot: Ashgate.

Gilliat-Ray, Sophie. 2003. 'Nursing, Professionalism, and Spirituality.' *Journal of Contemporary Religion*, 18, 3: 335–349. DOI: 10.1080/13537900310001601695.

Gilliat-Ray, Sophie. 2010. *Muslims in Britain: An Introduction*. Cambridge: Cambridge University Press.

Gilliat-Ray, Sophie. 2012. 'Muslims.' In *Religion and Change in Modern Britain*, edited by Linda Woodhead and Rebecca Catto, pp.110–121. London: Routledge.

Gilliat-Ray, Sophie, Stephen Pattison and Mansur Ali. 2013. *Understanding Muslim Chaplaincy*. Farnham: Ashgate.

Glendinning, Tony and Steve Bruce. 2006. 'New Ways of Believing or Belonging: Is Religion Giving Way to Spirituality?' *The British Journal of Sociology*, 57, 3: 399414. DOI: 10.1111/j.1468-4446.2006.00117.x.

Goodhew, David. 2012a. *Church Growth in Britain*. Farnham: Ashgate.

Goodhew, David. 2012b. 'Church Growth in Britain 1980 to the Present Day.' In *Church Growth in Britain*, edited by David Goodhew, pp.3–20. Farnham: Ashgate.

Goodhew, David. 2012c. 'From the Margins to the Mainstream: New Churches in York.' In *Church Growth in Britain*, edited by David Goodhew, pp.179–192. Farnham: Ashgate.

Goodhew, David. 2013. 'Church Growth in Britain: A Response to Steve Bruce.' *Journal of Religion in Europe*, 6, 3: 297–315. DOI: 10.1163/18748929-00602006.

Graham, David. 2012. 'Judaism.' In *Religion and Change in Modern Britain*, edited by Linda Woodhead and Rebecca Catto, pp.89–99. London: Routledge.

Guest, Mathew. 2007. *Evangelical Identity and Contemporary Culture: A Congregational Study in Innovation*. Milton Keynes: Paternoster Press.

Guest, Mathew, Kristin Aune, Sonya Sharma and Rob Warner. 2013. *Christianity and the Student Experience: Understanding Student Faith*. London: Bloomsbury Academic.

Habermas, Jürgen. 2005. 'Religion in the Public Sphere.' Address given on the receipt of the 2005 Holberg Prize. Available at http://www.holbergprisen.no/en/juergen-habermas/holberg-prize-symposium-2005.html. Accessed 12 August 2014.

Habermas Jürgen. 2006. 'Religion in the Public Sphere.' *European Journal of Philosophy*, 14, 1: 1–25. DOI: 10.1111/j.1468-0378.2006.00241.x.

Halsey, A.H. 1985. 'On Methods and Morals.' In *Values and Social Change in Britain*, edited by Mark Abrams, David Gerard and Noel Timms, pp.1–20. London: Marc Europe.

Hammond, Paul. Forthcoming. *Finding the Church in Fresh Expressions*. PhD in preparation at the University of St Andrews.

Hanegraaff, Wouter. 2009. 'New Age Religion.' In *Religions in the Modern World: Traditions and Transformations*, edited by Linda Woodhead, Hiroko Kawanami and Christopher Partridge, pp.339–356. London: Routledge.

Harris, Alana. 2012. 'Devout East Enders. Catholicism in the East End of London.' In *Church Growth in Britain*, edited by David Goodhew, pp.41–58. Farnham: Ashgate.

Harris, Margaret. 1998. *Organizing God's Work. Challenges for Churches and Synagogues*. Basingstoke: Palgrave Macmillan.

Harvey, Graham. 2009. 'Paganism.' In *Religions in the Modern World: Traditions and Transformations*, edited by Linda Woodhead, Hiroko Kawanami and Christopher Partridge, pp.357–378. London: Routledge.

Harvey, Graham and Vincett, Giselle. 2012. 'Alternative Spiritualities: Marginal and Mainstream.' In *Religion and Change in Modern Britain*, edited by Linda Woodhead and Rebecca Catto, pp.156–172. London: Routledge.

Hastings, Adrian. 1986. *A History of English Christianity, 1929–1985*. London: Collins.

Heelas, Paul. 1996. *The New Age Movement: Religion, Culture and Society in the Age of Postmodernity*. Oxford: Blackwell.

Heelas, Paul. 2008. *Spiritualities of Life: From the Romantics to Wellbeing Culture*. Oxford: Blackwell.

Heelas, Paul and Linda Woodhead, with Benjamin Seel, Bronislaw Szerszynski and Karin Tusting, 2005. *The Spiritual Revolution: Why Religion is Giving Way to Spirituality*. Oxford: Blackwell.

Hervieu-Léger, Danièle. 1999. *Le pèlerin et le converti: La religion en mouvement*. Paris: Flammarion.

Hervieu-Léger, Danièle. 2000. *Religion as a Chain of Memory*. Cambridge: Polity Press (translation of *La Religion pour mémoire*, 1993).

Hervieu-Léger, Danièle. 2001. *La religion en miettes ou la question des sectes*. Paris: Calmann-Lévy.

Himmelfarb, Gertrude. 2004. *The Roads to Modernity. The British, French and American Enlightenments*. New York: Knopf Publishing Group.

Hobcraft, John and Heather Joshi. 1989. 'Population Matters.' In *The Changing Population of Britain*, edited by Heather Joshi, pp.1–11. Oxford: Blackwell.

Hoggart, Richard. [1957] 1984. *The Uses of Literacy*. Harmondsworth: Peregrine.

Hornsby-Smith, Michael. 1987. *Roman Catholics in England*. Cambridge: Cambridge University Press.

Hornsby-Smith, Michael. 1989. 'The Roman Catholic Church in Britain since the Second World War.' In *Religion, State and Society in Modern Britain*, edited by Paul Badham, pp.85–98. Lewiston: Edwin Mellen Press.

Hornsby-Smith, Michael. 1999. *Catholics in England 1950–2000: Historical and Sociological Perspectives*. London: Geoffrey Chapman.

Hornsby-Smith, Michael. 2008. *Roman Catholics in England: Studies in Social Structure since the Second World War*. Cambridge: Cambridge University Press.

Hornsby-Smith, Michael. 2009. *Roman Catholic Beliefs in England: Customary Catholicism and Transformations of Religious Authority*. Cambridge: Cambridge University Press.

Hull, John. 2006. *Mission-shaped Church: A Theological Response*. London: SCM Press.

Hunt, Stephen. 2004. *The Alpha Initiative: Evangelism in a Post-Christian Age*. Farnham: Ashgate.

Huntington, Samuel. 1993. 'The Clash of Civilizations.' *Foreign Affairs*, 72, 3: 22–50.

Huntington, Samuel. 1996. *The Clash of Civilizations and the Remaking of the World Order*. New York: Simon and Schuster.

Jackson, Bob and Alan Piggott. 2003. 'A Capital Idea.' An unpublished report for the Diocese of London.

Jackson, Bob and Alan Piggott 2011. 'Another Capital Idea: Church Growth in the Diocese of London 2003–2010.' An unpublished report for the Diocese of London. Available at http://www.london.anglican.org/about/another-capital-idea/. Accessed 12 August 2014.

Jackson, Robert. 2012. 'Religious Education and Human Rights.' Contribution to the Westminster Faith Debate on 'What's the Place for Faith in Schools.' Available at http://faithdebates.org.uk/wp-content/uploads/2013/09/1330520267_Robert-Jackson-final-text-as-delivered.pdf. Accessed 12 August 2014.

Jackson, Robert. 2013. 'Religious Education in England: The Story to 2013.' *Pedagogiek*, 33, 2: 119–135. URN:NBN:NL:UI:10-1-100787.

Jawad, Rana. 2012. *Religion and Faith-based Welfare: From Wellbeing to Ways of Being*. Bristol: Policy Press.

Jenkins, Daniel.1975. *The British: Their Identity and Their Religion*. London: SCM.

Jenkins Philip. 2012. *The Next Christendom: The Coming of Global Christianity*, 3rd ed. New York: Oxford University Press.

Joas, Hans. 2002. *Do We Need Religion? On the Experience of Self-Transcendence*. Boulder, CO: Paradigm Publishers.

Joas, Hans and Klaus Wiegandt, eds. 2009. *Secularization and the World Religions*. Liverpool: Liverpool University Press.

Johnsen, Sarah. 2012. 'The Role of Faith-based Organizations in Service Provision for Homeless People.' In *Religion and Change in Modern Britain*, edited by Linda Woodhead and Rebecca Catto, pp.295–298. London: Routledge.

Kahl, Sigrun. 2005. 'The Religious Roots of Modern Poverty Policy: Catholic, Lutheran, and Reformed Protestant Traditions Compared.' *European Journal of Sociology*, 46, 1: 91–126. DOI: 10.1017/S0003975605000044.

Kershen, Anne and Laura Vaughan. 2013. 'There Was a Priest, a Rabbi and an Imam… : An Analysis of Urban Space and Religious Practice in London's East End, 1685–2010.' *Material Religion*, 9, 1: 10–35. DOI: 10.2752/175183413X1 3535214684014.

Kettell, Steven. 2013a. 'Faithless: The Politics of New Atheism.' *Secularism and Nonreligion*, 2: 61–72. DOI: 10.5334/snr.al.

Kettell, Steven. 2013b. 'Let's Call the Whole Thing Off.' *Public Spirit*. Available at http://www.publicspirit.org.uk/contributors/steven-kettell. Accessed 12 August 2014.

King, Peter. 2013. 'Faith in a Foxhole? Researching Combatant Religiosity amongst British Soldiers on Contemporary Operations.' In *The Defence Academy Yearbook 2013*, edited by Jane Volpi, pp.2–10. Shrivenham: Defence Academy of the United Kingdom.

Knott, Kim and Jolyon Mitchell. 2012. 'The Changing Faces of Media and Religion.' In *Religion and Change in Modern Britain*, edited by Linda Woodhead and Rebecca Catto, pp.243–264. London: Routledge.

Knott, Kim, Elizabeth Poole and Teemu Taira. 2013. *Media Portrayals of Religion and the Secular Sacred*. Farnham: Ashgate.

Koenig, Harold, Dana King and Verna B. Carson, eds. 2012. *Handbook of Religion and Health*. 2nd ed. New York: Oxford University Press.

Leaman, Oliver. 1989. 'Taking Religion Seriously.' *The Times*, 6 February.
Lee, Lois. 2015. *Recognizing the Nonreligious: Reimagining the Secular,* Oxford: Oxford University Press.
Leigh, Ian and Andrew Hambler. 2014. 'Religious Symbols, Conscience, and the Rights of Others.' *Oxford Journal of Law and Religion*, 3, 1: 2–24. DOI: 10.1093/ojlr/rwt048.
Levitt, Mairi. 1992. 'Parental Attitudes to Religion: A Cornish Case Study.' Unpublished paper presented at the BSA Sociology of Religion Study Group, St Mary's College, Twickenham.
Levitt, Mairi. 1996. *Nice When They Are Young: Contemporary Christianity in Families and Schools.* Aldershot: Avebury.
Lings, George. 2012. 'A History of Fresh Expressions and Church Planting in the Church of England.' In *Church Growth in Britain*, edited by David Goodhew, pp.161–178. Farnham: Ashgate.
Lövheim, Mia, ed. 2013. *Media, Religion and Gender: Key Issues and New Challenges.* London: Routledge.
McCrea, Ronan. 2014. 'Religion in the Workplace: *Eweida and Others v United Kingdom.' Modern Law Review*, 77, 2: 277–307. DOI: 10.1111/1468-2230.12066.
McLeod, Hugh. 2007. *The Religious Crisis of the 1960s.* Oxford: Oxford University Press.
Madge, Nicola, Peter J. Hemming and Kevin Stenson. 2014. *Youth on Religion: The Negotiation and Development of Faith and Non-Faith Identity.* London: Routledge.
Manow, Philip. 2004. 'The "Good, the Bad and the Ugly". Esping-Andersen's Welfare State Typology and the Religious Roots of the Western Welfare State.' Working Paper 04/03, Max-Planck-Institut für Gesellschaftsforschung, Cologne.
Marsh, Colin. 2012. 'The Diversification of Christianity: The Example of Birmingham.' In *Church Growth in Britain*, edited by David Goodhew, pp.193–205. Farnham: Ashgate.
Martikainen, Tuomas and Francois Gautier, eds. 2013. *Religion in the Neoliberal Age: Political Economy and Modes of Governance.* Farnham: Ashgate.
Martikainen, Tuomas, François Gauthier and Linda Woodhead, eds. 2011. 'Introduction: Religion and Consumer Society.' *Social Compass*, 58, 3: 291–301. DOI: 10.1177/0037768611412141.
Martin, David. 1969. 'Sociologist Fallen among Secular Theologian.' In *The Religious and the Secular*, pp.70–79. London: Routledge and Kegan Paul.
Martin, David. 1978. *A General Theory of Secularization.* Oxford: Blackwell.
Martin, David. 1990: *Tongues of Fire.* Oxford: Blackwell.
Martin, David. 1997. *Reflections on Sociology and Theology.* Oxford: Oxford University Press.
Martin, David. 2002. *Christian Language and its Mutations.* Farnham: Ashgate.
Martin, David 2004. 'The Christian, the Political and the Academic.' The 2003 Paul Hanly Furfey Lecture. *Sociology of Religion*, 65, 4: 341–356. DOI: 10.2307/3712318.
Martin, David. 2011. *The Future of Christianity: Violence and Democracy, Secularization and Religion.* Farnham: Ashgate.

Martin, David. 2014. *Religion and Power. No Logos without Mythos.* Farnham: Ashgate.

Meer, Nasar and Tariq Modood. 2012. 'How Does Interculturalism Contrast with Multiculturalism?' *Journal of Intercultural Studies*, 33, 2: 175–196. DOI: 10.1080/07256868.2011.618266.

Micklethwait, John and Adrian Wooldridge. 2009. *God is Back: How the Global Rise of Faith is Changing the World.* London: Allen Lane.

Mission-shaped Church: Church Planting and Fresh Expressions of Church in a Changing Context. 2004. London: Church House Publishing.

Mitchell, Claire. 2005. *Religion, Identity and Politics in Northern Ireland: Boundaries of Belonging and Belief.* Farnham: Ashgate.

Mitchell, Claire. 2012. 'Northern Irish Protestatism: Evangelical Vitality and Adaptation.' In *Church Growth in Britain*, edited by David Goodhew, pp.237–252. Farnham: Ashgate.

Mitchell, Claire and Gladys Ganiel. 2011. *Evangelical Journeys: Choice and Change in a Northern Irish Subculture.* Dublin: University College Dublin Press.

Modood, Tariq. 1990. 'British Asian Muslims and the Rushdie Affair.' *British Political Quarterly*, 61, 2: 143–160.

Modood, Tariq. 1994. 'Establishment, Multiculturalism and British Citizenship.' *British Political Quarterly*, 65, 1: 53–73. DOI: 10.1111/j.1467-923X.1994.tb00390.x.

Modood, Tariq. 2011a. 'Moderate Secularism: A European Conception.' *Open Democracy*, 7 April. Available at http://www.opendemocracy.net/tariq-modood/moderate-secularism-european-conception. Accessed 12 August 2014.

Modood, Tariq, 2011b. 'Multiculturalism: Not a Minority Problem.' Comment is Free at *The Guardian*. Available at http://www.theguardian.com/commentisfree/2011/feb/07/multiculturalism-not-minority-problem. Accessed 12 August 2014.

Modood, Tariq. 2011c. 'Is There a Crisis of Secularism in Western Europe?' The 2011 Paul Hanly Furfey Lecture. *Sociology of Religion*, 73, 2: 130–149. DOI:10.1093/socrel/srs028.

Modood, Tariq. 2011d. 'Civic Religion and Respect for Religion in Britain's Moderate Secularism.' In *British Secularism and Religion: Islam, Society and the State*, edited by Yahya Birt, Dilwar Hussain and Ataullah Siddiqui, pp.55–76. Markfield: Kube Publishing Ltd.

Modood, Tariq. 2013. *Multiculturalism*, 2nd ed. Cambridge: Polity Press.

Molendijk, Arie, Justin Beaumont and Christoph Jedan, eds. 2010. *Exploring the Postsecular: The Religious, the Political and the Urban.* Leiden: Brill.

Moorman, John. 1980. *A History of the Church in England*, 3rd ed. London: A&C Black.

Morris, R.M., ed. 2009. *Church and State in 21st Century Britain: The Future of Church Establishment.* Basingstoke: Palgrave Macmillan.

Muskett, Judith A. Forthcoming. 'Reflections on the Shop-windows of the Church of England. Anglican Cathedrals and Vicarious Religion.' *Journal of Contemporary Religion.*

National Council for Voluntary Organisations. 2011. *Participation: Trends, Facts, and Figures.* An NCVO Almanac. Available at http://www.ncvo.org.uk/images/documents/policy_and_research/participation/participation_trends_facts_figures.pdf. Accessed 12 August 2014.

Nye, Malory and Paul Weller. 2012. 'Controversies as a Lens on Change.' In *Religion and Change in Modern Britain*, edited by Linda Woodhead and Rebecca Catto, pp.34–54. London: Routledge.

Olson, Elizabeth and Giselle Vincett. Forthcoming. 'Researching Spirituality with and for Vulnerable Young People.' In *How to Research Religion: Putting Methods into Practice*, edited by Linda Woodhead. Oxford: Oxford University Press.

ONS. 2012. 'Religion in England and Wales 2011.' Office for National Statistics. Available at http://www.ons.gov.uk/ons/dcp171776_290510.pdf. Accessed 12 August 2014.

ONS. 2013. 'Full Story: What Does the Census Tell Us about Religion in 2011?' Office for National Statistics. Available at http://www.ons.gov.uk/ons/ dcp171776_310454.pdf Accessed 12 August 2014.

Orchard, Stephen. 2012. 'The Formation of the United Reformed Church.' In *Religion and Change in Modern Britain*, edited by Linda Woodhead and Rebecca Catto, pp.79–84. London: Routledge.

Osgood, Hugh. 2012. 'The Rise of the Black Churches.' In *Church Growth in Britain*, edited by David Goodhew, pp.107–126. Farnham: Ashgate.

Parris, Matthew. 2013. 'Scrap Tory Associations: Build a New Party.' *The Times*, 6 July: 21.

Paul, Leslie. 1964. *The Deployment and Payment of the Clergy*. London: Church Information Office.

Percy, Martin and Louise Nelstrop, eds. 2008. *Evaluating Fresh Expressions: Explorations in Emerging Church*. Norwich: Canterbury Press.

Pérez-Agote, Alfonso, ed. 2012. *Portraits du catholicisme: Une comparaison européenne*. Rennes: PU Rennes.

Perfect, David. 2011. *Religion or Belief*. Manchester: Equality and Human Rights Commission Briefing Paper. Available at http://www.equalityhumanrights.com/ publications/our-research/research-reports. Accessed 12 August 2014.

Perfect, David. 2013. 'Religion or Belief and the Law.' *Public Spirit*. Available at http:// www.publicspirit.org.uk/contributors/david-perfect/. Accessed 12 August 2014.

Pew Forum on Religion and Public Life. 2006. Pentecostal Resource Page. Available at www.pewforum.org/Christian/Evangelical-Protestant-Churches/Pentecostal-Resource-Page.aspx. Accessed 12 August 2014.

Pew Forum on Religion and Public Life. 2012. '"Nones" on the Rise.' Available at http://www.pewforum.org/Unaffiliated/nones-on-the-rise.aspx. Accessed 12 August 2014.

Prochaska, Frank. 2006. *Christianity and Social Services in Modern Britain. The Disinherited Spirit*. Oxford: Oxford University Press.

Robbers, Gerhard, ed. 2005. *State and Church in the European Union*. Baden-Baden: Nomos.

Robinson, John. 1963. *Honest to God*. London: SCM.

Rothgangel, Martin, Robert Jackson and Martin Jäggle, eds. 2014. *Religious Education at Schools in Europe, Part 2: Western Europe*. Vienna: Vienna University Press.

Rowe, Peter. *The Role of the Modern Cathedral*. Unpublished PhD thesis, University of University of St Andrews. Available at http://research-repository.st-andrews. ac.uk/handle/10023/1859. Accessed 12 August 2014.

Roxburgh, Kenneth. 2012. 'Growth Amidst Decline: Edinburgh's Churches and Scottish Culture.' In *Church Growth in Britain*, edited by David Goodhew, pp.209–220. Farnham: Ashgate.

Royle, Edward. 1980. *Radicals, Secularists and Republicans: Popular Freethought in Britain, 1866–1915*. Manchester: Manchester University Press.

Rushdie, Salman. 1988. *The Satanic Verses*. London and New York: Viking-Penguin.

Russell-Jones, Gethin. 2013. *Power of Ten: How Christian Partnerships are Changing the Face of Wales*. Cardiff: Gweini (The Council of the Christian Voluntary Sector in Wales).

Sacks, Jonathan. 1991. *The Persistence of Faith*. London: Weidenfeld.

Sandberg, Russell. 2011. *Law and Religion*. Cambridge: Cambridge University Press.

Sandberg, Russell. 2014. *Religion, Law and Society*. Cambridge: Cambridge University Press.

Sanneh, Lamin. 2004. *Whose Religion is Christianity? The Gospel Beyond the West*. Grand Rapids, MI: Eerdmans.

Savage, Sara, Sylvia Collins-Mayo, Bob Mayo, with Graham Cray. 2011. *Making Sense of Generation Y*. London: Church House Publishing.

Scorer, Peter. 2006. 'Current Developments in the Relationship between the Moscow Patriarchate and the Russian Orthodox Diocese in the UK.' Briefing Paper for Faith in Europe. Available at http://www.faithineurope.org.uk/moscow1.pdf. Accessed 12 August 2014.

Seenan, Gerard. 2006. 'Fury at Ferry Crossing on Sabbath.' *The Guardian*, 10 April. Available at http://www.theguardian.com/uk/2006/apr/10/religion. world. Accessed 12 August 2014.

Singh, Gurharpal. 2012. 'Sihkism'. In *Religion and Change in Modern Britain*, edited by Linda Woodhead and Rebecca Catto, pp.100–110. London: Routledge.

Smith, Christian. 1998. *American Evangelicalism: Embattled and Thriving*. Chicago, IL: University of Chicago Press.

Spencer, Anthony, ed. 2007. *Digest of the Statistics of the Catholic Community of England and Wales, 1958–2005: Volume I*. Taunton: Russell Spencer.

Statistics for Mission 2011. 2013. Archbishops' Council, Research and Statistics, Central Secretariat. Available at http://www.churchofengland.org/media/1737985/attendancestats2011.pdf. Accessed 12 August 2014.

Statistics for Mission 2012. 2014. Archbishops' Council, Research and Statistics, Central Secretariat. Available at http://churchofengland.org/media/1936517/statistics%20for%20mission%202012.pdf. Accessed 12 August 2014.

Statistics for Mission 2012: Ministry. 2013. Archbishops' Council, Research and Statistics, Central Secretariat. Available at http://www.churchofengland.org/media/1868964/ministry%20statistics%20final.pdf. Accessed 12 August 2014.

Stringer, Martin. 2013. *Discourses on Religious Diversity*. Farnham: Ashgate.

Sutcliffe, Steven and Marion Bowman, eds. 2000. *Beyond the New Age. Exploring Alternative Christianity*. Edinburgh: Edinburgh University Press.

Taylor, Charles. 1989. *Sources of the Self: The Making of the Modern Identity*. Cambridge: Cambridge University Press.

Taylor, Charles. 1991. *The Ethics of Authenticity*. Cambridge, MA: Harvard University Press.

Taylor, Charles. 2002. *Varieties of Religion Today*. Cambridge, MA: Harvard University Press.

Taylor, Charles. 2007. *A Secular Age*. Cambridge, MA: Harvard University Press.

Theos. 2012a. *Spiritual Capital: The Present and Future of English Cathedrals*. London: Theos.

Theos. 2012b (Nick Spencer and Holly Weldin). *Post-Religious Britain: The Faith of the Faithless*. London: Theos.

Theos. 2012c (edited by Nick Spencer). *Religion and Law*. London: Theos.

Theos. 2013a (Andy Walton, Andrea Hatcher and Nick Spencer). *Is There a 'Religious Right' Emerging in Britain?* London: Theos.

Theos. 2013b (Elizabeth Oldfield, Lianne Hartlett and Emma Bailey). *More Than an Educated Guess: Assessing the Evidence on Faith Schools*. London: Theos.

Theos. 2013c. *The Spirit of Things Unseen: Belief in Post-Religious Britain*. London: Theos.

Theos. 2014a (Ben Clements and Nick Spencer). *Voting and Values in Britain: Does Religion Count?* London: Theos.

Theos. 2014b (edited by Nick Spencer). *The Welfare Collection*. London: Theos.

Theos. 2014c (Nick Spencer). *How to Think About Religious Freedom*. London: Theos.

Thompson, David. 1989. 'The Free Churches in Modern Britain.' In *Religion, State and Society in Modern Britain*, edited by Paul Badham, pp.99–118. Lewiston NY: Edwin Mellen Press.

Todd, Andrew, ed. 2013. *Military Chaplaincy in Contention: Chaplains, Churches and the Morality of Conflict*. Farnham: Ashgate.

Totten, Andrew. 2013. 'Modern Soldiering and Soldiers' Morale.' In *Military Chaplaincy in Contention: Chaplains, Churches and the Morality of Conflict*, edited by Andrew Todd, pp.19–38. Farnham: Ashgate.

Trzebiatowska, Marta and Steve Bruce. 2012. *Why Are Women More Religious than Men?* Oxford: Oxford University Press.

Van Kersbergen, Kees and Philip Manow, eds. 2009. *Religion, Class Coalitions, and Welfare States*, Cambridge: Cambridge University Press.

Vincett, Giselle and Elizabeth Olson. 2012. 'The Religiosity of Young People Growing up in Poverty.' In *Religion and Change in Modern Britain*, edited by Linda Woodhead and Rebecca Catto, pp.196–202. London: Routledge.

Vincett, Giselle and Linda Woodhead. 2009. 'Spirituality.' In *Religions in the Modern World: Traditions and Transformations*, edited by Linda Woodhead, Hiroko Kawanami and Christopher Partridge, pp.319–338. London: Routledge.

Voas, David. 2003. 'Intermarriage and the Demography of Secularisation.' *British Journal of Sociology* 54, 1: 83–108. DOI: 10.1080/0007131032000045914.

Voas, David. 2009. 'The Rise and Fall of Fuzzy Fidelity in Europe.' *European Sociological Review*, 25, 2: 155–168. DOI: 10.1093/esr/jcn044.

Voas, David and Steve Bruce. 2004. 'Research Note: The 2001 Census and Christian Identification in Britain.' *Journal of Contemporary Religion*, 19, 1: 23–28. DOI: 10.1080/1353790032000165087.

Voas, David and Alasdair Crockett. 2005. 'Religion in Britain. Neither Believing nor Belonging.' *Sociology*, 39, 1: 11–28. DOI: 10.1177/0038038505048998.

Voas David, Siobhan McAndrew and Ingrid Storm. 2013. 'Modernization and the Gender Gap in Religiosity: Evidence from Cross-national European Surveys.' *Kölner Zeitschrift für Soziologie und Sozialpsychologie* 65, 1: 259–283. DOI: 10.1007/s11577-013-0226-5.

Walker, Andrew. 1985. *Restoring the Kingdom*. London: Hodder and Stoughton.

Walter, Tony and Grace Davie. 1998. 'The Religiosity of Women in the Modern West.' *British Journal of Sociology*, 49, 4: 640–660.

Waterman, Stanley and Barry Kosmin. 1986. *British Jewry in the Eighties*. London: Research Unit, Board of Deputies of British Jews.

Weber, Max. 1948. 'Politics as a Vocation.' In *From Max Weber: Essays in Sociology*, edited by Hans Gerth and C. Wright Mills, pp.77–128. London: Routledge.

Weller, Paul. 2004. 'Identity, Politics and the Future(s) of Religion in the UK: The Case of the Religion Questions in the 2001 Decennial Census.' *Journal of Contemporary Religion*, 19, 1: 3–21. DOI: 10.1080/1353790032000165096.

Weller, Paul. 2009. *A Mirror for our Times: 'The Rushdie Affair' and the Future of Multiculturalism*. London: Continuum.

Weller, Paul. 2011. *Religious Discrimination in Britain: A Review of Research Evidence, 2000-10*. Manchester: Equality and Human Rights Commission, Research Report 73. Available at http://www.equalityhumanrights.com/publi cations/our-research/research-reports. Accessed 12 August 2014.

Weller, Paul, Alice Feldman and Kingsley Purdam. 2001. *Religious Discrimination in England and Wales*. Home Office Research Study 220, Research, Development, Statistics. London: The Home Office.

Weller, Paul, Nazila Ghanea, Kingsley Purdam and Sariya Cheruvallil-Contractor. 2013. *Religion or Belief, Discrimination and Equality: Britain in Global Context*. London: Bloomsbury/Continuum.

Welsby, Paul. 1984. *A History of the Church of England 1945–80*. Oxford: Oxford University Press.

Welsby, Paul. 1985. *How the Church of England Works*. London: Church Information Office.

Wickham, Edward. 1957. *Church and People in an Industrial City*. London: Lutterworth.

Williams, Rowan. 2012. *Faith in the Public Square*. London: Bloomsbury/Continuum.

Wilson, Bryan. 1961. *Sects and Society*. London: Heinemann.

Wilson, Bryan, ed. 1967. *Patterns of Sectarianism: Organization and Ideology in Social and Religious Movements*. London: Heinemann.

Wilson, Bryan. 1982. *Religion in a Sociological Perspective*. Oxford: Oxford University Press.

Wilson, Bryan. 1990. *The Social Dimensions of Sectarianism*. Oxford: Clarendon Press.

Winter, Emily. 2013. *Christianity and Occupy: An Exploration into Christian Support for the St Paul's Occupy Movement*. Unpublished MA thesis, Lancaster University.

Wolffe, John and Bob Jackson. 2012. 'Anglican Resurgence. The Church of England in London.' In *Church Growth in Britain*, edited by David Goodhew, pp.23–40. Farnham: Ashgate.

Woodhead, Linda. 2007. 'Gender Differences in Religious Practice and Significance.' In *The Sage Handbook of the Sociology of Religion*, edited by James Beckford, and N. Jay Demerath III, pp.566–586. London: Sage.

Woodhead, Linda. 2011. *Recent Research on Religion, Discrimination, and Good Relations*. A Report for the Equality and Human Rights Commission. Available at http://www.religionandsociety.org.uk/uploads/docs/2011_05/1306247842_LINDA_WOODHEAD_FINAL_REPORT_MAY_2011.pdf. Accessed 12 August 2014.

Woodhead, Linda. 2012. 'Introduction.' In *Religion and Change in Modern Britain*, edited by Linda Woodhead and Rebecca Catto, pp.1–33. London: Routledge.

Woodhead, Linda. 2013a. '"Nominals" are the Church's Hidden Strength.' *Church Times*, 26 April: 16.

Woodhead, Linda. 2013b. 'What we Really Think.' *The Tablet*, 9 November: 12–13.

Woodhead, Linda. 2013c. 'Endangered Species.' *The Tablet*, 16 November: 6–7.

Woodhead, Linda 2013d. 'Neither Religious nor Secular: The British Situation and its Implications for Religion-State Relations.' In *Contesting Secularism: Comparative Perspectives*, edited by Anders Berg-Sørensen, pp.137–162. Farnham: Ashgate.

Woodhead, Linda 2013e. 'Telling the Truth about Religious Identity in Britain.' AHRC/ESRC Westminster Faith Debates. Available at http://static.westminster-abbey.org/assets/pdf_file/0009/69192/Telling-the-Truth-about-Religious-Identity-in-Britain-HANDOUT.pdf. Accessed 12 August 2014.

Woodhead, Linda. 2013f. 'A Gap is Growing within the Church.' *Church Times*, 20 September: 16.

Woodhead, Linda, guest editor. 2014a. 'What British People Really Think.' Special issue of *Modern Believing*, 55: 1.

Woodhead, Linda. 2014b. 'The "Fuzzy" Nones. Nonreligion and Secularity.' NSblog, 21 March. Available at http://blog.nsrn.net/tag/linda-woodhead. Accessed 12 August 2014.

Woodhead, Linda, ed. Forthcoming. *How to Research Religion: Putting Methods into Practice*. Oxford: Oxford University Press.

Woodhead, Linda and Rebecca Catto, eds. 2012. *Religion and Change in Modern Britain*. London: Routledge.

Woodhead, Linda, with Rebecca Catto. 2009. *'Religion or Belief': Identifying Issues and Priorities*. Manchester: Equality and Human Rights Commission, Research Report 48. Available at http://www.equalityhumanrights.com/publications/our-research/research-reports. Accessed 12 August 2014.

Woodhead, Linda, with Norman Winter, eds. 2013. *Religion and Personal Life* (Westminster Faith Debates). London: Darton, Longman and Todd.

Zavos, John. 2012. 'Hinduism.' In *Religion and Change in Modern Britain*, edited by Linda Woodhead and Rebecca Catto, pp.121–131. London: Routledge.

Zohar, Danah and Ian Marshall. 2000. *SQ: Spiritual Intelligence*. London: Bloomsbury.

Index

Note: Page numbers in *italics* refer to Figures; those in **bold** to Tables.